Phobias

by Gregory P. Korgeski, Ph.D.

ALPHA

A member of Penguin Group (USA) Inc.

To Skye

ALPHA BOOKS

Published by the Penguin Group

Penguin Group (USA) Inc., 375 Hudson Street, New York, New York 10014, USA

Penguin Group (Canada), 90 Eglinton Avenue East, Suite 700, Toronto, Ontario M4P 2Y3, Canada (a division of Pearson Penguin Canada Inc.)

Penguin Books Ltd., 80 Strand, London WC2R 0RL, England

Penguin Ireland, 25 St. Stephen's Green, Dublin 2, Ireland (a division of Penguin Books Ltd.)

Penguin Group (Australia), 250 Camberwell Road, Camberwell, Victoria 3124, Australia (a division of Pearson Australia Group Pty. Ltd.)

Penguin Books India Pvt. Ltd., 11 Community Centre, Panchsheel Park, New Delhi—110 017, India

Penguin Group (NZ), 67 Apollo Drive, Rosedale, North Shore, Auckland 1311, New Zealand (a division of Pearson New Zealand Ltd.)

Penguin Books (South Africa) (Pty.) Ltd., 24 Sturdee Avenue, Rosebank, Johannesburg 2196, South Africa

Penguin Books Ltd., Registered Offices: 80 Strand, London WC2R 0RL, England

International Standard Book Number: 978-1-59257-919-8
Library of Congress Catalog Card Number: 2009926597

11   10   09   8   7   6   5   4   3   2   1

Interpretation of the printing code: The rightmost number of the first series of numbers is the year of the book's printing; the rightmost number of the second series of numbers is the number of the book's printing. For example, a printing code of 09-1 shows that the first printing occurred in 2009.

Printed in the United States of America

Note: This publication contains the opinions and ideas of its author. It is intended to provide helpful and informative material on the subject matter covered. It is sold with the understanding that the author and publisher are not engaged in rendering professional services in the book. If the reader requires personal assistance or advice, a competent professional should be consulted.

The author and publisher specifically disclaim any responsibility for any liability, loss, or risk, personal or otherwise, which is incurred as a consequence, directly or indirectly, of the use and application of any of the contents of this book.

Most Alpha books are available at special quantity discounts for bulk purchases for sales promotions, premiums, fund-raising, or educational use. Special books, or book excerpts, can also be created to fit specific needs.

For details, write: Special Markets, Alpha Books, 375 Hudson Street, New York, NY 10014.

Publisher: *Marie Butler-Knight*
Editorial Director: *Mike Sanders*
Senior Managing Editor: *Billy Fields*
Senior Acquisitions Editor: *Paul Dinas*
Development Editor: *Lynn Northrup*
Senior Production Editor: *Megan Douglass*

Copy Editor: *Jaime Julian Wagner*
Cover/Book Designer: *Bill Thomas*
Indexer: *Celia McCoy*
Layout: *Ayanna Lacey*
Proofreader: *Laura Caddell*

Contents at a Glance

Contents

5 The Sky Is Falling!: Natural Environment Phobias   75

8 "Hell Is Other People": Specific Phobias Involving People   161

Introduction

When I was a very little boy, we had a set of white porcelain candle-holders on the wall over our couch. I don't remember ever having messed with them, but for some reason, my mother decided one day that she should give me a warning about the dangers of fire (even though the candles in them were never actually lit). So she told me to be careful and to never, ever touch them, because they were hot.

Now I'm sure that, in her mind, my mother assumed that it was clear to both of us that lit candles was the danger she was warning me about. When she looked at the candles and their holders, flames running down the cotton PJs of her oldest son was probably the image that she was trying to keep from turning into an actual "News at eleven" event.

But from my way-closer-to-the-floor perspective, her advice led in an entirely different direction. Since she wasn't actually pointing to a lit set of candles, and in fact I'd never actually seen those candles lit, I simply took Mommy's advice to mean that the white porcelain holders were hot—that they were, in fact, so hot that they would burn me. And so for the longest time, I never let myself touch them. In fact, I can still recall the day when, after sitting in a chair, staring at them, and thinking hard, it occurred to me that those things couldn't possibly be hot. I climbed up on the couch and carefully, with just one little fingertip, reached out and quickly brushed one of them—just to be sure.

They were cool. Eureka! My fears of singed flesh were groundless.

I share this story now, I know, at the risk of sounding like an idiot. But I don't think it was at all idiotic for a very little boy to have accepted his mom's warning about a danger at face value. After all, during those same couple of years I accepted all sorts of warnings and explanations from my parents on faith—that sticking my finger into an electric socket would shock me (whatever shocking was), that drinking certain things in bottles under the sink would make me or the puppy sick, or that those two smaller dudes were actually my brothers instead of some tiny strangers or elves who kept stealing my stuff. The existence of Santa Claus—I bought it. The tooth fairy, the whole shebang—whatever Mommy said, I believed.

The fact about "facts" like these is that, for the most part, we humans tend to believe a lot of things about the world that we haven't actually seen proof of, crept up on, and touched carefully with our fingertips. We are hard-wired to learn from a very early age to recognize what things, animals, and situations are dangerous. Because while a piece of porcelain on the wall won't hurt, a poisonous snake in the warm, squishy mud of a child's favorite riverbank certainly will. The very large striped kitty hiding in the tall grass certainly will. The strangers who hide behind the trees near your hut certainly will. And so, for tens of thousands of years, the little two-, three-, and four-year-olds who immediately accepted their mommies' and daddies' stern warnings about dangers that they didn't and couldn't understand survived. Meanwhile, the kids who needed hard proof often didn't.

So I wasn't an idiot, and neither are you. You are, in fact, descended from a thousand generations of the nonidiots—the toddlers who learned fastest that "Don't touch that!" was the advice to follow, even if it only looked like a harmless piece of porcelain or an amusing little hissing worm. They survived to have babies of their own, and so the process of selection in the gene pool continued on.

Of course, the downside of this ability to learn to fear innocent things is that we can sometimes become too fearful. In fact, we may start to pile up lists of dangers that seem to threaten us all the time. We become, in a word, phobics.

A *phobia* is a fear—but not just any fear. Like my fear of the candle-holders, a phobia is a fear of something that is out of proportion to the actual danger. While there may be some real, objective truth to the danger, the actual risk does not match the intensity of our emotional reaction. We are, in short, overreacting—and we know it.

If you have a phobia, by definition it means you recognize that your fear is too intense. (If you don't know that, then you may actually have a *delusion*, which is a totally different and more severe psychological problem.)

In this book, we will explore the mysterious world of phobias. Far from being simple or obvious, phobias actually turn out to be both interesting and complex. They may be minor or even amusing things to learn about, but phobias can also disrupt lives and trigger severe psychological and even medical problems.

How This Book Is Organized

The Complete Idiot's Guide to Phobias is divided into three sections:

Part 1, "Phobias 101," explores the science of phobias. We'll explore the long history of phobias, talk about how they are defined, discuss how common they are, and learn how they can affect your life. Then we'll discuss the cause of phobias and end with a state-of-the-art summary of the best ways to control or eliminate the phobias that get into your head.

Part 2, "Specific or 'Simple' Phobias," is a listing of the kinds of things most people think of when they use the term *phobia*. Specific phobias involve a fear of a particular thing. Whether it's a fear of a certain kind of animal (such as a cat), a natural event (such as lightning), or a situation (such as public speaking), you'll probably find your favorites in these chapters.

Part 3, "When Phobias Get Serious," discusses three kinds of phobia problems: agoraphobia, social phobias, and phobias in children. Not all phobias are focused on simple, specific objects or situations. There are several types of phobias that affect millions of people that are more complex.

You'll also find two helpful appendixes. If you only know the phobia by its technical name, or if you don't know where the discussion of "clown phobia" is located, check out Appendix A, an index of phobias. Appendix B is a list of resources for further information or for assistance in understanding or managing phobias.

Extras

Supplementing the main text of *The Complete Idiot's Guide to Phobias* are four kinds of extras that will give you additional information or insight into our topics. These are:

def•i•ni•tion

Short explanations of terms used in the book that may be unfamiliar to you.

Phobia Science

Cool facts or additional points about phobias, often from the world of psychological or medical research.

 Real Danger!

Truly dangerous situations or warnings to know about when navigating the phobia world.

 Try This!

Handy ideas, suggestions, or things to try that will help you cope with phobic anxieties.

How to Use This Book

When planning this book, the thing that most impressed me was that the people I talked to seemed to have two very different attitudes about phobias. On the one hand, everyone recognized that phobias are a serious topic and that phobias can be painful psychological problems.

Yet there was also, generally in the same group of people, a kind of amused fascination about phobias. Because there is something—I hesitate even to say the word but shall—*entertaining* about the topic of phobias. After all, haven't phobias been the topic of popular books, movies, and even TV shows? (I'm writing this paragraph in a hurry because the next episode of *Monk* is nearly on—the show about the detective who has so many phobias that there is even a website devoted to lists of all his phobias!)

And speaking of websites, there are many, many websites and blogs devoted to phobia lists and discussions. (I even found that some of the most valuable sources of data for this review included the reports of people who blogged about how phobias affect them; on the other hand, there is also a ton of "blog spam" about phobias and phobia lists all over the web. Clearly, this is a topic of interest to thousands of readers.)

The Complete Idiot's Guide to Phobias is designed to appeal to two different kinds of readers. It is a serious reference work for persons struggling with phobias, and it's an educational book for people who just want to learn and understand more about these mysterious problems—these fascinating glitches in the human mind in which you can know something isn't all that dangerous, and yet it terrifies you.

Avoiding "Medical Student's Disease"

I have two pieces of advice for you as you prepare to read, or to flip through, this book. The first concerns a topic that is often referred to as "medical student's disease," or talking yourself into having a phobia or other mental or physical condition.

As with my childhood candleholder phobia, it's important to recognize that our mind can play tricks on us. One trick that is familiar to anyone in medical school or psychology graduate school is our ability to "catch" diseases or conditions we read about. Since phobias are, by their very nature, a matter of imagination and emotion trumping rational thought, it's worth noting that when you read about something like social phobia, you may start to feel a bit of it. Imagining how you might feel frightened of making a speech may even begin to trigger your fears of those feelings getting a bit out of control. You can literally talk yourself into anything—including a phobia. (And did I tell you how one of those teensy little spiders, like the kind in your shower, once actually managed to bite me?) So suggestion number one is, beware of "medical student's disease."

Suggestion number two: if you think you may be prone to talking yourself into phobias or other such things, you might want to read Chapter 3 first. If you know some things about how to manage and control your fears, you should be fairly immune to self-induced phobias.

If You Really Need Help ...

Understanding how phobias operate may be enough to help you to immunize yourself against ever developing one. It may even help you to overcome a phobia that has been troubling you.

But reading is no substitute for actual treatment, if that becomes necessary. If you or a loved one have an actual phobia (or if you're worried that you *might* have a phobia, another anxiety disorder, depression, or what have you), it may be worthwhile getting a consultation from your friendly neighborhood psychologist, psychiatrist, physician, psychiatric nursing professional, or from another type of therapist. They won't bite—honest.

Acknowledgments

Thanks are due to Paul Dinas of Alpha Books, for offering me the chance to delve into the world of phobias; and to Marilyn Allen, for her always helpful and supportive work as agent. Thanks also to Megan Douglass, Production Editor, and to Jaime Julian Wagner, Copy Editor, for their careful reading and much helpful feedback; and especially to Lynn Northrup, Development Editor, for her many helpful questions, her feedback, and, increasingly as we worked through the book, her patience and "you're almost done!" e-mails of encouragement.

My wife, best editor, best friend, and partner in professional crime, Dr. Skye Payne, deserves more than the usual wifely thanks. As an expert in child developmental psychology, school psychology, and just about every other kind of psychology, she contributed more than her fair share to the book, but particularly to the chapter on phobias in children. In fact, our only "marital disagreement" while doing this book has been that I think she should be listed as a coauthor, but she prefers the humbler role of simply being mentioned here. It's only with the greatest reluctance that I have finally agreed to her wishes in this matter, and so must acknowledge that much of the thinking, expertise, and well over half of the first draft writing of the final chapter of this book was done by Skye. But for that, and much more, my eternal gratitude and appreciation.

Trademarks

All terms mentioned in this book that are known to be or are suspected of being trademarks or service marks have been appropriately capitalized. Alpha Books and Penguin Group (USA) Inc. cannot attest to the accuracy of this information. Use of a term in this book should not be regarded as affecting the validity of any trademark or service mark.

Part 1

Phobias 101

Phobias are fascinating and really rather mysterious things. Think about it: in a phobia, one part of you is absolutely terrified of something that another part of you knows is not really all that threatening! It's like having two entirely different minds happening inside your head at once!

In this part, we'll explore the whys and wherefores of phobias: what they are, how they start, and what you can do about them.

Chapter 1

What Are Phobias?

In This Chapter

- ◆ Phobias in history
- ◆ How phobias are defined
- ◆ The main kinds of phobias
- ◆ The impact of phobias

Human behavior is not always logical. Sometimes we do things we've promised ourselves that we would absolutely not do—no siree! I won't reach for another cookie today. Nope! No way! ... and we watch our hands reach up and snag that chocolate chip cookie anyway.

One of the strange things our minds can do is to become afraid of things that we logically know are not dangerous. That little garter snake can't hurt me! Getting a shot is safe—nothing to faint about! Airplanes are safe! Right?

Tell that to your mind. The fact is, many of us have strong, even uncontrollable fear reactions to harmless (or just slightly threatening) things. These reactions are uncomfortable and may even disrupt our lives.

These reactions are called phobias. Most of the time, people define a phobia with the phrase "fear of ___" [fill in the fear]. Most phobias have technical terms that start with a Greek or Latin phrase and end in the suffix -*phobia*, as in *ophidiophobia* (fear of snakes), *trypanophobia* (fear of injections), or *aviophobia* (fear of flying).

A Look at Phobias in History

Phobias are actually rich, varied, and complex. We know that people have had phobias for thousands of years. But it's only been recently that we've known much about those fears—or even known enough to *call* them by the term *phobias*.

def•i•ni•tion

A **phobia** is a strong but irrational fear of something.

The first written reference to phobic problems that we have is in the works of the ancient Greek physician Hippocrates (470–410 B.C.E.). Hippocrates wrote about the many ailments and problems of his patients, and we can still read many of his volumes of observations today. In one of his works (called *The Seventh Book of Epidemics*—you can find it online), Hippocrates described a condition in a man named Nicanor. Whenever Nicanor went out drinking, he would get terrified of the flute (or maybe the flute music?) played by the musicians. As Hippocrates wrote, "When the piper began to play, the music immediately threw him into such a great fright, that he was not able to bear the disorder of it." (Oddly, the flute music only bothered Nicanor at night—for some reason, in the daylight he was fine.)

Phobia Science

Hippocrates is often called "the father of medicine." He wrote many volumes in which he discussed the diseases and medical treatments of his time, in the process launching many of the ideas about the importance of careful observation and getting good clinical data in order to advance medicine. His oath, the famous Hippocratic oath, is still taken today by new doctors.

But Hippocrates didn't actually come up with the term *phobia*. That word wasn't used until nearly 500 years later, when a Roman doctor,

Celsus, used the word *hydrophobia* (literally, water fear) to describe someone who seemed to have a horror of water due to rabies. (People with advanced rabies may have tremendous thirst but be unable to drink and averse to water.) But where did the Roman sawbones Celsus get the term *phobia* in the first place? From a Greek god.

Phobos was the son of Aries, the Greek god of war. The story goes that Phobos was a frightening and formidable guy—so much so that warriors would paint his picture on their shields to give their enemies a real fright and to get them to run away in terror. So a phobic reaction resembles someone terrified of something.

The first relatively modern use of the word *phobia* wasn't until 1786, when (according to the *Oxford English Dictionary*) an unknown writer in the *Columbian Magazine* defined the word as meaning "A fear of an imaginary evil, or an undue fear of a real one." The word doesn't pop up again in print (as far as we know) until 1801, but by the late 1800s, people were starting to use the term a lot.

In the late 1800s, medical scientists were busy creating clear, scientific categories of psychological problems. In our modern era, accustomed as we are to knowing the psychological facts about ourselves and others (for example, are you an introvert or an extrovert?), it may surprise you to know that just over a hundred years ago, there were no clear, tidy categories for psychological problems. So your phobia might have been ignored or misunderstood as some vague kind of craziness, but nobody would have been able to tell you much about it.

That all began to change as doctors started to recognize that many psychological problems that *seemed* to be quite different from each other were, in fact, the same basic problem. One person might be too scared to leave their house, another merely avoided public speaking, and a third would not even dream of going into their garden for fear of snakes.

In 1895 Sigmund Freud (1856–1939), a Viennese neurologist who founded the science of psychoanalysis, noticed that while some things squick (gross out) most people at least a little (such as snakes, death, or getting sick), other things only bother a few people (such as fear of leaving the house). Years later, Freud wrote about a little boy named Hans who, after being terrified by a horse in the street, developed a strong fear of horses. (Freud believed that the fear was actually, unconsciously, a fear of the boy's father, related to his loving feelings about his mother.) Other researchers of the time also began to speculate that phobias were distinct mental conditions.

Many modern psychoanalysts believe that psychological problems such as phobias can be caused by conflicts in the mind—usually conflicts that the person is not even aware they are having. So a phobia could be caused by a clash of desires and fears that were too uncomfortable for the person to let themselves be consciously aware of ... so the feelings would "go underground" and emerge as an apparently pointless problem such as a phobia.

But it wasn't until 1947 that phobias became a separate diagnostic category in the *International Classification of Diseases*. (They were classified by the American Psychiatric Association in 1951.) In the 1960s, it was observed that phobias basically divide themselves into three rather different kinds or categories: agoraphobia, social phobia, and specific phobias. That set the stage for the phobia classifications that we still use today (including in this book).

def•i•ni•tion

The **International Classification of Diseases** (now called the International Statistical Classification of Diseases and Related Health Problems, or ICD) is an international system for classifying diseases and health problems. The ICD provides a way for scientists, physicians, and policymakers worldwide to track health statistics by ensuring a fairly uniform set of definitions of medical conditions.

We now know much more about phobias and similar conditions than we did in ancient times—even more than we knew just a few decades ago. In particular, we've come to understand much more about the kinds of biological and psychological processes that can cause phobias. As you'll see, phobias make a great deal of sense from the perspective of survival. In fact, it may be that the same things that create phobias also ensured that our species survived long enough so that you could be reading this book!

How Phobias Are Diagnosed

We know people have had phobia problems for thousands of years. But the term *phobia* has only been widely understood to mean a fear problem for about a hundred years—and it's only been an "official" diagnostic term for a few decades. But to really understand what we're talking about when we say *phobia*, you need to understand two things:

♦ Why we have diagnoses at all

♦ Why the word *phobia* really means several different things at different times to different people

The very idea of having systems of *diagnoses* is not as obvious or intuitive as it may seem. For thousands of years, our ancestors made sense of the odd problems or afflictions of others in fairly vague or superstitious terms—which probably made little difference in the centuries before there was any kind of organized treatment for diseases anyway.

def•i•ni•tion

Diagnoses are terms used in medicine, psychology, and related fields to signify what specific kind of disease or other condition a person has. Saying someone is feeling poorly is not a diagnosis, but saying someone has pneumonia or a major depression is.

Medicine as we know it today began to evolve a few thousand years ago. Even the ancient Greeks, Egyptians, Romans, Chinese, and others had basic knowledge of herbal treatments, rest, exercise, diet, bone-setting, wound treatment, and simple surgeries. Once those things were known, diagnosis became more important, because if you have some useful treatments, diagnosing the right problem is essential. That's why the old medical giants like Hippocrates were so valuable. They started writing down very clear descriptions of different kinds of illnesses, observing what treatments helped what conditions, and organizing these observations into categories. This process of observing and recording is really what launched medicine as a science.

Phobias are a really good example of why diagnoses help. As we'll see, many phobias are quite similar to each other in their effects, and treating them is a fairly straightforward process that you can adapt to almost any of the phobias you might have. Yet phobias may, on the surface, look quite different from each other. It's taken decades of research to develop a scientific understanding of phobias. During that time, researchers have pored over all the available data—everything from statistical studies of behavioral problems to psychological testing results to brain studies—to identify the common elements of problems that can seem as different as a child avoiding school, a woman afraid of getting a flu shot, or a man who would rather walk 50 flights of stairs than step into an elevator.

The other problem in talking about phobias is that people may mean very different things by the term:

◆ In the medical use of the term as a diagnosis, *phobia* can refer to a relatively severe psychological problem, one that has a big impact on your life.

◆ *Phobia* can also refer to fears that don't actually interfere much, or at all, with a person's life. People may not even be all that disturbed by these more minor versions of phobias.

◆ To complicate matters further, in medicine (not psychiatry) the word *phobia* can mean an aversion to something for physical, not psychological, reasons. For instance, a person who avoids the pain caused by bright lights during a migraine will be described in their medical chart as having "photophobia."

◆ Finally, the word *phobia* is often used colloquially to mean a dislike, feelings of annoyance, or a preference to avoid something. For instance, you might refer to your "Todd-phobia" if Todd is a co-worker whom you really, really feel squicked by and so try to avoid. Or a politician might be accused of having a "tax phobia" because she resists voting for any new taxes.

Anxiety Disorders

In psychiatry, particularly in the United States, the American Psychiatric Association's manual, the *Diagnostic and Statistical Manual of Mental Disorders* (usually abbreviated "DSM-IV," referring to its current fourth edition) is the official list of mental disorders. This manual lists each diagnosis along with basic information about each condition—the *symptoms* and *signs* of the disorder, information on who is most likely to get the disorder, how long it tends to last, and similar facts.

def•i•ni•tion

Here are two terms people (including shrinks) often mix up: symptoms versus signs. Briefly, **symptoms** are the complaints the person tells to the doctor (e.g., "it hurts when I walk") while **signs** are what the doctor actually observes when she or he examines the patient (e.g., "the patient had swelling in the ankle").

A big section of the DSM-IV manual is devoted to a category of mental disorders called anxiety disorders. In all anxiety disorders, the problem symptoms all revolve around anxiety.

So what's anxiety? Only probably the worst thing you can feel—especially when it's intense.

Anxiety is an uncomfortable feeling. It can include feeling apprehensive, afraid, fretful, stressed, edgy, or ill-at-ease. There are often both psychological and physical parts to it—everything from dry mouth to shaking to upset stomach to headaches to perspiring ... and on and on. Anxiety can make you pace or freeze in your tracks; it can make you bite your nails or compulsively repolish them; it can make you over-study for a test or avoid studying altogether. It can shorten your life, or it can keep you out of jail—depending on how it affects you and how you use it.

Psychologists often distinguish between *anxiety* and *fear*. Sometimes it's not easy to tell them apart, but the rule of thumb is that fear is usually defined as a realistic, reasonable feeling of apprehension or worry that you have when there is some real thing to be afraid of. Real, in this case, means that if you asked the average objective person, they'd agree—yep, that's something to be scared of. Anxiety, on the other hand, is a feeling that doesn't necessarily match up to any real threats or dangers or that is out of proportion to the size of the threat. The average person would be more likely to ask, "Why are you so scared of *that?*"

So for example, it would be normal and appropriate to be afraid if you were trying to walk across a super-busy, multilane highway at rush hour. (It would also probably be nuts to even try to do that, but that's a different discussion.) But it would be less reasonable to be that afraid when walking on the sidewalk on a safe, quiet street on a pleasant spring day. The first feeling would be fear; the second, anxiety.

Anxiety is actually a common everyday experience for most people. Just having an anxious moment or fretting some about a problem you're dealing with (or not dealing with, but just worrying a lot about) is also normal. In order to have a diagnosable anxiety *disorder*, your anxiety has to be quite a bit above and beyond.

When your anxiety problem is so wide-ranging or creates so much difficulty in your life that it seriously starts to bother you or interfere with your functioning in some part of your life, that pretty much always qualifies as an anxiety disorder.

Based on years of research, the authors of the DSM-IV have identified a collection of different kinds of psychological problems that fit under the anxiety disorder umbrella. These include:

◆ Panic attacks

◆ Agoraphobia

◆ Social phobia

◆ Specific phobias

◆ Obsessive-compulsive disorders

◆ Post-traumatic stress disorders

◆ Acute stress disorders

◆ Generalized anxiety disorders

◆ Various other anxiety disorders

Since this is a book on phobias, we'll be concentrating on just a few of these: specific phobias (covered in Part 2), agoraphobia (Chapter 11), social phobia (Chapter 12), and phobias and anxiety that affect children, including things such as school phobias (Chapter 13).

The "Big-Ticket" Phobias

You may be interested in reading about specific phobias, such as a fear of spiders or fear of the dark. But there's also a chance that you're interested in (or suffer from) more broad and disruptive phobias. That's why I'm including in this book three kinds of anxiety problems that can reasonably be called phobias that are fairly complex. All three can cause severe problems for a person, including impaired school or work functioning, difficulty living a "normal" life day to day, and general mental and even physical health issues. These are "big-ticket" problems because, unlike specific phobias that are focused on fairly limited concerns, these three problems can sweep across your whole life and leave only wreckage in their wake. They are agoraphobia, social phobia, and childhood phobias.

In agoraphobia, a person may be afraid of leaving their home or of going into public places. A person with agoraphobia may avoid going places where they might feel unable to escape, or where they fear embarrassment. Often, their major concerns include the fear that they will have an out-of-control reaction such as a *panic attack* if they are in that situation or away from the safety of home.

def•i•ni•tion

A **panic attack** is a severe or even overwhelming anxiety reaction that happens in the absence of any real external threat. A panic attack can include symptoms such as heart palpitations, severe sweating, trembling, and a fear of dying or going crazy.

In social phobia, a person's major fear is of social situations. Social phobics may avoid going to parties, public speaking, answering questions in class, or even answering the phone, depending on their particular fears. Often, the real fear of a person with social phobia is that other people will observe and evaluate or criticize them.

School phobia is a term that many parents and teachers use to describe the problem that some children have when they seem afraid to go to school or perhaps to leave home to go anywhere without their parent. This term is used in this book, but the current diagnosis for this condition in DSM-IV is generally "separation anxiety disorder," because it's felt that most often what the child is really afraid of is separation from home or from the persons they are attached to (usually their parents).

Specific Phobias

When most people talk about phobias, they are referring to specific phobias. If you have a specific phobia, you are afraid of a particular situation, object, or experience.

Specific phobias are different from the other anxiety disorders in that they don't involve pervasive anxiety. Generally, if you're not actually near whatever you fear, you won't be feeling anxious or frightened. For instance, a fear of heights (*acrophobia*) might bother you when you have to climb a ladder or take a stroll along the edge of the Grand Canyon, but it might not be something you think about at other times. So you can go years and years and never experience the fear. (Remember how Indiana Jones was a pretty calm dude except when he was around snakes? That kind of thing.)

You can also have a wide range of fear intensities, from a mild feeling of discomfort around your feared thing to total panic. In some cases, such fears may cause you to restrict your life. You may avoid driving, flying, or going to the dentist or doctor even when you really need medical attention. Other times, the feared object or situation doesn't get in your face very often, and so the impact on your life will be minimal. Because specific phobias are less pervasive, can be fairly mild, and often can be worked around, fewer people seek professional help for dealing with these fears.

Specific phobias can involve fears of everything and anything, from snakes to clowns to sex (or fear of sex with clowns who have snakes).

DSM-IV divides specific phobias into several categories:

- ◆ Animal phobias (like fear of snakes, dogs, etc.)—see Chapter 4
- ◆ Fears of things in the natural environment (like lightning or floods)—see Chapter 5
- ◆ Fear of medical stuff (like fainting at the sight of blood or when getting a shot)—see Chapter 6
- ◆ Situational fears (like public speaking, flying, etc.)—see Chapter 7

Technically, in order to qualify for an official DSM-IV specific phobia diagnosis, your fear of heights or mice has to be severe enough that it either interferes with your life in some way or else really bothers you a lot. If it's not that severe, it can still be called a phobia, but it doesn't warrant an actual anxiety disorder diagnosis.

Let's say your fear of mice (your *musophobia*) keeps you from ever going into your basement—you can't go down there to do the laundry, at least not without taking ten minutes to put on high rubber boots and tucking your pants in and being wet with perspiration. That mouse phobia would qualify at your doctor's office as an anxiety disorder—which would mean, among other things, that it would be severe enough that your health insurance might cover its treatment. (I say "might" because health insurance companies often have a fear of actually paying for legitimately needed treatment, but in all fairness, they should cover it.)

If you just feel that mice are "icky," but it would never stop you from bopping down to the basement or going anywhere else, you might still have a mouse phobia—just not one that is severe enough to merit an anxiety disorder diagnosis. (You could still get it treated and probably make it go away, but good luck getting the insurance company to pay for it!)

In short, some fears, like being hit by a car when trying to cross a busy freeway on foot, are totally realistic and adaptive and not phobias at all. A fear of driving, even on a quiet street in a safe car when you know how to drive just fine, would be a phobia. But that phobia might not merit an anxiety disorder diagnosis unless it caused you either very intense discomfort or disruption or you worry a lot about having it. (If you're just recovering from a car accident and are feeling extra squeamish but manage to drive to work all right, it wouldn't necessarily qualify for the diagnosis. It would be a normal reaction to the accident.)

Fears That Aren't Phobias

Not all fears are, or should be, called phobias. For one thing, nearly all phobias are harmful to the person who has them, while many fears, however uncomfortable, are sometimes quite advantageous. Fear of a mugger's gun may save your life, and fear of flunking out of school has been the motive driving many successful students.

In fact, sometimes the *absence* of fear is more of a problem than its presence. People may take risks, fail to think through major decisions, or otherwise wreck their lives when they aren't fearful enough. Not being afraid of the consequences of smoking, for instance, has been the cause of millions of premature deaths.

Other Causes of Fearfulness

Some fear that is not logically warranted can also be the result of other conditions than basic phobias. For example, a person who has had traumatic experiences in war or related to gunshots may jump or have flashbacks when he or she hears loud pops (like from a car engine backfiring). Or a woman who has been sexually assaulted can develop phobialike discomfort in situations similar to where the assault happened (at night or in parking lots), or she may develop a strong fear response to being around men, to sexual situations, and so on. Since the core problem here is technically *post-traumatic stress disorder,* it may not be diagnosed separately as a phobia.

def•i•ni•tion

Post-traumatic stress disorder is the term for a psychological condition that sometimes results from experiencing a highly frightening or terrifying experience where a person's life was threatened or where they felt extremely helpless; it can lead to persistent re-experiencing of the event through flashbacks or nightmares and distress when re-exposed to similar events, as well as problems like insomnia, depression, poor concentration, anger outbursts, and the like.

People may also become temporarily fearful due to stressful situations, such as being fearful of police cars for a few weeks after they've been pulled over for a speeding ticket. If the fear persists, it can become a phobia, but a short-term condition isn't necessarily a phobia.

I've already mentioned how the word *phobia* can mean something different in medicine than it does in psychology. That's another kind of confusing use of the term *phobia.* But perhaps most confusing is the way the word *phobia* gets used to refer to some fears that may not even exist as such:

◆ **Mild phobias**—Many times we use the word phobia colloquially to refer to reactions that by no stretch of the imagination could be called anxiety disorders. I've already mentioned the humorous example where you tell co-workers that you feel uncomfortable or grossed out by that guy named Todd by joking that you have "Todd-phobia." Often, people call things phobias that are actually fairly minor fears or things that they just find irritating.

◆ **Superstitions**—People also confuse phobias with superstitions. I'll talk in Chapter 9, for instance, about the term *triskaidekaphobia*, which refers to the fear of the number 13. (By the way, don't let it trouble you that there are 13 chapters in this book—that's a coincidence and not intentional, I assure you!) This is seldom actually a phobia in the technical sense; nevertheless, people's discomfort with that number is such a common occurrence that many buildings don't have thirteenth floors! Likewise, some people are afraid of walking under ladders, breaking mirrors, or having a black cat cross their paths (which my black cat, for one, finds ridiculous).

◆ **Spam phobias**—Spam phobias refer to phobia names that are actually generated by Internet search sites when people ask about them. I've even made up nonsense words and done Google searches for "fear of [insert nonsense word here]" and gotten occasional hits. Other terms (for example, *octophobia*, or fear, allegedly, of the number 8) are often mentioned in search engines, but there are no actual descriptions of the conditions, reasons why or how one might experience them, or references to them in the medical and psychological literature.

But here's the interesting thing about phobias: if you can think it, you can probably develop a fear of it. There may be no rational reason to fear the number 8—fair enough. But that doesn't mean a person *couldn't* develop a powerful fear of the number. It happens all the time.

In fact, in a classic psychological experiment done many decades ago, it was shown that it's sometimes amazingly simple to *create* a phobia of a harmless thing in the laboratory, which I'll discuss in Chapter 2.

Real Danger!

Be wary of definitions and descriptions of the phobia from websites that purport to have "fear of [you name it] Clinics." Although these sites always seem to have a vivid description of the symptoms of the phobia, the alert reader will note that all the descriptions are the same and are, in fact, generic lists of anxiety symptoms: "[you name it] phobia can include rapid breathing, increased heart beat ..." etc. (I got over 300 Google hits for the term I made up called *fakephobia*, including sites defining and offering clinics to cure it.) While they may offer standard phobia treatments, I'd personally be cautious about using a clinic if their advertising suggests they have an ongoing "clinic program" for phobias that don't even exist!

The Phobias in This Book

In the chapters that follow, we'll review both specific phobias and the more complex topics of agoraphobia, social phobia, and childhood phobias. Specific phobias are sorted into several different chapters (such as animal phobias or phobias of natural events), and then listed alphabetically in those chapters by the particular fear. For example, in Chapter 4 on animal phobias, if you look up "elephants" and "otters," "elephants" is discussed first.

While there are hundreds of different kinds of phobias that have been named, it's not always clear that there are really many people who may actually have them. Sometimes the term *phobia* is used to refer to something more like a feeling of distaste or aversion for something. Whenever possible, I've made it clear when the term *phobia* is actually referring to something such as an aversion or dislike, and not a true psychological or medical condition (in other words, a diagnosable anxiety disorder).

It's not always easy to tell if a phobia is an actual fear that people really have, and if so, if it is severe enough to qualify for a medical diagnosis. The problem is that we really have *three* things that are quite different from each other, but that are all called phobias:

◆ The severe psychological conditions that really cause people a lot of distress and interfere with their lives

◆ The "colloquial" terms for things or made-up phobia words

◆ Something that is more in the middle—phobias that bother people, but that don't severely mess up their lives, or that they may only notice on rare occasions

Sorting out these distinctions is not always easy, and was not easy when preparing this book.

One problem is that there is often a lack of research on phobias, even though they may be quite troubling for many people. Only a small percentage of phobias have been carefully researched. But many named phobias are real, even though they don't turn up often in the medical or psychological research. Whenever possible, I did consult the vast amount of research on phobias that exists in medical and psychological research databases. But often, phobias I looked for did not turn up in any of these databases—yet it seemed reasonable that they might actually exist.

In those cases, I used another tactic: reading blogs. Using Google blogs, I was often able to find discussions of phobias that had not been mentioned in the thousands of medical and psychological sources I'd searched. I don't mean the "spam blogs" that generate an automatic definition of just about any *-phobia* term, whether it's real or not. (Put any term, like *catnip*, before the suffix *-phobia* and Google it, and you'll probably find a page or two full of online businesses that purport to treat it "in just one session!") But I found that people do write about having many phobias that have not been written about in the scholarly journals. Whenever possible, I've mentioned when phobias seem to be real and when they seem not to have anyone claiming to be troubled by them.

How Big a Deal Are Phobias?

It's part of being human to have fears and anxieties—most of us do. Phobias are part of the human condition, but when they become intense, they can have a serious impact on a person's life.

How common are phobias, and how serious an impact do they have?

The Statistics on Phobias

Most research on phobias is concerned with the most intense level of phobia severity: phobias that actually interfere with a person's life.

Severe phobias are fairly common. The most recent studies done in the United States and other countries have fairly consistent results. At any given moment, between 4 and 9 percent of the population have phobias severe enough to qualify for the most severe diagnosis level (anxiety disorders).

Worse still, just because a person is momentarily phobia-free doesn't mean they won't develop one later. The *lifetime prevalence* of phobias is between 7 and 11 percent. In other words, the odds are between 7 and 11 in 100 that, at some time in your life, you'll have a severe phobia. (The odds are much higher that you either will or already do have a mild phobia or two. Or ten.)

def•i•ni•tion

Researchers use two different terms to describe how common a medical condition is. **Prevalence** means how many people in a population (such as in a community) have the condition at any one point in time. **Lifetime prevalence** refers to the number of people in that population who will have the condition at some point in their lives.

The odds of developing phobias are slightly different and are dependent on many factors. Most commonly studied are how gender, social/cultural background, and age affect your odds of having a phobia. There are many different studies of these risk factors. Here are some of the most commonly studied:

◆ **Gender**—Most studies show that women are more likely to develop specific phobias by a margin of nearly two to one. This varies a lot depending on the kinds of phobias studied. For instance, many more women get animal phobias, but the blood-injection-injury rates are closer to being equal. And like many other mental health concerns, it's also likely that more women than men are willing to admit to having phobias or to seek help with them, thus skewing the statistics.

♦ **Age**—Many phobias start in childhood, while others don't develop until later in life. For instance, most animal phobias and fears of blood-injection-injury may begin in early childhood. (And many children may have brief bouts of fears that don't "stick" as phobias.) Other fears, such as social phobia, tend to start in early adolescence. Still others, like fear of driving, fear of heights, or fears of being trapped in enclosed spaces, don't develop until late teens or early twenties.

♦ **Cultural background**—Overall rates of phobias in the United States are lower among Asian and Hispanic individuals. Some phobias, such as social phobia, occur in higher percentages of Native Americans. Different phobias may occur more often in some cultures than others; for instance, cultures where beliefs in magic or witchcraft are common may have higher rates of phobias about these beliefs. In times/places where certain diseases are more visible or rampant, there will be more fears of them. (People seldom develop phobias of leprosy if they've seldom or never seen it and so don't know much about it or feel threatened by it.)

♦ **Other mental health conditions**—You are more likely to have a particular kind of phobia if you already have another phobia of the same type. For instance, research shows about seven out of ten people who develop an injection phobia will also develop a blood phobia. Likewise, the odds of developing other mental health problems, such as clinical depression, tend to be higher among people who struggle with phobias.

How Phobias Affect People

If a phobia is severe enough that it can merit an official anxiety disorder diagnosis, it's severe enough to be very unpleasant and to disrupt your life.

A phobia will trigger an anxiety reaction. Anxiety reactions include strong emotions, as well as physical or bodily responses, changes in your thinking, and changes in your behavior—they pretty much hit you on every level.

Emotions can include everything from vague uneasy feelings to severe, out-of-control panic feelings. Fear, dread, or even terror can be part of it.

Physically, depending on the reaction, an anxious person can experience trembling, faintness, heart palpitations, perspiration, dizziness, rapid heart rate, dry mouth, and so on. With some phobias (such as the blood-injection-injury kinds), you can have a vasovagal response in which an elevated heart rate and increased blood pressure suddenly shift into a slowed heart rate and decreased blood pressure such that the brain suddenly is deprived of oxygen and you faint.

Thinking is also affected by anxiety. When you are anxious, you may tend to focus only on the thing you are afraid of—a snake phobic will only see the snake or will be totally engrossed in scanning the lawn for signs of snakes. This "tunnel vision" effect can interfere with judgment and perspective and can increase your anxiety still further.

As for behavior changes, the strong urge to avoid or escape a fear-inducing situation is the primary response. At times, this can lead to very unsafe actions, such as when a bee-phobic person driving a car suddenly sees a bee inside and swerves around on the road or even crashes. Another common problem caused by phobias is avoiding situations that a person ought not to avoid. Not attending a friend's or relative's wedding, missing school or work, or avoiding certain jobs or errands because of fears of one kind or another can be very disruptive.

It's estimated that millions of people miss out on, avoid, or have difficulties in school, work, and social situations due to phobias. In addition, phobias tend to increase people's vulnerability to developing other mental health problems, which in turn take their toll on people's functioning.

The Least You Need to Know

- Phobias have probably always existed—there are descriptions of phobias in ancient medical texts. But the term "phobia" has only been used regularly since the 1800s.

- Phobias are considered anxiety disorders in the world's medical diagnostic systems (such as the International Classification of Diseases, or the American Psychiatric Association's *Diagnostic and Statistical Manual,* or DSM-IV).

◆ A phobia is defined as a marked and persistent fear of an object or situation that is excessive or not justified by the reality of the feared thing. To be diagnosed as an anxiety disorder-level phobia, it has to be very disruptive of your life or bother you a great deal.

◆ Some phobias are not severe enough to be diagnosed as anxiety disorders, though they may still bother you a little bit. Other so-called phobias are more like superstitions—or may not exist at all!

Chapter 2

What Causes Phobias?

In This Chapter

- ◆ Why we emote
- ◆ Our built-in fear system
- ◆ How thinking and learning create fears

A former vice-president once said, "It's a terrible thing to lose one's mind." It's frustrating and scary to lose control. When our minds don't behave, it can throw us. Losing control over our memories, thoughts, or especially our feelings can leave us feeling vulnerable, disoriented, or "crazy."

This is one reason that phobias are so uncomfortable. Most of us aren't too bothered if we're afraid of things that are objectively, clearly frightening: hissing king cobras and falling off ladders *should* terrify us. But when those fears extend to garter snakes or step stools, it's a sign that our fears are out of control. Try as we might, we can't make ourselves go near, touch, or think about the feared object or situation. At that point, we have lost control of the closest and most important thing about ourselves: our own minds.

One way to regain some control is to understand what's going on. So let's use this chapter to explore the whys and wherefores of emotions and the causes of phobias. Once you understand what's going on, regaining control is much easier. And understanding how fears and phobias work is a key part of understanding some of the biggest truths about human psychology.

What Good Are Emotions, Anyway?

If you're afflicted by a severe phobia (or maybe a case of depression, sadness, or just garden-variety grumpiness), you may be wondering why we need emotions at all. Sometimes they seem like nothing but trouble and aggravation. Wouldn't we all be better off if we could be as logical as Mr. Spock or Data of *Star Trek* fame?

It sounds nice, maybe, once in a while—particularly when your feelings and anxieties are making your life miserable. But the truth is, not to feel would leave most of us more dead than alive. And that's true both psychologically and physically. It's true psychologically because a big part of feeling alive comes from having emotions. Good feelings just feel good—happiness, relief, joy. But even negative emotions (fear, anxiety, anger) can help us feel engaged, involved, alive. Plus, we feel *so* good when the bad feelings stop, right? But feeling things keeps us alive physically, too. Without emotions, we might literally not survive a day in the "jungle" of life on Earth.

The world is often a dangerous place. It can be too cold, too hot, too wet, or too dry, and there are things everywhere that bite, sting, and maybe even eat us. In order to survive, every animal, insect, and even single-celled organisms like amoebas must rely on built-in defensive systems. For humans, one of the most important defensive systems are our emotions.

Fear is one of our most powerful defenses. We all fear many things, and most of those fears are healthy. Like little guides or motivators, our fears are often quiet little background noises, just loud enough to keep us on track and safe.

For instance, we generally fear getting sick just enough to dress warmly and take vitamins. We fear car wrecks just enough to drive safely and wear our seatbelts. We fear social disapproval just enough to be polite to others and wear clean clothes when out in public. And how many banks have you robbed lately?

These fears persist because they work for us. Our fears ensure that we avoid physical threats and manage social dangers. We get our work done on time because of the fear of losing our jobs if we don't; we return our library books and keep our tires inflated because of the consequences if we don't.

So fears and anxieties are often good for us. Your fear can be your friend.

The problem, of course, is that too much fear can backfire. Instead of helping you to drive more carefully, your fear of car crashes may prevent you from driving at all. Instead of protecting you from the rare dangerous rattlesnake, your fear of snakes may prevent you from going anywhere outdoors that isn't covered in asphalt. And a normal respect for the need to get along with others might turn into a social phobia that keeps you from developing friends or romances.

Simply put, phobias are just a matter of too much of a good thing. This raises the question of how healthy fear responses can develop into phobias.

Fear Is in Our Genes

Psychologists studying this question have approached it from two directions. One approach is to focus on the *physical* origins of phobias— the way fear has been wired into our bodies and brains. The idea is that if we can understand how that wiring went awry, we can repair the problem physically.

The other approach to understanding phobias is to look at them from a *psychological* perspective. In other words, how do our experiences, memories, and the things we think and do contribute to creating phobias? If our experiences, whether they are traumas or just the lessons we are taught as kids, affect our fear "set points," we can easily modify these and so keep our kids from becoming phobic. If what we think about or imagine affects our fears, we can change that.

Phobia Science

When doing research, psychologists may try to isolate and study only one factor at a time, whether it's physical or mental, that contributes to a problem like phobias. In real life, though, we know that there are few simple, either-or causes of phobias. Genes, environment, experience, and how we think are all factors in creating our fears.

Our "Fight or Flight" System

Humans have a defensive system called our "fight or flight" system. When threatened by anything from a charging rhino to a slithering snake to a bullying co-worker, our nervous systems automatically respond. Sometimes we react by literally fighting back; other times, with a very sensible urge to run away. Still other times, we may react by freezing up or feeling paralyzed, in which case our bodies may literally shut down (which can be very useful in not provoking an angry, club-wielding maniac).

Our fear system is a built-in, genetic part of our makeup. Our brains and endocrine systems are both designed to respond to threats, danger, or pain. When you become aware of a threat, such as by hearing a sudden loud crack of thunder or touching a hot stove, signals from your sensory system (your ears, eyes, sense of touch) travel up nerve pathways to your brain. These signals are instantly processed in various areas of the brain (depending on the kind they are—for instance, visual information is handled in a different place than smells or touch or other senses).

If the information includes signals that are associated with bodily threat (such as pain from that stove), the fight or flight system is activated. Immediately, a number of things happen in your body, such as:

◆ Your heart rate increases.

◆ Your stomach and intestines become less active in digestion, freeing up energy (e.g., from blood flow to those areas) for use in your large muscles (the ones you will have to fight or run with).

◆ Blood vessels in many parts of your body may become constricted, while the blood vessels in your large muscles become dilated.

◆ Pupils may dilate.

These changes, and many more, enable you to cope with a physical threat or emergency. Virtually every body system may, in fact, become involved in the emergency response. You become more alert, more "charged up" to fight, or you may become scared and anxious, ready to back off or run.

Our emergency response system evolved to help us survive, and it's served us well. Being able to rapidly recognize and respond to threats kept our ancestors alive. You are here today because your ancestors got frightened just fast enough to escape when animals attacked or when floods or fires threatened. (And so they got to live long enough to be fruitful and multiply, while their less fearful brothers and sisters ended up as tiger food before they could pass on their genes.) So congratulations are in order to you and your ancestors!

When Healthy Fears Go Wild

Our emotional self-defense system protected us from common dangers back in prehistoric times. But in modern times, these ancient fears may not be so useful. For instance, most people in the developed world live nowhere near truly dangerous snakes, yet the fear of snakes is common. (In fact, some researchers point out that more than eight in ten of people who have phobias of snakes have never even seen or had contact with an actual, living snake.) On the other hand, as pointed out by Helen Saul in her book *Phobias: Fighting the Fear* (see Appendix B), few of us develop phobias of more modern objects or situations that truly are dangerous, such as moving automobiles or IRS audits.

When healthy fears go wild, get out of control, or persist when they are no longer needed, that's a problem. They may become minor phobias or full-blown, severe phobias that merit an anxiety disorder diagnosis.

Is there a biological explanation for the fact that our built-in fear reactions get out of control? Absolutely. In fact, a bit of reflection would show that it's almost inevitable that many people would be biologically prone to such overreaction.

People vary on all sorts of biological traits, whether it's height, eye color, or the speed of their reflexes. The biological parts of any fear reaction depend on a complicated set of brain and hormone responses in the body, and some of us will just be naturally better at triggering those responses. While 30,000 years ago that skill might have meant that those more responsive-to-danger people survived the dangers of the African savannah, nowadays it just makes them more likely to become "anxiety disordered."

Part of what is happening in that case is that your fight-or-flight system is, for some reason, overly active. Just as an allergic response happens when your immune system overreacts to harmless substances and treats them as dangerous toxins, your nervous system overreacts to harmless events and treats them like life-threatening dangers. So seeing a picture of a snake or flying in an airplane triggers the full-bore "Danger!" areas of your brain, and you're afraid.

For instance, there is evidence that socially anxious individuals may have higher levels of activity in a brain area called the amygdala, a part of the limbic system that is activated when we feel fear. People with public speaking anxiety also seem to have higher levels of amygdala activation than other people do. Other areas of the brain associated with anxiety reactions include the anterior cingulate cortex (which helps control emotions, heart rate, and thought), the hippocampus (related to memory and spatial ability), and the insular cortex (another part of the limbic system, related to experiences of emotion). Certain differences in neurotransmitters, such as dopamine, may function differently in people with higher propensities to become anxious.

Are Phobias Inherited?

Some of us, then, may just have a physical tendency to react more strongly with fear or anxiety—meaning that the parts of our brains that recognize and respond to danger signals have lower thresholds for responding to threat. This fits well with the fact that the *comorbidity* of anxiety disorders and phobias is fairly high: people who get one phobia or other anxiety disorder are more likely to develop other such fears or reactions as well. The fact that many people who develop phobias also have relatives with phobias, and that even

def•i•ni•tion

Comorbidity refers to having more than one disease or illness at the same time. High levels of comorbidity between one disorder and another might suggest that the two conditions are somehow related, share the same medical cause, or affect each other in some way.

identical twins reared apart tend to develop similar anxiety problems, tends to support the idea that there is something inheritable in phobias and other anxiety conditions.

Many of our fears may be at least partially hard-wired into our nervous systems. Scientists now speculate that there was an evolutionary, survival advantage to some fears and that our ancestors may have evolved these fears as protective devices. For instance, ancestors who tended to feel more squicked or uncomfortable than others in areas of the world infested by poisonous snakes would have avoided snakes more than their peers—and so would have survived in higher numbers to pass along their "easily squicked by snakes" genes.

Partially genetically-programmed fears in humans may include fears of snakes, spiders, thunder and lightning, darkness, blood, heights, and angry people. In addition, most infants show signs of fears of strangers, a fear which starts to be apparent at about the time the infant is able to crawl. (This makes sense: when you're old enough to move around, there's a greater survival need to avoid adults who are not your safe, reliable mommy or daddy.)

There is also evidence that people who have family members with anxiety disorders are more likely to develop them as well. Of course, lots of anxiety among family members may just reflect the fact that children growing up in an anxious environment may pick up the vibes of their anxious parents or siblings. Studies of biologically identical twins who have been raised in different environments have suggested that some kinds of anxiety, such as generalized anxiety disorder, don't seem as likely to be inherited. Other kinds of phobias, such as panic disorder, agoraphobia, and blood-injection-injury phobias, may be more likely to be at least partially genetically based.

Fear Is in Your Mind

While it's likely that phobias are partly biological, genetic and physical causes only account for a part of the problem. A big part of the cause of phobias seems to be psychological.

One way to think about this is that you probably can't inherit a phobia or anxiety disorder. At most, you might inherit a biological

def•i•ni•tion

Negative affects (not "effects" — it's spelled with an "a") is a psychological term for unpleasant emotions, such as depression or sadness. Negative affectivity is the tendency to experience higher-than-average amounts of negative feelings.

vulnerability, or tendency, to become more anxious. Some parts of our personalities, such as our general anxiety or depression-proneness, or our tendency to experience *negative affects*, appear to be biological. But even if you have the genes or this biological vulnerability, that doesn't mean you are guaranteed to develop a phobia or other anxiety disorder.

An example of how your psychology and your genetic makeup work together is in the area of sports. Some people have the genetic talents needed to excel in one or another sport. You may be naturally able to run fast or to swim faster than other people. Your leg length, musculature, or cardiac capacity may be better suited than average to a particular sport. But you won't always make it to the Olympics even if you have that fine bod going for you—it depends on whether you happen to get interested in running or swimming, if you get the support for practicing that you need, and whether you actually keep at it on the track or in the pool day after day for the years it takes to become a major athlete. Inborn talent takes you only so far.

The same principle applies to your vulnerability to anxiety, depression, or most physical diseases. Your blood pressure may be inclined to be high, but if you exercise and eat sensibly, you can almost certainly manage it reasonably well. Likewise, your anxiety system may be more vulnerable, but that doesn't guarantee you'll develop a phobia. It all depends on some psychological factors, including your experiences, your thinking, and other factors.

Learning, Experience, and Phobias

The little boy—he was only 11 months old—sat happily on the mattress and watched the fuzzy white laboratory rat sniffing around. Without fear, the boy reached out and played with the animal. There was no reason to think the boy was at all frightened of the rat—he looked relaxed and happy to play with his fuzzy new friend.

The next time he touched the rat, a researcher standing behind the boy hit a suspended metal bar with a hammer, startling the boy with the loud clang. The boy became visibly upset and began to cry. After that, every time the boy touched the rat, the researcher clanged the gong.

Within a short time, the little boy would become upset and cry every time the rat came near. He also became afraid of furry dogs, fur coats, and researchers wearing bearded Santa Claus masks.

The little boy was the subject of a famous study done in 1920 by psychologist John B. Watson. "Little Albert," as the boy was called in the report of the experiment, went down in history as an example of the way we can become conditioned to fear harmless objects. In short, Little Albert has often been considered to be the first example of an "experimental phobia."

Phobia Science

The Little Albert experiment was done in 1920, well before our modern concern with the ethical treatment of participants in psychological experiments. Nowadays, the Little Albert experiment would be considered highly unethical, since neither poor Albert nor his mother were aware of the experiment and so could not give informed consent to be made the subject of a fear-causing procedure.

Nobody knows what ever happened to Little Albert; his mom (an employee of the hospital where Watson worked) apparently heard about the experimenting on her baby and so quit her job and moved away— no forwarding address or anything! The fate of Little Albert and his rat phobia was lost to history.

In fact, we don't know whether the boy actually developed a phobia to rats, to anything fuzzy, or even to psychologists. But we do know that the basic model or theory of phobia-creation that was kicked off by Watson's research has been one of the major models of phobia creation in the field of psychology.

The idea is fairly simple and intuitive: we learn from experience. If we have had mostly positive experiences with something, we tend to feel good when we have the experience. Ditto negative experiences.

So if your first exposure to kittens and cats is of pretty, fuzzy little animals that purr softly and cuddle in your lap, and if your mom has an enthusiastic reaction to the "pretty kitty" and pets it with you, you will probably learn to like cats. But if the first cat you meet hisses, scratches, and bites you, or if your mom starts screaming about the "dirty filthy cats!," you may learn to fear Tabby and all the other tabbies you meet.

There are two major learning theories of phobias. In one version, which is basically the Little Albert model, phobias are emotional responses that are conditioned by experiences you have. In this model, negative, frightening experiences that are paired up with innocuous objects train you to fear those objects.

A second learning model is the operant conditioning model, in which you learn to be afraid of something because you have somehow (maybe accidentally) been rewarded for the fear response. For example, if you are scared of being hit by a baseball, and so your gym teacher lets you sit out the inning and read instead, you may feel rewarded for the fear. After awhile, every time you don't take the risk of being hit by the ball or don't get back on the horse that scared you, you are rewarded by your body's reactions—the drop in anxiety, the feeling of calm that you get once you know you don't have to get back on the horse. The operant conditioning model might account for fears that have to do with avoiding unpleasant activities or situations.

In addition to these two types of learning, it's thought possible to "absorb" a phobia by observing someone else's phobic behavior. This makes a certain amount of sense, if you figure that we all learn what's dangerous in our worlds from others.

Last but not least is trauma. Extremely powerful, overwhelming, threatening experiences will often trigger a conditioned response in a person, which can include or lay the groundwork for phobias. For instance, being in a mild fender-bender accident on an icy road will sometimes make a person frightened of driving again. This reaction can even begin to expand or become more powerful—a kind of "spreading phobia" effect that often results in a situation where one frightening situation starts to get bigger and more frightening. Eventually, a person may become afraid not just of driving on the kind of icy road that caused their accident but also of driving on dry roads—and even of being driven places by someone else.

The Unconscious Bits

Fifty years ago, your best hope for getting cured of a severe phobia might have been to go consult with your local psychoanalyst. According to the school of psychology called psychoanalysis, founded by Sigmund Freud in Vienna in the early parts of the twentieth century, psychological problems were mostly the result of conflicts in the parts of our minds that we aren't even aware of—our unconscious.

How would Freud explain a phobia in his theory? Well, to start with, Freud might have said that the thing you *think* you are afraid of (rats, for instance—Freud also treated a man with a rat phobia) isn't what you *really* fear. The rats (or spiders or horses) might unconsciously represent something entirely different—something it would be too painful for you to face or even think about ... or maybe just something that was hard for you to articulate or identify.

For example, Freud guided a father by mail in the treatment of the man's young son, who had a fear of horses. "Little Hans" developed this fear after seeing a horse collapse in the street. After the incident, Hans became afraid that a horse might bite him or come into his room and collapse. He had several other fears as well.

Freud analyzed the case as having to do with some of Hans's normal little-boy fears, such as the insecurities related to his parents having another baby, fears about sexual feelings, and related things. His approach to treatment was to encourage the father to talk with the boy, listen to his fears, and help him understand some of the things he was afraid of. While Freud's notions of the specific fears Hans had might not be as popular today, his basic approach to helping a distressed child—a more patient, comforting, and soothing process of listening to the child and helping him or her understand their fears—would still be considered excellent psychological work by many therapists.

The unconscious model of phobias is not as popular among therapists and researchers today as it once was. More contemporary models, including learning models, biological models, and cognitive models of phobias are probably more useful in most cases. But sometimes it can be really helpful to recognize that your phobia is somehow connected to something else, something that has been frightening or bothering you. For instance, a fear of driving might turn out to be a fear that, if you take the wheel, your spouse (who always drives) will criticize you—so the fear isn't of driving but of being criticized.

Cognitive Models of Phobias

Over the past quarter-century, new research and models for understanding phobias have evolved. One of the most popular is called *cognitive behavior therapy*, or CBT.

def•i•ni•tion ⎯⎯⎯⎯⎯⎯⎯⎯⎯⎯⎯⎯⎯⎯⎯⎯⎯⎯⎯⎯⎯⎯⎯⎯

Cognitive behavior therapy (CBT) is a form of therapy for depression and anxiety disorders that assumes that these conditions result from the things we tell ourselves. Treatment involves becoming aware of our "automatic" or habitual thoughts, analyzing them, and learning how to tell ourselves new and more effective things—to change what we think and how we think about it.

Most of the time, we tend to think in habitual, familiar ways about our experiences, problems, and concerns—which is fine, unless our habitual thinking patterns cause us to develop psychological or other kinds of problems. In that case, the trick is to take conscious control of your thinking process and do some things differently.

Cognitive therapy researchers have studied the thinking processes of people with anxiety disorders and phobias. They have found that phobic or anxious people often think differently than other folks (or than they do when they're not thinking about their phobias).

One thing phobics do is to maintain what they term a "cognitive bias" toward threatening situations. If, for instance, you have a fear of flying, you will tend to have a kind of bias in which you pay more attention to news about plane crashes. You will think more about things that could go wrong on a flight. At the airport, you may focus your attention more than other people on whatever it is about flying that most scares you. So if it's the risk of crashing, you'll really tune in to the flight attendants' little speeches about safety (the thing most people ignore after their first couple of airplane rides). If it's the fear of being cooped up in a tight, airless airplane, you'll notice how crowded the airport is, your gate is, and the planes are.

This bias tends, then, to create a mental state of hypervigilance, in which you are more aware of threats than others. Now, the problem with being super watchful for the bad news is that you start to filter out, or fail to notice, the good news. Pretty soon, you will have managed to convince yourself that the news is *all* bad, the dangers are overwhelming, and there are no ways to cope. Your bias toward the negative, toward threats, tends to get stronger because you are, in effect, rehearsing your anxiety over and over again.

Real Danger!

Beware of creating a self-fulfilling prophecy! If you are afraid of falling on the ice, you'll become so aware of the slipperiness and danger that your body will stiffen up, your gait will become awkward, and you'll be much more likely to fall. If you're afraid of panicking when out in public, your constant tuning in to how anxious you get when out will merely serve to crank up your anxiety levels further.

CBT therapists say people develop "schemas," which are basically collections or networks of beliefs about the world. A person with anxiety disorders may develop a complicated set of beliefs about the dangers they face, and these beliefs will make it more difficult for the person to be objective about their fears. Their biased schemas, or expectations and beliefs, about the things they fear affect every stage of their experience: their first impressions of the situation, how they experience being around the thing they fear, and their memory of what happened afterward. So even if you manage to get through a frightening airplane flight or horseback ride, you may tend to remember the experience as worse than it actually was!

It's been found that different kinds of phobias or anxiety disorders have different characteristic cognitive processes that fuel them. For instance, people with social phobia tend to be hyperaware of any hint that others might be viewing them critically. Agoraphobics (see Chapter 11) may be super tuned in to any hint that they are feeling anxious while out in public.

As we explore the specific phobias, and later, the major phobias of agoraphobia, social phobia, and school phobia, we'll examine the thinking processes that tend to go along with each type of phobia.

The Least You Need to Know

♦ One difference between phobias and other fears is our experience that, in the phobia, we've lost control of our reactions—this makes us doubly uncomfortable with phobias.

♦ Emotions such as fear are usually healthy and valuable in protecting us from dangers and keeping us on the ball. But when the fears are excessive and unreasonable, we may be sliding into phobia territory.

♦ There are different explanations for how phobias develop. It's most likely that a combination of genetic, biological, and psychological causes combine to create phobias.

♦ Mental causes of phobias can include learning experiences, traumas, or cognitive behavior (habitual patterns of thought), such as being hypervigilant to possible danger.

Getting Help with Phobias

In This Chapter

- ◆ Basic phobia treatments: how to desensitize yourself to your fears
- ◆ Cognitive therapy for phobias
- ◆ When to bring in the pros

When I was in graduate school getting my doctorate in clinical psychology, the very first thing we were taught was how to treat specific phobias. This was not an accident—new therapists are often taught how to tackle phobias before more complex problems such as depression or psychoses because phobia treatment makes a great "basic therapy" skill builder.

The reason for this is simple: specific phobias are relatively easy to treat. Most people can eliminate, or at least greatly reduce, a phobia with modern therapy methods. Even better news is that these treatments aren't all that complicated. If you take them step-by-step, you can often reduce a phobia in a fairly short period of time—even without professional help.

Of course, not all phobias are simple, and so your treatment mileage may vary. But even complicated phobias such as agoraphobia or social phobia, or phobias involving children, can be treated a step at a time using these same basic methods.

In this chapter we'll survey the basic phobia treatment approaches. We'll start with the most "classic" approach—systematic desensitization. Then we'll look at the newer techniques of cognitive behavior therapy and other approaches to phobia treatment. Finally, we'll talk about the pros and cons of getting professional help for your phobias.

Systematic Desensitization Therapy

When a person is bothered or troubled by some situation and then they stop letting it get to them, they often say they're less sensitive about that topic or situation. They may even say they've gotten desensitized to the topic—as in, "It used to bother me at the health club when I'd see my overweight bod in the big mirror, but since I've gone regularly, I've gotten desensitized to it."

In the treatment of phobias, desensitization works something like that. *Systematic desensitization* is a treatment method that was invented by psychologist Joseph Wolpe over fifty years ago. It has been proven effective as a phobia treatment in hundreds of studies. It's simple to use (with practice and maybe some guidance), and it's useful for treating virtually all phobias.

def•i•ni•tion

Systematic desensitization is a treatment for phobias that helps people become less anxious about a feared situation or object, using a combination of relaxation training and gradual exposure to the feared situation, so that the scary situation triggers a less powerful fear reaction over time.

How does it work? The idea is actually fairly simple and even familiar to most people. The core of the idea is that a person becomes less emotionally reactive (or sensitive) to the things they fear by systematic exposure to the feared object or situation. In addition, the treatment involves practicing a different, calmer emotional reaction whenever they are exposed to the things they fear.

In other words, if you learn to relax when you're around those horses, riding in the car, or looking down from that high space, you'll gradually have more and more experiences of being calm in the face of your phobia and will generally melt the phobia away.

It's the same basic idea that parents use when they have a child who gets water up her nose in the swimming pool or gets splashed. Perhaps the child starts to cry and is suddenly afraid of being in the water. Most parents know that the key to preventing a lifetime of fear of water is to gradually, gently help the child back into the pool so they can have new, more positive experiences in the water that erase the bad memory.

There are several standard steps to systematic desensitization therapy:

1. Training in relaxation techniques

2. Learning to rate your anxiety level

3. Building an "anxiety hierarchy" list of fears

4. Pairing each item on the hierarchy with relaxation—the opposite of fear

Let's look at each of these steps in greater detail.

Learning Deep Relaxation

When he was inventing desensitization therapy, Joseph Wolpe speculated that one key to overcoming fear was to break the link between the feared object and the feelings of fear. This was based on the idea that a phobia consists of two things that have gotten linked in your mind:

♦ The object or situation (whether it's heights, horses, blood, etc.)

♦ Feelings of fear

This was viewed as a conditioned pairing of the two things in your mind. You may recall from Chapter 2 that John Watson, in a classic (if ethically shoddy) experiment, clanged a loud gong whenever the toddler named Little Albert touched a fuzzy white rat. The gong was paired with the rat in the boy's mind, so he developed a laboratory phobia of white rats.

In order to break that link between the object and the fear emotion, Wolpe introduced a new emotional reaction or feeling that was not compatible with the fear. The idea is logical: it's usually very hard to feel two highly different feelings at the same time. If you are sleepy, you can't also be super alert. If you're sad, it's hard to be happy. If you're relaxed, you can't be terrified at the same time. The relaxation tends to shut down the fear.

This was not a totally new idea. For centuries, yoga instructors and other teachers, not to mention good animal trainers, bartenders, and moms everywhere, have known that helping a person (or a horse) to be calm tends to reduce their fear. And yoga teachers, horse trainers, bartenders, and moms all have their ways of doing that. Likewise, in desensitization therapy, the first step is to teach yourself how to relax.

Now, you may be saying, "Hey, I already know how to relax ... but I still have my phobias!" Not so fast—we are talking about being skilled at relaxing in a new way, not just falling asleep in the recliner! In desensitization therapy, the real key is learning to switch on relaxation feelings fairly quickly, reduce your body's muscle tension, slow your breathing, and trigger peaceful feelings whenever you need to reduce your stress level. This takes technique and practice. If you know anything about high-performance athletes or dancers, you'll know that they often have to work for months or years in order to learn to manage their bodies' and minds' states of relaxation. Relaxation is not always easy to switch on or to maintain.

In systematic desensitization, we assume that it may take at least a few weeks of daily practice sessions to learn to control your relaxation well enough to even start the rest of the therapy. The goal is to get to the point where you can drop from, say, a 9 or 10 on a "how anxious am I?" scale to a 2 or 3, meaning very relaxed, in just a few moments.

There are several ways to develop this skill. Some people prefer meditative approaches, such as sitting quietly and visualizing a lit candle or a peaceful scene (the bubbling brook in the woods, the beach, etc.) Others take deep, slow breaths and focus on something such as the feeling of the breathing itself. Some may imagine a single number, like "1," with each exhalation; others may count each deep abdominal breath.

Therapists often teach a person to relax using an exercise involving tensing and relaxing every muscle group in the body, one at a time. For instance, you might start by focusing on one simple thing: your hands. The "script" the therapist reads as you recline in a chair or on a couch might go this way:

1. "Focus on your hands. Make a fist. Make it a very, very tight fist—as tight as you can. Hold that tension—harder! Harder!" (The therapist silently counts to five …)

2. "Now … relax! Open your hands. Just let them open. Feel the heavy, warm, relaxed feeling in your hands and fingers, in your forearms, as the warm blood rushes into your hands … Just relax …" (The therapist silently counts to ten and repeats the hand tension instruction, then moves on to the upper arms, shoulders, feet, legs, etc.)

If you do this kind of exercise with a therapist, they may tape record it and give you the tape to play for yourself at home in your practice sessions. Or, you may find a script for this on the Internet and create your own recording—some people prefer to hear their own voice as they do the exercise.

> **Try This!**
>
> The key is practice, practice, practice! As you rehearse this kind of exercise, you get better and better at inducing fast, deeper relaxation in your muscles and stronger peaceful feelings emotionally. You will need this skill for the next part of the desensitization. Remember, professional athletes practice relaxation daily for the same reason—it takes skill to do it fast, deep, and well.

Learning to Rate Your Anxiety Level

Think of the last time you felt really, really scared of something. Recall the feeling, and the situation, as vividly as you can for a few moments.

Rate how scared you felt in that situation, on a scale from 0 to 100, with 100 the "highest possible fear" end of the scale. Your rating should be near 100, if we assume that 100 is the most fear you can imagine ever feeling. Write the rating down.

Next, remember the most peaceful, wonderful, relaxed moment you can recall. That day in the sun at the beach? After lovemaking? When dancing with your love? Remember that feeling as well … the most peaceful you've ever felt. Now rate that on the 0–100 scale as well. Write the rating down.

Most people rate their most feared situation at about 100 (or in the high 90s, anyway); they rate the most peaceful, relaxed memory in the low numbers—0 or 1, or no greater than 10. What really matters is that you write these ratings down so that you will remember them.

What you've just done was to create a personal rating scale that has two "anchor" ratings, one at the high and one at the low end. If you are fairly clear on the difference between your high fear level ratings and your most-relaxed ratings, you can begin to use this scale for rating phobia situations.

Try This!

Just for practice, rate how anxious you are feeling right now on a 1 (low) to 10 (high) scale. High end? Low end? Practice this a few times through the day.

Rating your emotion level is another important skill you learn in desensitization therapy. It's useful for the therapy exercises, but more importantly, knowing how to rate your emotions helps you understand your phobia better. Once you have a familiar rating scale, you have a measuring tool—your own personal "mind dipstick." You can use it to do experiments and learn a lot of important things about how your fears operate.

In desensitization therapy, you may find it helpful to keep a little note-book or log where you write down what your feeling ratings are. You can use it in the next step—building your own personal list of terrors and fears.

Building Your Anxiety Hierarchy

All fears are not created equal. Even if you have a single, specific phobia, you may actually have many different little "subfears" that make up that one big fear. Knowing what the many little parts of your fear are can help you develop a list of targets to work on in the therapy.

Suppose, for instance, you are afraid of dogs. You may have been attacked while doing your mail route by someone's large, snarling Doberman pinscher—and so now you fear running into dogs on your mail route.

But not all dogs are created equal, right? If you recall the Doberman attack, you may recall that on a 0–10 scale, you felt a 10+ as the Doberman leapt at you. And imagining *any* other dog attack you say, would give you that same 10+ rating.

Hold on! What if the dog in question was only a little beagle puppy, sleeping on a carpet in the sunshine inside a locked screen door? Do you *really* pull such a high anxiety rating imagining Baby Snoopy?

I didn't think so. Maybe that's only a 3 or 4 on your anxiety scale, right?

The fact is, few people are equally scared of every possible situation involving their phobias. A fear of heights may make standing on the top rung of a 15-foot ladder seem impossible, but standing on the first rung may not be so awful. And the fifth rung is probably somewhere in between.

So what you do next in the treatment is build a list of fears. Brainstorm 'em and write 'em down. List as many fears or examples of your phobia as you can. As you do, rate how frightening each item is to you. (Hint: the best way to do this may be on index cards so you can shuffle them around.)

For example, let's go back to the Doberman situation. You might imagine the dog leaping for your throat at a 99+; as you recall that episode, your heart starts to pound and you feel really awful.

When you're a little calmer, make a list of some other situations, and rate them. You might, for instance, come up with these:

- Standing right next to a large, growling dog—85

- Standing 10 feet away from a medium-size dog whose tail is wagging—65

- The Doberman is barking at me and running toward me, but is still a half a block away—90

- Beagle puppy sleeping on porch—15

- Small dog on a leash, tail wagging, sniffs my hand—25

… and so on. Try to come up with about 20 items—more is better (I've had clients generate 100!). Most importantly, try to get items that are fairly evenly scattered along the 0–100 scale. You will need some that are really easy starter items and some that are at the top of your fear chart.

Just for a quality check, toss in one cat. As in:

- Cat sleeping on couch—(rating)

Unless you have a cat phobia, your rating on the cat item (or whatever you pick that is totally different from your phobia items) should be a zero. If you somehow spike a 50 on the item that isn't even a phobia, you're making some error in your ratings.

Review this list a few times and see if the ratings hold. Tinker with it until you have a list of between 10 and 20 items.

Working Through Your Anxiety Hierarchy

Once you have practiced your relaxation skills and have a reliable set of about 20 anxiety items arranged by how much fear they create from low to high, you're ready for the core of the treatment. The steps are simple:

1. Get yourself in a comfortable position, and do your relaxation exercises till you are relaxed.

2. While relaxed (rate how relaxed you are on your scale), pick up the card with the lowest-rated fear hierarchy item. Close your eyes and just visualize that item for a few seconds. It's important that, while doing so, you do your best to maintain your level of relaxation. Don't expect to stay totally mellow, but as you visualize the "easy" item, just keep doing your deep breathing and calming techniques.

3. Do the visualization for a few seconds—perhaps just ten seconds or so. Then stop and go back to your relaxation exercise.

4. After a few seconds of resting, pick up that same card and give it another ten seconds of visualization. If your anxiety level stays low, put it down, rest, then pick the next highest card.

In a first session, do only a few cards. Take your time. Give yourself time to really visualize each situation thoroughly, and always try to end up fairly relaxed.

In later sessions, you may again start with a few easy anxiety hierarchy items, but you can make progress by working slowly up the hierarchy. How fast should you go? It depends on your response. If you find yourself feeling fairly calm with higher-rated items, you may use just a few sessions to work through them. With daily practice, and being careful to not overwhelm yourself, you may find that you can dramatically reduce or eliminate a phobia this way.

If you find your anxiety increasing, back off and practice the basic steps for a bit more. If that doesn't do it, consider blending this approach with some of the others in this chapter or, better still, consult with a professional.

More on Desensitization Treatment

The basic systematic desensitization technique that I've just discussed has been used effectively by thousands of people for decades to reduce or eliminate phobias. In our example, you use visualization of the feared object in order to work through your anxiety hierarchy items. But is that enough?

Actually, yes. Many people find that just thinking about the thing they fear is enough to get them past their phobia. But other people, or their therapists, prefer a more in-person approach. A live

> **Try This!**
>
> If possible, try out your phobia-shrinking skills on easier, more minor fears first. It's easier to overcome a fear that you don't react too strongly to, and once you have done that, you'll find that tackling a scarier phobia will be much easier.

exposure to a phobia stimulus is called *in vivo* exposure. This is also a common, and often very powerful, approach to dealing with a phobia.

For example, many therapists and even airlines have programs designed to help people overcome fear of flying that involve actual visits to airports and even trips up into the air. The process is done the same way—gradual exposure, such as by visiting the airport briefly on a first visit, getting closer slowly to a feared animal or the edge of a cliff, or going up onto a height a bit at a time. You can also combine visualization and in vivo exposure.

Finally, therapists may now provide you with "virtual" exposure to many phobic stimuli. Using computers, software, and 3-D goggles, you can sit in your living room and be at the edge of the Grand Canyon, in an airplane, or near a barking digital dog.

Whether you imagine the phobic stimulus, go near it in person, or work with computer-generated images, the keys are the same: you have to expose yourself to the thing you fear, you want to do it gradually, and you should be in a relaxed mental state if possible (even if you can't relax to perfectly calm, push yourself just a bit to expose yourself anyway).

Cognitive Behavior Therapy for Phobias

When behavioral psychologists were first inventing treatments for phobias, they paid little attention to the thoughts people had about the things they feared. Whether your fear of snakes involved being bitten or seeing them as slimy, it didn't much matter to those early psychological pioneers. Like John Watson's experiments pairing the noise of a loud gong with Little Albert's touching the rat, they basically assumed that fears were caused by a simple matter of pairing up a painful or aversive feeling with the feared object.

More recently, therapists have learned much about how the things we tell ourselves, or the images we hold in our minds, affect our emotional reactions. As I mentioned in Chapter 2, cognitive behavior therapy (or CBT) is the field of therapy that combines behavioral techniques, such as systematic desensitization, with newer techniques that involve working with the thoughts you have about a fear.

CBT is a well-researched and effective approach to dealing with phobias or other psychological problems. First designed by Dr. Aaron Beck to treat depression (Beck's version was originally called "cognitive therapy"), in recent decades CBT has been refined and extended to help people with a wide range of problems.

Phobia Science

While cognitive behavior therapy is a fairly new field, many of its concepts are similar to those used for centuries. Ancient Greek and Roman philosophers and many teachers of Eastern philosophies such as Buddhism taught that our experiences, and whether we are happy or suffer emotionally, are the results of how we think and what we think about.

I've described the basic theory of CBT a bit in Chapter 2, but it bears repeating here because it's an important, even revolutionary, concept. (It was seen as "revolutionary" in psychology when CBT was invented, and it may not actually be as obvious as it may at first seem to be.) The core idea is that your thoughts are just like any other behavior, such as waving your hand or saying "yes." That is, what you think is largely under your voluntary control—thoughts don't "just happen" any more than waving your arm "just happens." You decide what you think, and so you can change what you think.

This seems like a simple idea, yet it's surprising how nonobvious it is to most people. Most of us grow up being taught how to behave or how to do things by our parents and teachers. Whether it's using basic table manners, learning to say "please," or tying our shoes, we are used to the idea that we control our *actions*. Later, we may go out for a sport or learn a work skill where we get coached in the "best" or "correct" way to hit a baseball, operate a computer, or write a term paper. Again, we are used to the idea that we can learn skills for *doing* things better.

But our thinking? Nah! Mostly, we tend to assume that what and how we think about things is pretty much automatic.

Not so! In CBT you learn that the things you think, say to yourself, or imagine, *are* in fact under your voluntary control. With practice, you can make dramatic changes in your mental landscape. (And yes, "thinking practice" is as important as practice in a sport or other skill.)

For example, one person may have to make a speech to classmates or co-workers, and he focuses on how he will be judged by others. He's not ready. He won't know enough and everyone will know it. (These thoughts, while under the person's control, will generally be well-worn habits, and they will *seem* to the person to be "obvious" and to be "just the facts.") As a result of these thoughts, the person's anxiety level goes up. He overprepares for two weeks before the talk and so buries the audience in too much information. He stammers at the podium. He looks nervous, sweats, and makes jokes that don't work. Result? His talk is awful, and people do, indeed, think less well of him—another self-fulfilling prophecy in action.

Another person makes a speech. She is a bit nervous, but she reminds herself that she doesn't have to be perfect and that it's her friends in the audience who will appreciate her efforts. She focuses less on over-preparing and more on making eye contact and connecting with the audience. As long as she gets her main points across, she tells herself, she'll be fine. So she relaxes, focuses on how her friend Marge seems to be enjoying her talk, and she stays fairly calm. Result? She does great. People like her talk. But the most important "talk" she has given is the one she gave herself, in her own head, before she ever got to the podium.

That's the essence of CBT: learning how to talk to yourself. In managing fears, the real key is finding less scary ways to think about things.

Changing Phobic Thinking

There are many approaches to doing CBT, but the basic idea is to learn to identify your thoughts and to take control of them. If you think differently, you'll feel different.

A first step is to clearly state what, exactly, your fear is about. Next, write these thoughts down so they are easier to keep clear in your mind, and begin to identify the specific dangers you are reacting to. Next, treat each danger as a theory or hypothesis in your mind— something to look into more carefully. As you do, examine other possibilities, other ways of thinking about that danger, and ways to cope with it. The idea is to come up with some new ways to think about the dangers—ways that help you feel less anxious.

So the steps, in brief, are:

1. Make a list of every thought, fear, or image you have of the phobia situation. (Write them down on the left half of a sheet of paper, or better yet, give each fear its own sheet.)

2. For each item on the list, write out answers to these three questions:

    A. What is my evidence that this is actually true? (Are snakes really all over my yard, waiting to lunge at me? Does that bridge collapse often? Has it *ever* collapsed before? Are the odds of a dog biting me on the park trail very high?)

    B. What are some other possibilities besides the most awful one I've been imagining? (I might not see a snake in the yard all summer; besides, they're more scared of me than I am of them! The bridge could last 500 more years. If I did see a dog, it'll be on a leash and won't get near me anyway.)

    C. If the worst is true, how will I cope? (I'd do first aid and call 911—they know how to treat snakebites and I'll be fine. If a bridge collapses, I can learn how to escape a car in the water. If a dog bites, I'll report it to the police and see the doctor.)

This exercise is really a kind of fishing expedition. Your goal is to come up with some things you can focus on that trigger less fear than the thoughts you've been having.

Real Danger!

The goal of this exercise is not to get iron-clad proof that the best things will *always* be guaranteed to happen. That's impossible. But that's not necessary—because we are dealing with phobias here. Remember, by definition a phobia is an *irrational* fear. You already know that it's not an *actual* danger—it's an out-of-proportion *feeling* of danger. (Otherwise, we're not talking about a phobia.) You can't use this technique to make yourself bulletproof. CBT is a technique designed to help you refocus your attention on more positive ideas about planes, dogs, snakes, making speeches, or whatever you have an exaggerated fear of.

Usually, if done patiently a few times, you should be able to come up with at least one or two different ways to think about the thing you fear.

Once you have some more positive thoughts or images about your feared object or situation, spend some practice time focusing on these rosier possibilities. Write them down in a notebook and review them daily. Write out new stories about the situations you fear—stories in which things work out just fine. Reread and rewrite those stories, imagining yourself managing things better than you had expected.

Most of the time, life is full of self-fulfilling prophecies. Using this kind of cognitive approach, you deliberately rewrite the story of your fears until they may be fears no more. If you combine this cognitive part with the behavioral part of being exposed to the feared object (using the gradual approach described above in the desensitization section), you will be combining two powerful approaches to fear reduction.

Other Ways of Managing Phobias

In addition to the approaches discussed above, other therapy approaches have been successful in helping people with phobias.

The first psychotherapies were based on the work of Sigmund Freud. Current practitioners of therapies derived from Freud's work are called psychodynamic therapists. In psychodynamic therapy, as it's practiced nowadays, a therapist may help you understand more about the context in which your phobia arose. Sometimes, for instance, you may realize that the fear started during a stressful period in your life, during a marital conflict, or some other emotionally difficult period. Particularly if more direct approaches (such as desensitization) seem to have missed the boat in understanding your fears, a psychodynamic approach might help you get a better handle on some underlying fears or other issues that are the real subject of your fear.

Other approaches to counseling or therapy may also have something to offer. Sometimes, the simple act of talking through a fear can go a long way toward reducing it or giving you some better tools for handling it. Most counseling or therapy includes some form of catharsis or expressing your feelings (such as fear). This is a powerful way to reduce the intensity of some fears (unless you end up dwelling on and, in effect, "rehearsing" the intense feelings with the counselor).

Other things in counseling or therapy that help include the typical encouragement to come up with solutions to a fear or problem and to find the support to confront the fear. Problem solving, brainstorming solutions, etc., may also be helpful.

Finally, many people find help from others who have the same fears. This can include both in-person and online support groups.

Addressing the Context of Phobias

All phobias are not alike. In order to have the best chance of defeating a fear, it's helpful to consider the "big picture" situation of your life in which the fear arose. If you were to consult a therapist about your phobia, he or she would generally spend some time asking you about your life, the stresses you are experiencing, your childhood fears and traumas, your strengths, and other things that might help the two of you develop the fullest picture of how your phobia came to be.

For example, some phobias may have more of a genetic basis than others. Some phobias, such as fainting at the sight of blood, may be strongly influenced by your family genetic background (they can run in families).

Other phobias may be based in not having enough of certain skills. For instance, not all parents think to teach their children the basics about being around animals. There are basic skills involved in knowing how to approach dogs that are usually effective in getting a dog to wag its tail and be friendly. Kids who aren't taught this skill, or whose parents are themselves highly anxious around dogs, may get growled at, barked at, or bitten much more than other kids.

Similarly, if your mom or dad shows you how to fix a flat tire and you have a cell phone that you can use to call a tow truck if you have car troubles, you may be less frightened of driving alone. Knowing that you can pop the wheel off can help you not develop driving phobias.

> ## Phobia Science
>
> Kids who are taught how to solve new problems, whether they involve dogs or trucks or credit cards, generally approach life with more confidence. They feel free to take more risks, but they also have better judgment about which risks to take—so their attitudes are more likely to be "I can figure this out." Such persons develop wider ranges of skills and so have fewer phobias than people whose basic attitudes in life are to feel vulnerable and be overly cautious—and so who restrict their life experience.

Other contextual factors in phobias include your self-esteem level, your general social skills or comfort level, and the presence of other emotional difficulties such as depression, generalized anxiety levels, high stress levels, physical illness, etc. Any of these factors can set you up for possible phobias. Make a list of the stress factors in your life right now—do they have anything to do with the fears that trouble you?

Finally, you would want to consider the effects of negative or even traumatic experiences. For instance, a fear of driving is normal after a person has been in a recent car crash. If you just fell off a horse, being afraid of horses isn't uncommon. Your phobia may be related to these traumatic events, or even to a scary movie you watched recently. (I was afraid of showering for a few days after the first time I watched *Psycho!*) Knowing that these fears are normal, but that you shouldn't give in to them, can nip some phobias in the bud.

Not Freezing Up

Many phobias may start or be made worse if you freeze up in a new or scary situation. This happens for a few predictable psychological reasons. Understanding this process can be a first step to phobia prevention.

In a new situation, a child may react in several ways. One is to "reach out and touch." For instance, many small children will naturally grab for something they see that they're curious about. Whether it's a plastic toy or a writhing snake, these children will start out pretty fearless.

Whether for reasons of temperament, prior scary experience, or not having enough support from a parent, other children do something different. They freeze up in the presence of something new. This reaction may be a primitive response that helped our ancestors survive. Freezing may prevent predators from noticing you, for instance. (It's the secret of survival success of many backyard bunnies and other critters.)

This kind of response may carry over into adulthood. Faced with a new situation, many people have an automatic freeze response—they don't look at, much less handle or confront, a new situation or object. This freezing may stop them from handling that situation in the present or from developing skills for handling this kind of situation in the future.

The best solution to this is to deliberately develop knowledge and competence in this new situation. For instance, if you are unsure how to deal with dogs, it's easy to find information on the best ways to approach a dog. Look it up online or find a friend or animal trainer who can help you learn these skills.

Whether it's knowing how to navigate in a foreign country, ride a bike, or make a speech, you can develop new skills that will help you keep your fears in check.

Make a list of all the things you should know about a new adventure or situation. If you're traveling to a new country, get some travel guides and study them. Learn some of the language. Find someone to go with, or make a list of the sources of information, resources, and help you'll need. If it's getting on horses that spooks you, find a riding instructor and ask her or him to help you get used to being around horses.

The more active you are in learning about the feared situation, the better you'll cope and the less fear you'll feel.

Getting Professional Help

Most people never get professional help with their phobias in large part because their fears don't interfere all that much with their lives. In other cases, the problem with their fears only comes up briefly—they may feel like they should get some help, but then the fear shrinks or the situation is done with (they get through the speech despite their fear, or the vacation ends and so there are no more snakes around), and so the need for help passes.

Unfortunately, others go for years without help when the help is actually very much needed. For instance, persons with agoraphobia—a very severe, complex phobia that may dramatically interfere with living (see Chapter 11)—endure that phobia for an average of 10 years before seeking help!

In many cases, you should be able to use some of the techniques in this chapter to reduce or even eliminate your fears. But sometimes that may not be enough. A good rule of thumb is that you should consider getting expert help with a phobia if ...

- ◆ You notice that the phobia interferes with your life in an important way, such as keeping you from doing things you like to do.

- ◆ The phobia interferes with your job, relationships, or safety.

- ◆ You can't overcome the phobia yourself.

> **Real Danger!**
>
> Many people let serious phobia problems go untreated because getting help feels to them like getting too close to the thing they fear. For example, they may think, "If I get help with my fear of flying, then I'll be forced to start flying and I can't because I'm phobic about flying!" A better way to think about it is, "Nobody will make me fly even if I get over the fear, but it's possible that after getting help, I might actually want to fly somewhere!"

If you need help, it's available. Psychologists, psychiatrists, psychiatric nurses, social workers, counselors, and other professionals are often skilled in helping you to work on phobias. And most of these folks make sure they are listed in the Yellow Pages or online (type in "psychologists" and the name of your town and state, country, or other location). Your doctor or clinic can probably suggest someone you can see, or you can consult your health insurance company's directory of approved providers, if you have one. You can also check with your state psychological or psychiatric society to see if they can refer you to someone. (Also see Appendix B for some resources you can contact for help.)

Therapists may work with phobias in different ways, and it's important to find a person whom you basically trust. Feel free to ask how they plan to help you with your phobia before starting the treatment, and discuss what kinds of help you think would be best or most comfortable. (But consider their suggestions and input, too. Some clients sabotage their treatment by wanting to run everything instead of getting the input and new perspectives they really need!)

In some cases, medications can also help you with a phobia. Most specific phobias are generally not treated with medications, but if you have a separate problem such as depression or generalized, severe anxiety, medications may help. More complex phobias such as agoraphobia may also benefit from medications, which can help reduce or manage the panic attacks that are part of that condition. Of course, if you think medications are needed, you should discuss this with your doctor (or nurse practitioner, etc.), with a psychologist who knows about medications and who can help you find a doctor to prescribe them (in a few states, psychologists can also prescribe medications for mental health problems), or with a psychiatrist. (Psychiatrists are medical doctors who specialize in mental health treatment; psychologists generally have Ph.D.s or Master's degrees instead of medical training.)

The Least You Need to Know

♦ There are a number of highly effective phobia treatments, including systematic desensitization and cognitive behavior therapy.

♦ Systematic desensitization therapy involves learning to tolerate gradually higher levels of exposure to the thing you fear based on learning relaxation skills and pairing your relaxed state with contact with the feared situation.

♦ In cognitive behavior therapy, you also learn how to control and guide your thoughts or images of the feared situation, so that you will trigger a less powerful fear response.

♦ Other forms of therapy, developing skills for coping with feared situations, and understanding the context of your fears are important.

♦ Seek professional help with your phobia if it significantly interferes with your life or if you can't overcome the phobia on your own.

Part 2

Specific or "Simple" Phobias

Specific phobias are what most people mean when they use the word *phobia*. In this kind of phobia, you develop a strong, illogical fear response to perfectly innocent or mostly harmless animals, things, or situations. Whether it's a fear of otters, or fainting at the sight of a hypodermic needle, you'll probably find your favorite simple phobias in the following chapters.

This part includes fears of animals, things in the natural environment, medical phobias, situations that terrify, and specific phobias that involve people. To wrap this up, we list some imaginary or humorous phobias that often turn up on everyone's list of cool phobias.

Chapter 4

Slither and Roar: Animal Phobias

In This Chapter

- ◆ Why we fear animals
- ◆ List of animal phobias

You may recall that specific phobias are fears of very particular events, situations, or things. One of the most common types of specific phobias is animal-related phobias. In the *Diagnostic and Statistical Manual of Mental Disorders* (DSM-IV), animal phobias are one of the major subcategories of specific phobias.

In this chapter we'll look at the possible reasons for developing fears of the beasts. Next, we'll review some of the most common animal phobias. One thing's for sure: if it purrs, barks, tweets, or slithers, somebody somewhere is deathly afraid of it.

Why Do We Fear the Beasts?

It's not unusual for people of any age to have animal phobias (though generally, unless there is a trauma of some sort, they tend to start in childhood, before age 7 or 8). We may be prewired to fear animals, which would make sense if you figure that animals probably represented one of the most lethal threats for prehistoric children (and adults). Being biologically ready to respond powerfully to animal-based threats was no doubt a survival tool that helped our ancestors live long enough to, well, become our ancestors.

You may develop an animal phobia for any of several reasons. Some animals may trigger fears of being attacked, bitten, or stung; in those cases, you may develop the phobia after you've personally been stung by a bee. More commonly, you may just have learned that bee stings are painful (or that rattlesnake bites are painful and deadly) and so build the fear up in your mind. Other phobias may be related to the fear of germs or feelings of disgust—like the disgust you might feel around some slimy or slithery animals.

There may be as many different kinds of animal phobias as there are animals. That's because you can develop a fear of just about any animal. In fact, animal phobias are probably the most common kind of specific phobia. People who develop one animal phobia have a greater than average chance of developing several.

Most people who have animal phobias are concerned with just one (or more often, just a few) different kind of animals. So you might be afraid of cats, but very comfortable around snarling pit bulls. You may fear tiny spiders but not mind seeing rattlesnakes while hiking in the mountains.

Fears of spiders, mice, and insects are among the most common specific phobias. Other animal phobias are less common.

Like other simple phobias, a person's reaction when confronted with a feared animal is to have the usual anxiety reaction or response, which may include:

- Increased heartbeat, shallow breathing, feeling ill or faint, trembling, and related physical reactions

♦ The strong urge to get away from, avoid, or maybe just not to look at the feared animal, possibly accompanied by taking drastic or even panicky action to avoid the animal (like swerving in your car while driving when you have a bee phobia and a bee enters the car)

♦ Intense mental focus on the animal, including perhaps terrifying images of the animal attacking, coming near, biting, or engaging in some other kind of awful behavior

♦ Panicky reactions, fleeing the scene, or attempting to flee

While surveys show us that animal phobias are fairly common, not many people seek treatment for them. In my nearly three decades working as a psychologist, I can recall having treated only one animal phobia in a client—a dog phobia in a mail carrier who had been attacked by a pit bull. That example actually fits the pattern: people generally seek help for phobias that interfere with their day-to-day life, relationships, mobility, or jobs. A mail carrier needs to function around strange dogs, but most of the time, people can cope with animal phobias simply by avoiding the animals. Remember that most snake phobics, for instance, have never even seen a real snake!

Animal Phobias

Amphibians (*batrachophobia*)

From the Greek *batracho-*, meaning frog. *Batrachophobia* is the fear of amphibians such as frogs, toads, salamanders, newts, etc. The fear of amphibians has occurred in many cultures. The specific fears can include the fear that frogs are a bad omen (not so common a fear as it once was, perhaps), that contact with frogs may cause warts (likewise a fading fear), or that physical contact with frogs may be poisonous (and in some places in the world, this is true). Amphibian phobias may sometimes stem from feelings of disgust at "icky" and slimy things. (*See also* Toads.)

Animal skins or fur (*doraphobia*)

Fear of animal skins or fur is called *doraphobia*, from the Greek *dora* meaning hide or skin. It's sometimes defined as the fear of touching animal skins or fur. Presumably, people may feel discomfort or disgust at possibly unclean or disease-bearing skins or have other fears of fur associated with animals, but there are few, if any, actual cases of *doraphobia* described in the medical or psychological literature.

Animals (*zoophobia*)

This is a general term for fear of animals. It's not likely that there are people who actually fear all animals, though. *Zoophobia* can include the fear of being bitten, attacked, eaten, or overwhelmed by animals. It can also include strong feelings of revulsion or disgust triggered by animals.

Ants (*myrmecophobia*)

Fear of ants. This can include feelings of being "creeped out" by ants (with the person imagining that the ants are crawling all over them or up their pant legs), the fear of having to kill an ant that gets on the person, the fear of ants such as fire ants (whose bite can be painful or toxic), or the fear of "home invasions" by large swarms of ants in warmer or semitropical climates—where ants may be plentiful and some (like carpenter ants) may actually do a lot of damage to property.

Bacteria (*bacteriophobia*)

Fear of bacteria. A certain amount of fear (though not a phobia) of bacteria is probably healthy. Bacteria-caused infections are among the leading causes of death worldwide. On the other hand, there's no getting away from bacteria, no matter how much scrubbing you do. There are tens of millions of bacteria in even a pinch of dirt or a teaspoon of water and on virtually every surface you touch. A huge percentage of the *biomass* (the total weight of all organic stuff on Earth) on the planet is actually bacteria. And there are ten times more bacterial than human cells in your body. That's right: you are basically a walking casserole of bacteria with a little bit of "human" on the side.

Bees (*apiphobia* or *melissophobia*)

Fear of bees. *Api-* is the Latin for bee and *melissa* is the ancient Greek word for bee. Most people with this phobia fear being stung; a bee or wasp sting is painful. Many people with the fear have never actually been stung personally but know about the danger, or perhaps they have seen others be stung (or more likely, are reacting to the fears of others). The approach of a bee or wasp can cause people to bolt from a picnic table, and some people may swerve dangerously in their cars if a bee gets inside. Some find the fear quite disabling in the summertime, and in some parts of the United States, fears of swarms of killer bees have grown more common as some strains of bees have spread northward. A small percentage of people can develop truly life-threatening allergies to bee stings, which of course adds still more intensity to people's fears. (*See also* Wasps.)

Birds (*ornithophobia*)

Fear of birds. This fear can take different forms. There are fears of fierce birds such as birds of prey or of loud, strange-seeming birds like parrots, but sometimes people fear any bird, even the small ones like parakeets. Some people have fears of feathers or of seeing dead birds, which are probably disgust-related phobias. A person may have fears of being attacked by birds, like in Alfred Hitchcock's film *The Birds*— though it's sometimes pointed out that, at least in the film, the characters' fears would not be phobias because the birds really *were* attacking them. But it's not uncommon for children to be scared by encounters such as birds getting into a house and thrashing around as they try to get out, and this can trigger fears of similar experiences.

Bugs under the skin (*epidermal zoophobia*)

A belief that you are infested under the skin with creepy-crawly bugs. This condition tends most often to afflict older women who live alone and who have a history of other mental health problems (such as anxiety or depression). It may be a rare condition, and technically it's really a delusion, even though it has that *zoophobia* name.

Bulls (*taurophobia*)

Fear of bulls. The term comes from the Greek *tauro-*, meaning bull. Taurus is the bull constellation. Bulls in real-life pastures can be the most dangerous animal in a herd, and so it's not surprising that they've symbolized power and authority since ancient times. Bulls can be formidable and frightening animals, and a fear of bulls when crossing someone's pasture (or running from them in Pamplona, the site of the annual running of the bulls) can be healthy.

Cats (*ailurophobia, felinophobia, galeophobia,* or *gatophobia*)

Fear of cats. People have developed cat phobias since ancient times. Cat phobias can include fear of physical harm from cats (triggered most often in childhood by cat bites or being clawed), or their occasional hissing or threatening behavior. (Children are most likely to develop this kind of reaction.) But there have been many cat-phobes whose concerns flowed more from various superstitions, from cats as threats to cats as evil or mystical creatures. People have thus feared black cats, cats crossing their paths, being stared at by cats, etc. People with cat phobias may avoid visiting people who have cats or may even avoid going out because of the fear of encountering cats.

Interestingly, a cat phobic visiting someone with a cat may end up being singled out for the cat's attention and body-against-leg rubbing behavior—not because the cat wants to torment the phobic, but because the phobic person will perhaps be the person most careful to avoid looking at the cat. Since cats feel anxious when they are stared at (they are perhaps stare-phobic), they may feel most comfortable around that one person in the room who is not looking their way and so gravitate to the phobic.

Chickens (*alektorophobia*)

From the Greek *alektor-*, meaning rooster. Fear of chickens can apparently include injury and disgust type fears. There is little or no scientific research on this fear, but people reporting it say their fears include any kind of image of chickens, seeing chickens, thinking about them, saying the word, or eating them. The disgust elements may be related to the idea of chickens as being dirty (eating from the ground, chickens being in proximity to their own feces, etc.); feathers, eggs, or other chicken parts may be part of the fear images. The fear of injury images can include images of being pecked or swooped on by the birds.

Dogs (*cynophobia*)

Fear of dogs. Generally, this is fear of being attacked or threatened by dogs. A fear of being bit by a yelping little poodle can be as powerful for some people as the fear of larger, more dangerous dogs. It was the aggressive barking of a dog that developed my temporary fear of the neighbor's collie. That fits with the general pattern on dog phobias—about two thirds of dog phobias are triggered by dog attacks or other aggressive behavior by dogs. Of the other third, half appear to be triggered by observing others experience problems with dogs. Most dog phobias start during childhood, though adults can also develop the fear. One group of adults at high risk for dog phobia are mail carriers.

Exposing children early on to more positive, peaceable experiences with dogs seems to help prevent phobias from taking root and so may psychologically "immunize" children from dog phobias. Likewise, teaching children some dog-handling skills (such as knowing how to approach a dog) can help them feel more competent and relaxed around dogs, which will reduce their anxiety and minimize the risk that they'll trigger dog-aggression.

Fish (*ichthyophobia*)

Fear of fish. This can include different types of fears, ranging from being bitten or otherwise hurt by fish while swimming in piranha-infested rivers (not a phobia if they're really there, but kind of excessive if you have the same fear at the YWCA pool) to seeing dead fish or eating fish. The causes of these fish phobias vary—fears of eating fish, for instance, can be related to the fear that the fish may be in some way contaminated or unhealthy (whether due to mercury poisoning, the strong flavor of some fish, or the fear of choking on a fish bone). Many people won't eat raw-fish meals such as sushi for these same reasons; though again, simple caution doth not a phobia make.

Frogs (*batrachophobia* or *ranidaphobia*)

From the Greek *batracho-*, meaning frog. (*See also* Toads, Amphibians.)

Germs (*verminophobia, bacillophobia,* or *mysophobia*)

Fear of germs. In practice it can be hard to distinguish between a phobia and a case of obsessive compulsive disorder (OCD) involving germs; this is often the case, but in this disorder the fine line may be washed away entirely. Fears can range from the vague, ill-defined or disgust-triggered notions about germy dangers through the avoidance of places, objects, or situations that might lead to contamination. It's probably reasonable to suggest that if the person's major problem is avoiding places, things, or actions that might lead to contamination, along with feelings of fear or strong discomfort, it's better slotted as a phobia, whereas if their main issue is having to wash their hands or get things cleaned up after exposure, it's closer to a compulsion. (*See also* Bacteria.)

Horses (*equinophobia* or *hippophobia*)

Fear of horses. *Equus* is Latin for horse, while *hippo-* is the Greek prefix derived from their word for horse. (The word *hippopotamus* originally meant river horse.) Since horses are large and may seem rather mysterious or even fearsome to some people and cultures, a fear of horses is, to some extent, ancient. Modern people with little exposure to horses (except for watching cowboy flicks) may develop fears when they suddenly find themselves exposed to the actual animals. Fears of horses can result from actual experiences, such as falling off a horse while riding, being bitten by a horse (particularly at a young age), or encountering an aggressive horse. People unfamiliar with horses may also be taught to fear being kicked or having their feet crushed by horses, and indeed, some caution when around horses is not particularly foolish—at least until you learn how they behave and how not to get yourself hurt around 'em, pardner.

I mentioned in Chapter 2 Sigmund Freud's case of Little Hans, the small boy who developed a fear of horses. Hans's fear meant it was hard for him to even go outdoors, since he lived in a city where it was still common to see horses on the street. Nowadays, that's not the case for many people (unless you live in a rural area where they are more common), so the phobia may have less impact on your life.

Insects (*acraphobia, entomophobia,* or *insectophobia*)

Fear of bugs or insects. Fears can include aversion/disgust, which might include reactions to particular insects as ugly or disgusting due to their unusual shape or color, the concern that they spread diseases (e.g., flies), reactions to swarms or clumps of insects, or images of those swarms in disgusting situations (outhouses, on roadkill, etc.). People may fear being bitten and so avoid touching or holding even harmless bugs (meaning most of them). Fears of specific insects such as mosquitoes may be related to fears of contracting diseases (malaria, West Nile infections, etc.).

Itching (*acarophobia*)

Fear of either itching or of insects that cause itching. The buggy culprits can include ticks, worms, mites, or other small insects, whether real or imagined.

Lice (*pediculophobia* or *phthiriophobia*)

Fear of being infested by lice. *Pediculus* is the Latin word for louse (the singular of lice). *Pthiriasis* is an infestation of lice.

Mice or rats (*musophobia, murophobia,* or *suriphobia*)

Fear of mice or rats. Humans have long feared the loss or contamination of food supplies by mice or rats, and there is some basis for concern about the risks of bites, particularly when small children might be exposed to rats. But the concern can easily overflow into a phobia, and it's reported that fear of mice is the third most common phobia in the United States.

Microbes (*bacillophobia* or *microbiophobia*)

Also sometimes called *bacteriophobia*, this is the fear of small, invisible organisms such as bacteria or viruses. Often, the fear of contamination by these organisms leads to a fear of contact with dirt or things the person perceives as dirty. (*See also* Bacteria, Germs.)

Moths (*mottephobia*)

Fear of moths or butterflies. Some written sources say the fear is of being attacked, though most people who confess to the phobia (and there seem to be quite a few) describe their discomfort with the motion of moths or butterflies (including their rapid flying and their whirling or twirling around) and their appearance (on screens, indoors at night, and the fuzziness and potentially large size of moths). Sometimes moth phobias spread to fear of butterflies or vice versa. People sometimes report the onset of the fear occurring after dreams of moths (perhaps in overwhelmingly large numbers, clumps, etc.). The disgust dimension seems most powerful in these descriptions, including the vague fears of bodily invasion (e.g., moths flying into their ears). Many people with this fear volunteer how debilitating it can be, particularly in the summer, and also mention how embarrassing they find the fear to be.

Otters (*lutraphobia*)

Fear of otters. *Lutrinus* is the Latin word for otter. Otters are those adorable little, furry animals that spend their days floating on their backs, sunning themselves, holding hands with other otters, and being entirely harmless. While dutifully listed as a legitimate phobia by various books and websites, the existence of the phobia is questionable—I found no references to *lutraphobia* or to otters in either the medical nor the psychological databases, nor did I find any blog posts by apparently real people who apparently really lose sleep over otter attacks. (However, the term *lutraphobia* may lead the list of phobias that trigger blog posts of the "Are you kidding me?" sort.) While not wanting to offend anyone who may actually have the phobia, and bearing in mind that, theoretically, you can develop a phobia of anything, this one seems dubious.

Parasites (*parasitophobia*)

Fear of parasites. Parasites, from bacteria to tapeworms to leeches to ticks to vampires (bats or Transylvanian), survive by taking nutrients from others. People may fear that they will become infested or be attacked, or they may come to believe that they already are infested. People may believe (sometimes realistically) that they've done something that puts them at risk for parasite infestation (such as drink potentially infested water) and so may become preoccupied with the fear that they have been infested. In some cases, the fear can develop after medical treatment for an actual infestation. People may develop fears of going outdoors or swimming in potentially leech-infested lakes. They may become so afraid of tick bites that they avoid going into the woods—though again, whether this is a phobia or simply cautious behavior (blended with anxiety) is not always clear. Most likely, these phobias can be blends of fear of actual harm and the disgust response.

One unusual parasite phobia-related condition is Ekbom's syndrome, which is a belief that you are infested under the skin with parasites. This condition tends most often to afflict people with a history of other mental health problems such as anxiety or depression. It is a rare condition, possibly more often seen by dermatologists than mental health practitioners (not because people need to see a skin doctor, but because when they think they have these imaginary bugs, they will go to a dermatologist, not a psychiatrist). Technically it's really a delusion, not a phobia—though of course, as with many phobias, there may be some overlap in the two psychological conditions.

Rats (*musophobia, murophobia,* or *suriphobia*)

See Mice or rats.

Reptiles (*herptophobia*)

Fear of reptiles. (The term is also used to refer to more specific reptilian fears, particularly fear of snakes.) *Reptilia* is a class of animals that includes everything from snakes to lizards to crocodiles to turtles, so a general reptile fear may include fear of one or more such creatures. Reptiles are cold-blooded, air-breathing, scale-covered animals, and some are dangerous to mammals—so a certain generalized fear of "those things" may make psychological or even evolutionary sense. Most research has addressed fear of snakes. Both threat and disgust can be involved in reptilian fears.

Sharks (*selachophobia*)

Fear of sharks. *Selachos* is the Greek word for shark. One study done in 1991 showed that the fear of sharks revolves around the belief that sharks might attack, so it's a danger, not a disgust, fear. Shark attack fears were heightened in the popular imagination after the 1975 film

Jaws, but there have been many legends and true stories about the dangers of sharks throughout recorded history that have kept the fear of sharks prominent in the minds of people venturing onto or into the seas.

Shellfish *(ostraconophobia)*

Fear of shellfish. In ancient Greece, an *ostrakon* was a shell. This can include a fear of any shellfish: lobsters, crayfish, crabs, clams, etc. There is little or no medical or psychological research on this fear, though people do report fears ranging from the more intense, "can't even look at a clam" kind to fears of consuming shellfish. The latter kinds of fears are most likely either the disgust fears that can be related to the "ick" factor in strange-looking animals (or the belief that shellfish are unclean) or learned fears that one might become ill from eating bad shellfish. In several religious traditions, including Jewish, some Islamic, and Seventh Day Adventist traditions, eating shellfish is forbidden.

Snakes *(herpetophobia, ophidiophobia, ophiophobia, ophiciophobia, or snakephobia)*

Fear of snakes. This is one of the most common fears and one of the most well-researched simple phobias. There is some speculation that a fear of snakes is hard-wired into humans and some other mammals; this is suggested by animal studies showing strong reactions in animals and humans with no histories of prior experience with snakes. Children seem to show no fear of snakes until they are a few years old (two to three, depending on the study). Fear type, as with most animal phobias, seems divided into the fear of injury by snakebite and reactions to the "ick" factors, including the belief that snakes are slimy and reactions to their weird, writhing style of moving. Studies show that most snake phobics have never been in contact with actual snakes.

Snakes have been seen as magical, have been involved in legends and mystical beliefs, and have been used as symbols since ancient times. The caduceus, the ancient medical symbol, is a picture of a snake twined around a rod. Moses could turn his rod into a snake and vice versa. Psychoanalysts sometimes saw snakes as penis symbols; others see dreams of snakes as symbols of transformation, and in some Eastern traditions, the snake symbolizes *kundalini*—the life energy that flows through the body's chakras, or energy centers, during meditation.

Spiders (*arachnephobia* or *arachnophobia*)

Fear of spiders. This is one of the leading animal fears, sometimes topping number one in the charts, and there are literally hundreds of published research studies on all sorts of aspects of spider phobias and their treatment. Some evolutionary psychologists and biologists believe there may be an inherited component to this fear, which would plausibly have resulted from the need of our ancestors to avoid dangerous spiders (and so those cave boys and girls who freaked out lived to mate, while those who wanted to pick up the pretty poisonous spiders didn't). There is something of a realistic element to that theory; spiders have been known to bite (as a boy I got a painful bite by a tiny spider that was not any bigger than the head of a pin—so I know they hurt!). The bites of certain spiders can be quite dangerous. Spiders seem to share both the danger and disgust triggers, given their appearance (all those legs, that occasional fur, etc.) and their sometime association with dirt or dirty places. Spiders are virtually everywhere on Earth, so escaping them is nearly impossible (and if you kill all the spiders, you'll soon have all those other bug phobias to deal with, since spiders keep the population of other critters down). Spiders' webs also add their sinister element to the mix, whether the fresh version, taut and holding, perhaps, a trapped bug, or the old, dust-covered, Dracula's castle cobweb versions.

Fear of spiders can result in fairly impaired functioning. In extreme cases, people may feel they must check out a room before entering, undertake dramatic bouts of cleaning in their homes, or avoid entering places or situations where they fear they might come in contact with spiders.

Tapeworms (*taeniophobia* or *teniophobia*)

Fear of tapeworms. Tapeworms are parasitic flatworms that can live in the intestinal tract of mammals, including humans. You can acquire your own personal collection of tapeworms by eating undercooked pork, fish, or beef that contains the larvae of the worm or by eating food prepared by someone who has an infection and who practices poor hand-washing hygiene. Once inside you, the larvae are freed by your digestive juices, and the baby tapeworms can attach themselves to your intestinal lining. Surgery or medications will be needed to make you tapeworm-free again. The largest tapeworms—get ready—can grow as long as 100 feet. Tapeworms don't suck your blood, and they are painless—but they survive off intestinal nutrients, which can lead people to develop severe nutritional deficiencies. Once upon a time, people would deliberately ingest tapeworms in order to lose weight. Tapeworm infections mainly occur in areas of the world where there is inadequate sanitation—tapeworm infections are not very common elsewhere. Phobias of tapeworm infections are probably less common, though people have reported phobias after seeing films about or photos of tapeworms (or perhaps, after reading descriptions like this one). Since tapeworms are pretty high on the disgust meter, impressionable persons who see films or photos of them may begin to develop signs of the phobia.

Termites *(isopterophobia)*

Fear of termites. *Isopteros* is late Greek for swift as flight, and the *isoptera* is the order of white ants or termites which have four large equal wings. (*Iso-* means equal and *pteros-* means wings.) Fear of termites chewing away the base of your home is rational and not a phobia. Some people may develop constant worries that their home will collapse on top of them due to termite damage, which can slide into phobia territory. However, there are no reports of this phobia in the scientific literature, and if it exists outside of cartoons, it seems to be fairly rare.

Toads *(bufonophobia)*

Fear of toads. During toad season (such as after it rains in areas where toads may be drawn out into the open by wet weather), people with this fear may have difficulty going out, cutting the grass, etc. Running into toads can lead to the typical phobic responses of panic, dizziness, and hyperventilating. (*See also* Amphibians.)

Wasps *(spheksophobia)*

Fear of wasps. The term comes from the Latin word for wasp, *sphekso*. People may fear the pain of being stung or may believe (accurately or not) that they may have an allergy to the wasp's venom and may die if stung. There is one case report in the psychological journals of a person whose phobia improved after she was given an allergy test that showed she was not, in fact, allergic to wasp stings. People with this fear may have difficulties functioning outdoors in the summer, particularly if they see wasps or believe wasps may be present. Panicking if a wasp gets into their car may be a dangerous reaction. They may also fear bees or other flying/stinging insects, and of course, one phobia may flow over into the others. (*See also* Bees.)

Wild animals (*agrizoophobia*)

Fear of wild animals—lions, tigers, bears, the works. People may have specific fears (like being eaten), but they may be even more afraid of the unknown element, such as when they hear scary sounds coming from the woods at night.

Worms (*scoleciphobia* or *vermiphobia*)

Fear of worms. This fear may be due to the disgust kind of phobic reactions triggered by slimy things. Some people may fear going places where they may see worms (such as on lawns after rain). Baiting hooks with fat juicy nightcrawlers may be out of the question, and even thinking about it may trigger considerable anxiety.

5

The Sky Is Falling!: Natural Environment Phobias

In This Chapter

♦ Our dangerous world

♦ List of natural environment phobias

Since prehistoric times, we have had to contend with the world around us. And let's face it: much of the world around us can be terrifying.

All snug and safe in your cozy cabin or mansion, you may not spend much time thinking about this. But just go outside in a thunderstorm—or even in the dark, for that matter—and you may start to feel your hackles rise. Whether it's earthquakes, lightning, floods, or just trees, there's always something to be afraid of in the natural environment.

From an evolutionary point of view, this makes sense. *Evolutionary* means *survival*. Our ancestors survived because they had enough healthy fear of things they didn't understand to stay away from dangers.

Loud noises, large things that move (whether it's falling rocks, trees in a storm, or waves at the beach), or unfamiliar situations—these could all spell danger. Those who felt some kind of fear reaction and so stepped back or avoided the big waves would have survived long enough to pass their genes along. They were our ancestors. Those who were fearless in the face of lightning and rolling rocks were ... well ... their genes aren't around anymore.

When the World Seems Dangerous

In the modern world, most of those ancient dangers are either well managed or well understood. Lightning rarely causes barns to catch fire anymore—we have Ben Franklin and his lightning rod to thank for that. We can't prevent tornadoes, but we know where to hide to be fairly safe if one passes nearby. Darkness is scary, but we have flashlights.

But despite our mastery, fears of the natural environment are fairly common. The *Diagnostic and Statistical Manual of Mental Disorders* (DSM-IV) says that, in adult clinical settings, this is still the second most common category of phobias.

There is only a limited amount of research on how *natural environment phobias* develop. Statistics vary on how common they actually are, and not all researchers have found that they are as common as the DSM-IV reports (not an unusual discrepancy in psychology research). Some groups, and people in some countries, have higher amounts of natural environment phobias than others. And of course, some phobias in this category are more common, while others hardly ever develop in anyone.

def•i•ni•tion

The DSM-IV defines **natural environment phobias** this way: "This subtype should be specified if the fear is cued by objects in the natural environment, such as storms, heights, or water. This subtype generally has a childhood onset."

As you have seen from earlier chapters, the reasons people develop phobias can vary a great deal. Sometimes people develop a phobia out of a fear of losing control emotionally; other times they are afraid of being hurt, criticized by others, or just have physical reactions like fainting.

In most cases of natural environment phobias, the fear people have—the toxic image in their minds—is of being injured.

The list of natural environment phobias is divided fairly evenly between things that do have the potential to cause us harm and things that are almost never dangerous or threatening. For instance, fearing floods or lightning makes sense to most people—but what about fear of trees? Or lakes? If you glance through the following list of natural environment phobias, you'll notice that a lot of harmless things make the list: darkness, trees, snow, empty spaces. (Empty spaces? What, you may ask, could be dangerous in a space where there is nothing present?)

It may be that, as with other phobias, natural environment phobias are like fingerprints—everyone's reactions may differ. If you grew up around lakes, for instance, you may find them to be pleasant places; someone else may find them scary. On the other hand, some people's childhood experiences in their particular lake may have included a capsized boat, a dead fish rotting on the surface, or some other stressful situation that left them permanently uneasy around large bodies of water.

Natural Environment Phobias

Air *(anemophobia)*

Fear of air in the form of wind or other moving air. This fear can range anywhere from drafts to tornadoes. The specific fears vary but can include many things: fear of getting dust in one's eyes due to wind gusts, being knocked over by the wind, wind damage to property, etc. More generally, the fear may relate to a sense of loss of control due to violent weather, fear of injury or damage, fear of storms, or fear of the ominous sense one may get when a strong wind or storm is approaching.

Celestial spaces (*astrophobia*)

The fear of things related to "outer space." *Astrophobia* is most often defined as the fear of stars, outer space, or celestial space, but the term is also sometimes used to refer to a fear of just about anything connected to space, such as fear of space travel or space aliens. Some people may develop a fear reaction when they read, hear, or think about astronauts who get stranded in space (such as the Apollo 13 story), and both children and adults may have been traumatized by witnessing the *Challenger* space shuttle disaster on TV. Science fiction contains examples of people (or maybe aliens) who supposedly have *astrophobia* as part of the plots of the stories, and other definitions include fear of things like space aliens. This fear does not appear to have been studied or described in the medical or psychological journals, so while some websites assert it's "often" treated in clinical settings, that seems unlikely.

Clouds (*nephophobia*)

Fear of clouds. From the ancient Greek *nephos*, meaning cloud. Children in particular (and maybe sailors) who have experienced frightening storms or tornadoes may develop an intense fear of storm clouds. So the fear may actually be of an associated threat (storms, etc.). Some people are said to fear cloudy days because it may make them more vulnerable to depression.

Cold (*cryophobia, cheimaphobia, cheimatophobia, psychrophobia,* or *psychropophobia*)

Fear of extreme cold, ice, or frost. *Cryos-* comes from the Greek *kryos*, meaning frost or icy cold. People may dread the cold, or cold weather, especially if they've had experiences of being really cold either during a long winter or after being exposed to frostbite. This can include fear of being in a cold climate, cold season, or of having a too-cold home (e.g., fear of running out of heat in the winter). Some people may also associate prolonged cold (such as very long, cold winters) with depression.

Comets (*cometophobia*)

Fear of comets. Comets are small bodies in space that orbit the solar system and have a familiar "tail" when seen from Earth. Throughout history they were mysteries and were, in many times and places, considered bad omens.

Cosmic phenomena (*kosmikophobia*)

Supposedly, the fear of cosmic (outer space-related) objects or entities. This is a broader term than fears of specific kinds of objects such as comets, black holes, etc. It's dubious that *kosmikophobia* exists in the cosmos, other than as a metaphor.

Darkness or night (*achluophobia, lygophobia, myctophobia, noctiphobia, nyctophobia,* or *scotophobia*)

Fear of darkness or night. As might be guessed from the sheer number of terms used for this fear, it's fairly common. Fear of the dark often begins in children around the age of two and is more common among children and adolescents. This may be a fairly natural fear in humans, and it's been found that darkness tends to increase the intensity of startle reactions in humans. It also can trigger anxiety related to a lack of control, because it can cause a feeling that things aren't familiar or leave you feeling ungrounded in reality. Darkness itself, then, may trigger some of the fear, but darkness also creates a situation in which other dangers either are, or seem to be, suddenly present. Some of the dangers of darkness are concrete and tangible, such as not knowing where things may be in a room or the greater danger and difficulty of seeing to drive at night. Darkness may also be associated with potential dangers such as robbers and muggers, and for young people, superstitious people, or people who never got over scary movies, the potential dangers may include ghosts, goblins, witches, etc.

Dawn or daylight (*eosophobia*)

Fear of dawn or daylight. This fear has not been reported in the medical or psychological research, so it's not clear whether or how often it actually occurs. Supposedly, some people with agoraphobia are more bothered by going out in the daylight, and some social phobics may feel more exposed or vulnerable to criticism in the light—of course, with phobias, the rule of thumb is that anything can happen, so this may be true. Daylight is a known fear of vampires, though that would technically be for medical, not psychological, reasons.

Daylight or sunshine (*phenogophobia* or *phengophobia*)

Fear of daylight or sunshine. This fear may be related to the fear of being observed or scrutinized (social phobia). It is rarely mentioned, even in blogs, other than in the usual lists of possible phobias.

Floods (*antlophobia*)

Fear of floods. *Antlia* is Greek for pump. Floods can be life-destroying events, and people whose homes have been submerged may be particularly vulnerable to lifetime concern about being caught in a flood again. People who have been caught in a flash flood may develop a fear of storms and may even cancel outings in order not to travel if they live in areas that are prone to flooding. In some low-lying countries and islands, the threat of melting glaciers and rising sea waters has triggered some worry over eventual flooding. Fear of tsunamis—tidal waves caused by disturbances under the ocean—would fit in this category as well.

Fog (*homichlophobia* or *nebulaphobia*)

Fear of fog. One may fear becoming lost, disoriented, or injured in the fog or may react to the sense of being closed in by the fog (which would perhaps be a variant of claustrophobia). Specific fears of injury due to walking or driving into obstacles, fears of dangers such as threatening animals or dangerous humans, or supernatural fears associated with fog (ghosts, vampires, etc.) may all be present. Even the dampness and cold associated with fog may add to one's discomfort.

Forests or woods (*xylophobia* or *hylophobia*)

Fear of forests or woods. Forests can be mysterious and frightening places for children and adults; myths and stories abound about the dangers of forests, whether they include becoming lost or disoriented, being injured due to difficult terrain, or being threatened, pursued, bitten, or eaten by strange animals (from bears to reptiles to annoying bugs). Some people feel claustrophobic in forests and only feel comfortable in open areas such as prairies or fields. Traditionally, people feared robbers, unfriendly inhabitants or natives, or other unknown dangers in forests. This is not the same as the fear of being in dark woods at night, which is *nyctohylophobia* (see next listing).

Forests or woods at night (*nyctohylophobia*)

Fear of forests at night or of dark, wooded areas. People may fear forests at any time (*see* Forests, above), but nighttime brings special dangers and threats, from further disorientation or injury to mysterious, unknown sounds to increased danger from nocturnal predators. A safe forest in the daytime can feel like an entirely different and more dangerous world after dark.

Frost, ice, or cold (*cryophobia*)

See Cold.

Gravity (*barophobia*)

Fear of gravity.

Hurricanes or tornadoes (*lilasophobia*)

Fear of hurricanes or tornadoes. People may fear loss of control, injury, death, or loss of their property. Those who have lived through hurricanes or tornadoes may retain vivid memories of the events and may have lingering post-traumatic stress symptoms, but some people with these phobias get them simply by watching films or news reports about tornadoes or hurricanes. If you have this phobia, you may feel fine unless there are signs or forecasts of a pending storm, at which time your fears may switch into high gear. People with this fear may be constantly checking weather reports, and many own special weather radios so they can have constant weather updates. Coping with such fears can involve everything from avoiding going or even looking outside during a storm to being hypervigilant about the weather during storm periods—or even relocating to a new part of the country that is perceived as safer.

Lakes (*limnophobia*)

Fear of lakes. Like most phobias of large, ordinarily harmless environmental objects, it may involve any of a number of particulars, whether it's fear of being on the water, fears of a disgust sort (e.g., because a lake may "smell like fish"), fear of boating on a lake, or may be related to fears of drowning or of fish in the lake, etc. (Like many phobias, the term seems to be used for any general fear or discomfort related to lakes, though the particular thing about lakes that people fear may vary quite a bit.) There are no research studies on how prevalent this fear may be.

Lightning or thunder (*brontophobia, cerauntophobia, karaunophobia,* or *tonitrophobia*)

Fear of lightning and/or thunder and/or thunderstorms. (*Astrophobia* usually refers to fear of thunderstorms.) This is a common fear in children (and household pets) as well as some adults. (Surveys show that about 3 percent of women and less than 1 percent of men have phobias for lightning or storms.) Fear of lightning and thunder was no doubt common back to prehistoric times. The psychological fear is likely related to fear of injury, feeling overwhelmed, and fear of something unknown or not well-understood. Actual experiences such as having seen a tree or something hit by lightning might make this fear more likely, though lightning is generally such an awesome sight that those kinds of traumatic experiences aren't needed to develop the fear. Survivors of lightning strikes may experience permanent neurological damage, along with severe burns and/or disfigurement, and disability; knowing these risks can add to the fear. Fear of being struck by lightning is actually a fairly normal and adaptive fear, but extreme fear that slides into phobic territory can lead people to become overly obsessed with the dangers of a storm and so hide indoors in interior rooms, experience severe anxiety reactions, or do other things to avoid storms. In some such cases, even seeing a cloud or hearing weather forecasts that mention a chance of thunderstorms can trigger hours of discomfort and apprehension.

Northern lights (*auroraphobia*)

Fear of the Aurora Borealis or auroral lights. Auroras are colorful displays of light visible in higher northern or southern latitudes. There are no studies or even reports of phobias of auroras in the scientific research, but it would not be unheard of for something as extraordinary as auroras to provoke fear in a very small number of people.

Ocean or sea (*thalassophobia*)

Fear of the ocean or the sea. From the ancient Greek *thalassa* for sea. The fear can involve anything related to the sea, from waves to wide open wet spaces to fears of undersea creatures. Fears of the ocean reportedly increased for a time after the release of the 1975 film *Jaws*. (*See also* Sharks in Chapter 4.)

Open high places (*aeroacrophobia*)

Fear of open high places. This phobia is similar to fear of heights (*acrophobia*), though it generally refers partly to the sensation of vertigo people may experience. (*See also* Heights in Chapter 7.)

Open spaces (*agoraphobia*)

Fear of open spaces. Agoraphobia is a very common and, often, a very disabling fear. It is discussed extensively in Chapter 11.

Rain (*ombrophobia* or *pluviophobia*)

Fear of rain. Practical reasons for fearing rain can include fear of flooding or dampness, particularly if one lives in an area where floods seem imminent; other reasons can include the ruination of crops for farmers or that rain may interfere with activities or plans, ranging from construction to picnics. Some people simply fear being caught in the rain for the loss of control it can inspire, while some may fear having outfits ruined or the discomfort of getting wet outdoors. Others can feel that rainy days bring feelings of gloom or may trigger depressions.

Rivers (*potamophobia* or *potamphobia*)

Fear of rivers. From the ancient Greek *potamos* for river. Can include fear of crossing rivers, currents or rushing waters, things living in the river, drowning in a river, or floods.

Snow (*chionophobia*)

Fear of snow. From the ancient Greek *chion* for snow. While not the kind of phobia that turns up in clinics very often, the fear of snow or snowstorms is probably not uncommon among people who live in climates where snowfalls occur. Snow can create a number of practical and sometimes life-threatening problems, and people do report being traumatized by experiences of heavy snowfalls when they are involved in severe difficulties driving or traffic accidents. Snowstorms bring cold, wet, hypothermia-inducing conditions. They reduce visibility, and this can disorient people. Snow can result in disrupted plans, shutdowns of travel in entire regions, power outages, slippery driving and walking conditions, and even avalanches. Snow shoveling is a leading cause of heart attacks. Snowmen can be scary, and snowball fights can put your eye out.

Stars (*siderophobia* or *astrophobia*)

Fear of stars. Mostly this phobia is linked to ancient superstitions or beliefs about the stars, such as in astrology.

Thunder (*ceraunophobia* or *cerauntophobia*)

See Lightning or thunder.

Thunder and lightning, or thunderstorms (*astraphobia*, *astrapophobia*, *brontophobia*, *ceranophobia*, *cerauntophobia*, or *keraunophobia*)

Fear of thunder and lightning, or thunderstorms. (*See also* Lightning or thunder.)

Trees (*dendrophobia*)

Fear of trees. Possibly a rare fear, but people who have it often say it began in childhood and may attribute it to having seen a scary movie in which trees were threatening or could talk or move (like the trees in the *Wizard of Oz* or *Lord of the Rings*). It's also possible that practical concerns—like falling branches or hidden dangers in trees—can trigger a fear response. People with this fear may have difficulty being under or near trees, may not be able to buy a house if the yard has trees, and may avoid being in the woods.

Water (*aquaphobia* or *hydrophobia*)

Fear of water. Generally this has to do with the fear of drowning; it can include fear of swimming, going in or near the water, being on a boat, or even of washing or contacting water. This is an ancient fear and was first recorded by the ancient Roman physician Celsus, who recommended throwing someone into the water or holding them under in order to cure their fear. (It would probably have had the opposite effect—generally forced and sudden exposure to feared situations or objects tends to further traumatize a person due to the shock and sudden loss of control; they generally also learn to fear and/or hate the person who subjects them to this fear.) (*See also* Lakes, Ocean or sea, Rivers.)

Hydrophobia is also an old medical term for rabies, which is based on the fact that when a person is suffering from this disease, they may develop both an extreme thirst but also a strong aversion to water. (Medical uses of the term *phobia* refer more to a physically-based aversion, avoidance, or discomfort than to an emotional reaction.) Hence, *hydrophobophobia* is the fear of getting rabies. (*See* Chapter 6.)

Waves or wavelike motions (*cymophobia* or *kymophobia*)

Fear of waves or wavelike motions. Comes from the ancient Greek *kymo*, or wave. In some cases, waves may be experienced as overwhelming; sometimes people recall childhood experiences of waves knocking them over or pulling them into the water. One may also associate waves with seasickness, illness, or nausea due to their motion and its effect on the body's balance/vestibular system in the inner ear, which, when disrupted, can cause nausea, vomiting, and seasickness. Even looking at waves, at a boat bobbing up and down, or similar things can trigger this feeling if a person has already experienced the sickness. Waves or the sight of the sea or seascapes can be anxiety triggers as well.

Whirlpools or dizziness (*dinophobia*)

The same term is used for both fear of whirlpools and fear of dizziness. People may be afraid of being injured or swept away, or of loss of control in a whirlpool, or may associate it with dizziness. (*See also* Dizziness or vertigo in Chapter 6.)

Wind (*ancraophobia* or *anemophobia*)

Fear of wind. This phobia can include fears of stormy or inclement weather, of being knocked over, or of property or personal injury due to wind damage.

6

Blood and Gore:
Medical Phobias

In This Chapter

- ◆ What are blood-injection-injury phobias?
- ◆ Other kinds of medical phobias
- ◆ List of medical phobias

Phobias come from feelings of vulnerability, and our bodies are perhaps the thing we tend to feel most vulnerable about. That's probably why there are so many fears related to medical topics, from fear of getting injections to fears of diseases.

The relationship between anxiety disorders and medical problems is strong, but not simple. Research shows that people with generally high levels of anxiety or depression tend to report many more medical concerns. Of course, that is not to say that the complaints of anxious patients are all in their heads. No doubt, many people with very faint signs of actual medical conditions may sense that something is wrong and so their worrying, and physical preoccupation, increases. Likewise, if you've had some actual physical problems such as a heart attack, or even have a family history of certain conditions, your sense of vulnerability and anxiety will often increase.

Nevertheless, it's a common fact known to most doctors that the "real" problem suffered by many of their patients with physical complaints is fundamentally psychological. Anxiety tends to increase our awareness of dangers of all sorts, and so awareness of bodily threats can swell disproportionately as our anxiety increases. (And note that psychological problems are no less real than physical ones! In fact, the more we learn about brain imaging, the harder it is to assert that there are *any* psychological problems that don't have at least some physical components.)

In this chapter we'll review the major body fears. There are two categories of medical-related fears that we will explore. The first are the "blood-injection-injury" phobias, which involve reactions such as fainting at the sight of blood; other medically related phobias involve fears of various diseases, medical complications or conditions, etc.

Fainting at the Sight of Blood and Gore

A nurse once told me, while poking me with pointy things to draw blood, that many of the patients who faint during such a procedure are the biggest, strongest, youngest, and healthiest guys and gals. This highlights the interesting and sometimes paradoxical nature of blood-injection-injury phobias.

The *Diagnostic and Statistical Manual of Mental Disorders* (DSM-IV) includes an entire category of specific phobias that revolve around the topics of blood, injections, and injury. According to DSM-IV, "This subtype should be specified if the fear is cued by seeing blood or an injury or by receiving an injection or other invasive medical procedure."

The experience of seeing yourself bleed, getting a shot, or seeing someone else get physically injured generally triggers a series of reflexive physical responses. This kind of reaction, whether in a mild or a full-blown phobic form, is different from other phobias.

For one thing, the usual emotional response to bloodshed is not feelings of anxiety or fear—patients surveyed don't say they feel afraid so much as squeamish. The physical reactions to blood or injury (which can affect a patient getting a flu shot or a nurse watching a surgery) happen in two separate and different phases. In the first phase, the person's heart rate goes up—this happens as they anticipate the shot or injury. After that, in the second phase, their heart rate slows dramatically (the so-called *vasovagal response*) and their blood pressure drops. This can lead to feelings of queasiness or even fainting. Three quarters of people with blood-injection-injury phobias have reported that they have histories of fainting.

def•i•ni•tion

The **vasovagal response** is a fainting episode triggered by stress, pain, prolonged standing, strong emotions, or other things. The episode may begin with lightheadedness, nausea, weakness, perspiration, or visual disturbances and may end in fainting due to reduced heart rate and blood pressure. The person usually recovers within a few minutes as blood flow to the brain is restored.

It's thought that this kind of physical reaction may have evolved as a natural bodily defense against injury. The sharp drop in blood pressure and heart rate would have helped protect injured people from too much blood loss, as might their being temporarily immobilized by fainting.

In a phobia, this protective reflex is triggered by either the actual injury or by the fear of this reaction happening. People begin to fear they may faint if they get injections, during dental procedures, etc. The result can be delaying needed medical care or great discomfort and inconvenience.

Blood-injection-injury phobias are thought to be partly inherited.

Other Medical Phobias

In addition to blood-injection-injury phobias, there are many phobias (or at least, phobia *names*) that focus on other kinds of physical injury or physical vulnerability. As with other kinds of phobias, it's sometimes not easy to spot the clear line between an obsessive concern with one's health and an actual phobia. Nor is it always clear that a phobia is severe or disabling enough to technically be considered an anxiety disorder according to the DSM-IV.

In some cases, the phobia may be named but not really be very prevalent, or it may not exist at all. For instance, a great many of the phobia-of-disease names that turn up in online phobia lists have not been researched, or even documented, in either the medical or the psychological literature of the past hundred years. This isn't to say one can't be afraid of getting kidney disease or joint immobility (two examples of such "phobias" in the following section, which have never been reported, as far as I can determine, in the thousands of medical and psychology references I searched).

In writing about these particular phobias, I've tried to strike a respectful balance between mentioning the fact that the phobia hasn't been documented in the professional research with the fact that people can, and probably have, developed phobias for just about anything. Searching blogs, a modern way of documenting just about any kind of human experience, shows that often people do write about having some of these phobias, though their actual descriptions may be fairly lighthearted, or not really match what is meant by a phobia. Still, it's sometimes been helpful finding in blogs that people do indeed suffer profoundly from phobias that have seldom been noted in the professional research literature. But these fears do have in common physical concerns, which are often severe enough to preoccupy a person, to trigger a lot of health-related avoidance behavior, and to disrupt their life.

Medical Phobias

Airsickness (*aeronausiphobia*)

Fear of becoming sick while flying. This fear can lead people to avoid flying, often at great expense and inconvenience to themselves. If they fly, they may obsess the entire time over whether they are feeling sick "yet," which may actually work like a self-fulfilling prophecy, resulting in nausea, vomiting, intense anxiety, or panic over being "trapped" in the in-flight situation. This phobia can develop as a result of actual airsickness triggered by the motion of flying, the experience of being sick in other situations (such as driving or amusement park rides), seeing others get sick, or some combination of these experiences. The presence of airsickness bags in every airplane seat may work as a kind of suggestion that triggers increased awareness of sickness in some people.

Amnesia (*amnesiphobia*)

Fear of amnesia or memory loss. It's worth noting that many people do develop a fear of getting Alzheimer's disease and so having memory problems, but it's generally not the case that people confuse Alzheimer's and amnesia. Amnesia is a popular device in movies and TV, used to allow characters to conveniently forget critical things about themselves or their experiences; this popularity might lead some people to dwell on amnesia as something to fear. However, like so many (most!) phobias that appear on phobia lists, there is little or no published research to show that anyone ever really develops a phobia of amnesia. It's not impossible, but neither is it likely.

Angina (*anginaphobia*)

Fear of heart problems such as angina pectoris. The origin of the word is the Greek term *ankhein* or *ankhone* (English spellings are only approximations), meaning either a choking, or to choke; here, that would refer to the idea of a choked-off blood vessel. People who have had heart attacks, older people, or those with generally higher levels of anxiety or depression may tend to fear heart attacks. Likewise, certain agoraphobia symptoms or panic episodes may be misinterpreted as a heart attack. (*See also* Heart disease.)

While it's important to never assume that your chest pain or other symptoms are just due to anxiety, the (maybe reassuring) fact is that many "heart" symptoms are, in fact, the result of anxiety. When in doubt, though, always seek prompt medical attention!

Blindness or blindness in a visual field (*blindness phobia* or *scotomaphobia*)

Generally, *scotomaphobia* is defined as fear of blindness in a visual field. This phobia is on the phobia lists and is plausible, but there are no reports of it existing in the medical or psychological literature. The term is generally defined (here we are talking about Internet definitions, since it does not seem to be in the medical literature) as referring to blindness "in a visual field," which would seem to imply a condition of partial blindness. More rarely, the term *scotomaphobia* is applied to a more general fear of blindness, though generally people just call that blindness phobia. However, as with most seldom-researched phobias, it's not clear whether this refers to the fear of going blind as an actual clinical phobia (a severe, disruptive preoccupation with going blind), or just a realistic fear people may have—such as the kind of fear photographers and other people whose life revolves around visual ability; or persons with diseases such as diabetes, which can cause blindness; or diabetic photographers.

Blood (*hemophobia*, *hemaphobia*, or *hematophobia*)

Fear of blood. Blood phobia, the strong physical reaction of nausea, anxiety, fainting, to seeing blood, is one of the most common phobias. Many people with the vulnerability to strong reactions to seeing blood don't actually report being afraid, and some may not even realize they have strong reactions to seeing blood until it happens. Physical reactions can include sudden squeamishness, closing the eyes, nausea, or fainting. Blood phobias can lead a person to avoid medical care, donating blood, etc. In rare cases, this can even lead to life-threatening situations when a person badly needs medical attention but is afraid of getting it. More common may be that a person doesn't actually anticipate or know that he fears seeing blood, but then getting nauseated or passing out when he suddenly sees his own or someone else's blood or injury.

Body odors (*osmophobia*, *osphreisiophobia*, or *bromidrosiphobia*)

Fear of body odors, other odors, smells. Some people fear their own body odors and can become preoccupied with them, or they may avoid social situations for fear of being noticed as having an odor. They may become obsessed with these concerns, over-use deodorants, or bathe repeatedly and obsessively. Related to this can be fears of various smells (associated with things such as uncleanliness, fears of disease, etc.). Sometimes people who get migraines may notice distinct smells or odors (or other signs such as flashing lights) before the migraines, and so might develop a fear of certain smells.

Bowel movements—painful (*defecaloesiophobia*)

Fear of painful bowel movements. People may develop this fear after actual painful bowel movements as a result of surgery or illness. (*See also* Constipation.)

Brain disease (*meningitophobia*)

Fear of brain disease. This fear is not listed in any medical or psychological research databases, so it's apparently rare (though of course, it's entirely reasonable and plausible that one might have such a fear). At a certain point in life, many people begin to notice fading memory skills, and so a certain level of preoccupation with Alzheimer's may plausibly fall under this title.

Cancer (*cancerophobia* or *carcinophobia*)

Fear of cancer. Cancer is one of the leading causes of death, and few people are untouched by the disease in either themselves or loved ones. Hence, it's not surprising that fear of developing cancer is one of the more common medical fears. As a realistic concern, fear of cancer can be responsible for many good self-care practices such as smoking avoidance and doing regular breast or testicular exams. But it can also lead some people to become preoccupied and to take extreme measures that are not helpful, such as being too afraid to go to a doctor to have symptoms checked out. Some people may avoid contact with others with cancer or may even avoid having children for fear that their children may develop the disease. They may habitually interpret minor symptoms as cancer symptoms, which can reinforce constant anxiety and require many doctor visits to seek reassurance for minor or routine symptoms (since almost everyone has "symptoms" of something or other virtually every day).

Childbirth (*maleusiophobia, tocophobia, parturiphobia,* or *lockiophobia*)

Fear of childbirth. This fear is fairly common, with estimates that it affects 6 to 10 percent of pregnant women. The fear may be present before pregnancy but increase to true phobic or anxiety disorder levels once a woman knows she is pregnant. Fear of childbirth may begin in adolescence or may be the result of a prior experience of a difficult childbirth or of a coexisting depression. The fear may be focused on one of several areas including fear of pain, fear of complications, fear of having a bad childbirth experience for other reasons, or fear of losing control or behaving in an embarrassing fashion. Women who are denied control over the method of childbirth (e.g., who request but are denied caesareans) may have an increase in fear as a result. This fits with the general rule of thumb about anxiety situations: the more control a person feels they have over the situation, the lower their anxiety tends to be. As such, more contemporary medical teams emphasize talking through fears with the woman, helping her to make choices and decisions, and affirming that her fears are normal and can be addressed in a supportive fashion.

Expectant fathers can also experience childbirth fears, particularly if they are planning to (or expected to) participate in the birth process.

Choking (*anginophobia*)

Fear of choking or of suffocation. The origin of the word is the Greek term *ankhein* or *ankhone* (English spellings are only approximations), meaning either a choking, or to choke. (Hence, the heart symptom of angina also refers to a choking or constricting of a blood vessel.) The fear of choking may originate in an experience of nearly choking while eating and may lead some people to restrict their eating to foods they think are safe or that they won't be able to choke on. Some have difficulties swallowing pills because of fear they'll gag or choke on them. The word *anginophobia* can also refer to fear of angina or to a fear of smothering. (*See also* Angina.)

Cholera (*cholerophobia*)

Fear of cholera. (It also refers to fear of anger, which I discuss in Chapter 8.) Cholera is a form of gastroenteritis that can be caught by drinking or eating contaminated food or water. Historically, many people died during cholera epidemics in Europe and the United States; currently, the disease is still more common in areas where sanitation is poor, including parts of south-central and southeast Asia, Central and South America, and Africa. Epidemics could be terrifying: severe cholera can be rapidly fatal. As with many disease phobia terms that address fairly rational fears of truly awful diseases, there are actually no reports of a cholera phobia in the medical or psychological research databases.

Constipation (*coprastasophobia*)

Fear of constipation. From the Greek *copro-* for dung and *stasi* for standing. Constipation is the inability to have bowel movements or having painful bowel movements. Sometimes as a result of having had painful bowel movements or constipation (perhaps combined with anxiety, depression, or a tendency to worry about one's physical symptoms), a person may develop the fear of ongoing or chronic constipation. In some cases this leads to an overreliance on laxatives, which can in turn increase the problem of constipation. (*See also* Bowel movements—painful.)

Dental surgery (*odontophobia*)

Fear of dental surgery. Contrary to what you may find on the Internet, it is not the "fear of teeth"—that's *odonophobia*. The term *odontophobia* is sometimes also used to refer to the broader areas of dental phobia, fear of dentists, etc. (*See also* Dentists.)

Dentists (*dentophobia*)

Fear of dentists, dentistry, or more specifically, of receiving dental care. Some degree of this fear appears to be very common, with 8 in 10 people in the United States admitting to at least some dental anxiety—and about 1 in 20 confessing extreme anxiety. As such, a great deal of the time and research of both dentists and mental health professionals has been devoted to studying and reducing dental fears, and hundreds of studies have been conducted on dental phobias. This fear leads many people to delay or forego necessary dental care or to experience extreme anxiety and discomfort while undergoing care. In other cases, people may have difficulty completing a dentist's visit due to their anxiety, which can actually interfere with the dentist's work. In addition to the usual anxiety symptoms such as sweating, pounding heart, panicky feelings, and the like, dental phobic reactions during treatment can include such things as gagging, coughing, choking, and intensified awareness of pain experiences, all of which may complicate treatment.

Recently, researchers have argued that dental anxiety might more accurately be classified as a kind of post-traumatic stress disorder (PTSD). This is because so-called dental phobia lacks one of the defining features of a true phobia, namely a recognition that one's fears are unreasonable or out of proportion. In fact, research does suggest that most people with dental fears actually have had some unpleasant, painful, or uncomfortable experiences in the dental chair, so that their fears are technically more similar to those of people with PTSD.

Aside from the pain, another factor that seems to contribute to dental anxieties is the experience of a lack of control. Further, experiencing one's dentist as cold, distant, or uncaring may trigger greater anxiety than actual pain experiences.

Dental fears can be related to the experience of needles and drills or to broader blood-injection-injury fears such as queasiness at the sight of blood. Somewhat more women than men have dental fears according to some surveys, and there is also evidence that some women's fears may be indirectly related to other traumatic experiences such as histories of sexual abuse, assault, or other traumas. (*See also* Dentists in Chapter 8.)

Diabetes (*diabetophobia*)

Fear of diabetes. Diabetes is a metabolic disturbance in which the body cannot process glucose (sugar) in the blood properly; it can lead to a host of complications including blindness, amputation, kidney failure, and early death, particularly if it is not properly managed by diet, exercise, medications and, often, injections of insulin. *Diabetophobia* is, however, another of those named phobias that turn up on all the phobia lists and seem to make sense (why *wouldn't* someone be afraid of this disease?) but seldom, if ever, are documented as existing. There is little or no evidence in the medical or psychological research literature—or, for that matter, in the popular literature (such as blog searches)—that very many people actually develop phobia-level fears of *getting* diabetes. Like most disease phobias, one may have a healthy fear of or respect for the dangers of the illness, but that's not really the same thing as a phobia.

The phobia issue that does commonly arise has more to do with the fears of currently diabetic patients. In addition to the anxieties and depression that may come with discovering that one has a serious, life-altering (and life-threatening) illness, the need to monitor blood sugar levels and to take injections stirs up blood-injection-injury phobias in a sizable percentage of diabetic patients. Research shows that many of these patients actually do poorly on measures of physical health because they may be reluctant to take injections or stick themselves in order to obtain the small blood samples needed to monitor blood glucose levels. Other common fears that may interfere with treatment involve fear of doctors, doctor visits, and the like, along with some degree of depression and embarrassment or shame at having the disease. Patients may develop a phobiclike reaction to letting their blood sugar levels go too low, since low blood sugar can result in a severe anxious reaction, shaking, weakness, and even loss of consciousness. Again, this can lead to poor self-care and reluctance to keep blood sugar in lower, healthy ranges. Many also report "diabetes fatigue," which is more like burnout at having to constantly manage and monitor their condition. (*See also* Blood, Injections, Needles.)

Disease (*nosophobia* or *nosmaphobia*)

Fear of contracting a disease. From the Greek term *nosos*, meaning disease. As with most phobias, this is connected with a sense of personal vulnerability. A person's fear of having some awful disease may increase when they have unexplained symptoms or get inaccurate and terrifying information about those symptoms (for instance, if they rely on Internet sites for health information without getting expert medical advice when it's needed). Some people classify "medical student's disease" (fear of getting every new disease they learn about) as a form of *nosophobia*. Some writers have noted that our culture may tend to foster a kind of group *nosophobia* because of the frequent warnings about seemingly limitless health dangers from almost anything that is in our food, water, or air fresheners—if you really pay attention to the news, you should be constantly terrified of an endless list of diseases.

Dizziness or vertigo (*dinophobia* or *illyngophobia*)

Fear of becoming dizzy or developing vertigo when looking down. Related to fear of heights (*acrophobia*). A person who is prone to vertigo or dizziness might also have some kind of inner ear disturbance, so medical check-ups might be in order. Dizziness can also occur due to hyperventilation and/or as part of a panic attack; this can in turn make a person more worried whenever she is in a situation where she has had such reactions, which can make future episodes of dizziness or panic more likely. Persons who have experienced dizziness-causing events such as seasickness or carsickness may develop fears of going on the water, driving, etc. (*See also* Heights in Chapter 7.)

Doctor visits (*iatrophobia*)

Fear of going to the doctor. People can find doctor visits uncomfortable for many reasons, including fear of injury or pain (needles, exams, etc.), fear of authority figures, or fear of humiliation or embarrassment (disrobing, having to reveal poor health habits or personal problems, etc.). Many people have recollections of painful visits to doctors as infants or children and so may associate not just doctors, but doctors' offices, nurses, disinfectant smells, etc., with their fears. Other people fear getting bad news about a disease. People with fear of doctors may avoid necessary medical care, which can have a serious impact on their health or longevity.

Double vision (*diplophobia* or *diplopiaphobia*)

Fear of developing double vision. Possibly a symptom of psychosis or delusion.

Dying or death (*thanatophobia*)

Fear of dying or death. The term *thanatos* is Greek for death. This is a fairly universal fear, and some experts say that many other phobias are really rooted in this fear. For instance, fear of diseases, choking, or the fears one feels during a panic episode are often really the result of the conviction that dying is imminent. Fear of dying is fairly common among people struggling with various other forms of mental illness. The fear often starts in childhood and can persist or increase throughout a person's life, or it may spring up among people who become ill with a physical condition.

Some writers and philosophers have speculated that the fear of death is a powerful force shaping cultures. By emphasizing youthfulness, many of the commercial enticements and advertisements used to sell everything from breath spray to garden supplies make use of our powerful desire to feel safe from anything that might suggest age, disease, imperfection, or personal limitation—all of which are associated with death. People avoid talking about death—or sometimes even saying the word—and may go to great lengths to avoid referring to it. In fact, one of the common difficulties faced by people with terminal illnesses is that their relatives and loved ones may avoid talking with them about their condition and death even when it is necessary to do so.

Erection, losing (*medomalacuphobia*)

Fear of losing a penile erection. Many males worry excessively about the possibility of having difficulty getting, or sustaining, an erection during sexual activity. Fears include primarily not being seen as virile, masculine, or adequate as a lover, which may be partially a form of social phobia or fear of critical evaluation or rejection by others. Issues of status, self-image, or medical concerns may have bearing on this phobia. Since erections are notoriously vulnerable to anxiety, such fears may become self-fulfilling prophecies—which is often the case with almost any kind of social or performance anxiety issue.

Erections (*medorthophobia*)

Fear of penile erections or erect penises.

Fainting (*asthenophobia*)

Fear of fainting. This can be a component of agoraphobia (see Chapter 11), in that it is a fear of an uncontrolled physical or emotional reaction; a person may fear going into open or public places due to this fear or due to related fears such as having strong panic reactions.

Fatigue (*kopophobia*)

Fear of fatigue or becoming fatigued. People may associate fatigue with weakness, vulnerability, or illness. This may have a basis in fact if they have some medical condition in which fatigue signals some kind of danger (such as someone with a heart condition becoming very short of breath). Other people may misinterpret symptoms or become overly focused on feelings such as fatigue, resulting all too often in increased feelings of discomfort and anxiety. Anxiety can at times be highly fatiguing, so of course anxiety about one's fatigue can become something of a vicious cycle: anxiety wears the person out, and then they notice this increased fatigue and become more anxious as they tell themselves there is definitely something wrong. People who have had actual fatiguing physical conditions may also develop an anxiety problem about their fatigue, possibly compounding both problems; in fact, some physicians might consider this to be the rule rather than the exception for many patients. Other people may view any fatigue as a kind of personal failure or sign of weakness and may neglect the need for adequate rest and self-care.

Gaining weight

See Weight, gaining.

Heart disease (*cardiophobia*)

Fear of heart disease. This is similar to *anginaphobia*, which is the fear of a heart attack. *Cardiophobia* is a broader term that includes fear of any sort of heart disease. More than just a specific fear, in medicine the term denotes a syndrome in which a person may have recurring episodes of abrupt pain and palpitations (or other heart sensations) and may have anxieties about heart problems—all without any physical evidence that they actually have a heart problem. This syndrome may be related to panic attacks. It may recur when the person is feeling stressed or aroused, and it may not disappear even when the person is reassured that their heart is fine. (*See also* Angina.)

Infection (*molysmophobia* or *molysomophobia*)

Fear of infection, dirt, or contamination. Fears of infection or contamination are probably related to the basic (and self-protective) human feeling of disgust. People may avoid contact with food, objects (toilet paper on the seats, anyone?), or people who seem unclean, dirty, or potentially infectious. In many cultures, divisions between "clean" and "unclean" can extend to whole groups of people or may add to the complexity and confusion of the culture's attitudes toward topics such as sexuality. Fear of infection or contamination may increase during periods of concern about disease (epidemics or plagues), certain times of the year, or in certain settings (e.g., hospitals). Phobias about infection or contamination can be hard to distinguish from obsessive-compulsive disorder (OCD) or hypochondriacal concerns. On the other hand, an essential part of public health education—particularly in cultures lacking fundamental hygiene education or resources—is often to deliberately develop a reasonable amount of fear of contamination due to unsanitary conditions (e.g., advertising campaigns that advocate hand washing or safe sex).

Injections (*trypanophobia*)

Fear of injections. Other terms sometimes used include *aichmophobia*, *belonephobia*, and *tryanophobia*, though these terms refer more to needles, pins, or other things that merely poke and stick, whereas *trypanophobia* is often reserved for the medical injection aspect of the fear. *Trypanophobia* is a very common fear, with an estimated 1 in 10 medical patients having the phobic reaction (and that number is thought to be low, since many people with the condition may avoid going to doctors even when needed). This phobia may or may not include a conscious awareness of a sense of fear of injections, but it can also include simply reacting when one is receiving or about to receive an injection—or even when one sees someone else injected or looks at syringes. The phobia dramatically interferes with much-needed medical and dental care; many people either refuse to go into medical settings or may have great difficulty participating in medical care once it becomes apparent they will be asked to receive a shot or vaccination, have blood drawn, etc. The condition also poses serious problems for people with conditions such as diabetes that require regular injections. Patients with those conditions are often expected to inject themselves, which also can pose severe difficulties that can even be life-threatening. (*See also* Diabetes, Needles, Vaccinations.)

This phobia falls in the blood-injection-injury DSM-IV category. It may also have elements of disgust reaction in addition to sensitivity to the sight and feel of injections.

There are actually several different kinds of injection phobias. Most people have the so-called "vasovagal" reaction in which seeing or anticipating injections can lead to initial heart rate and blood pressure increases and fear, followed by a drop in blood pressure and heart rate, with nausea, sweating, tinnitus (ringing in the ears) and fainting. According to Dr. James Hamilton, a physician who has studied this condition, there are a small number of instances in which the drop in blood pressure and heart rate from this response have been so severe that patients have died. (However, there aren't many statistics on this so far.)

Other categories of injection phobias exist, including cases in which previous traumas related to injections lead the patient to react not just to injection, but to other medical situations or objects associated with injections (alcohol on cotton balls, medical settings, etc.). Some patients, who as children were restrained and injured (or badly frightened) during injections, may develop resistive phobias—they may not just avoid the shots but become actively resistant, flail or pull away, or

even flee the doctor's office. Still others have hyperalgesic responses—
they feel not just anxious or faint, but experience the shots as extremely
or unbearably painful, far out of proportion to any actual tissue damage
that is done by needles. (In contrast, many patients—such as diabetics
who receive or give themselves multiple daily shots—may report that
they literally don't feel most of their shots.) Finally, there are people
who have strong phobic or fainting reactions to seeing other people
getting injections (in person or even in films, etc.).

Injection phobias may sometimes be dismissed or inadequately handled
by medical staff, either because it seems like such a common and mild
concern that they may just assume patients should respond without
complaint, or simply because slowing things down and responding
patiently and sympathetically (and with special skills) to patients with
these concerns is not cost effective. The result is that, often, dentists
or physicians who develop reputations for being especially sensitive and
skilled at working with needle-phobic patients become favored referrals
of therapists and other practitioners who have patients struggling with
these concerns.

Injury (*traumatophobia*)

Fear of injury. Often, the fear of injury is also the actual fear in many
other specific phobias, but as with other terms, this one has a name
of its own. Fear of injury can come from experience with injuries in
general or may be based on some kind of particular experience (for
example, if one has fallen while walking on ice and been injured). It
is one of the fundamental human fears; generally, fear of injury is an
important survival mechanism. (Without it, or when supplies of it are
low, people do tend to get into trouble more often.) Taken to extremes,
though, it can trigger avoidance of even normal activities because they
are linked in the traumatophobe's mind with the risk of getting hurt.

Insanity, dealing with (*lyssophobia*)

Fear of dealing with insanity or mentally ill people. Many people find it
frightening to interact with mentally ill, confused, or confusing people.
While the actual danger posed by individuals suffering from diseases
such as schizophrenia is quite low, the stereotype persists that people
who seem crazy or who act differently may be dangerous. Besides fear

of harm, it can be confusing and anxiety-provoking to try to understand someone who perhaps isn't acting in a typical manner, whose speech makes no sense, or who seems to be preoccupied with or trying to communicate things that don't fit with the conventional views of reality. Behavior that is different from the "norm" scares us. This may be partly the echoes of a genetically wired-in tendency to avoid "sick members of the herd" or may just flow from our uncertainty about how to respond. Psychoanalysts have sometimes suggested that we may fear the mentally unwell because their behavior unconsciously reminds us that we are all, at times, just a bit closer to the edge of madness than we might like to believe.

Joint immobility (*ankylophobia*)

Fear of immobility in the joints. There does not appear to be much (if any) medical or psychological research to verify that this phobia exists. However, there are a few studies showing that people suffering injuries or threats to limbs (lower limbs in particular) and people with joint hypermobility syndromes do have higher-than-average risk for anxiety disorders.

Kidney disease (*albuminurophobia*)

Fear of kidney disease. People with certain vulnerabilities (such as diabetics, who have high rates of kidney disease) can develop anxiety about this. Changes in urinary habits or vague back pain can lead some people to worry about this possibility. Medical evaluation and reassurance are often the treatments offered.

Leprosy (*leprophobia* or *lepraphobia*)

Fear of contracting leprosy. The term *leprosy* comes from the Greek word *lepi*, referring to fish scales. In addition to a fear of contracting leprosy, the term may refer to a healthy person being convinced that he actually has the disease. Leprosy is also called Hansen's disease; it is an infectious bacterial disease that affects skin and nerve tissue and upper respiratory tract mucosa. The fear of leprosy has been a widespread fear, both historically (e.g., the Bible has many references to the fear of leprosy; c.f. Leviticus 13:44–46) and still today in areas of the world where treatment of the disease is not available. Partly this fear is due to the mysterious and terrifying nature of the disease—it can result in significant physical disfigurement, often progressing to affect the skin, eyes, nerves, and limbs.

As a result of the intense fear of the disease, lepers would become outcasts, being forced to live—or perish—outside of towns. They sometimes gathered together in leper colonies that received little or no assistance from others. Indeed, people would not just shun but might actively repel lepers who attempted to enter villages or towns. While somewhat communicable, leprosy is in fact not particularly easy to catch—it's estimated that only about 1 person in 20 is actually capable of developing the disease.

Lockjaw or tetanus (*tetanophobia*)

Fear of contracting tetanus. Tetanus is a disease caused by infection by the *C. tetani* bacterium, which people or animals can get as the result of wounds (such as puncture wounds). The bacterium produces a neurotoxin called tetanospasmin, which causes skeletal muscles to contract. Among other things, this can create muscle spasms in the jaw (which is why it's called lockjaw) along with stiffness and spasms in other parts of the body. It has a fatality rate of about 11 percent and can be prevented by inoculation.

Medicine (*pharmacophobia*)

Fear of taking medications. Medications can be both powerful and mysterious, inspiring a range of feelings from hope to caution to fear. As evidence of that, consider the placebo effect, in which fake and chemically useless "medicines" can be as powerful (or even more powerful) than drugs in treating a wide range of medical conditions. Indeed, medicines generally interact powerfully with the human mind in all sorts of ways—so it's not surprising that people sometimes become fearful of taking medications. This can be due to a range of causes: general distrust of doctors, publicized concerns about the possible harm caused by certain medications, cultural beliefs about medicines and their dangers, or mental conditions such as general anxiety, a tendency toward hypochondria, or severe mental illness. One severe condition that can lead to a medicine phobia is idiopathic anaphylaxis, which is an allergic response that happens without a clear or identifiable physical cause. After having what seems to be an allergic response, a patient may decide that a certain medicine they took is something they are "allergic" to, and they can develop a phobia of it (and perhaps to other medications as well). This can cause other medical difficulties; the patient may be reluctant to take medicines that are perfectly safe because they are convinced the medicines are dangerous.

Medicines, new (*neopharmaphobia*)

Fear of taking new or experimental drugs.

Menstruation (*monophobia*)

Fear of menstruation. This may be present in both women and men and may flow (sorry) from various underlying fears. Young women may be unfamiliar with menstruating initially, or they may not have been informed and reassured by their parents or other family that it is normal and healthy; since blood is generally associated with injury and may also trigger fairly powerful blood phobia reactions, the sight of menstrual blood, or even the fear of it without seeing it, may be very frightening. Menstruation may also trigger feelings of embarrassment or shame in young or even older women—many older generations of women did feel shame and embarrassment at menstruation until recent generations developed movements to claim greater comfort with the facts of female sexuality. Still, in many historical and contemporary cultures, menstrual blood may be frightening. Young women may fear that boys or men know they are menstruating, and men may themselves find the topic of menstruation uncomfortable, similar to a blood phobia. The link between menstruation and sex—itself a frightening topic for many—may amplify fears, as does the association with pregnancy or the lack thereof. Many women and men find the thought of sex during menstruation uncomfortable or even repulsive, though in fact it is entirely harmless and healthy; in some cases, it's less the individual's own discomfort than their assumption that their partner may find sex at that time to be unpleasant, so they may tend to preemptively avoid it.

Microbes (*bacillophobia, baceriophobia, microbiophobia, microphobia,* or *mysophobia*)

Fear of germs, bacteria, microbes, or other microorganisms. This phobia can be related to disgust feelings or to fears of injury by infection. It can be related to, trigger, or be hard to distinguish from OCD, and it may lead to other phobias such as fears of getting, or having been exposed to, particular diseases. (*See also* Infection.)

Muscular incoordination (*ataxiophobia*)

Some sources define *ataxiophobia* as the fear of disorder (mess, clutter, etc.), while others use *ataxophobia* for that. A wide range of dictionaries such as the esteemed *Oxford English Dictionary* as well as relatively new online sources such as Wiktionary fail to list the term at all (not unusual). It seems most likely that *ataxiophobia* would be the best term since it includes the *ataxia* prefix the way that is most commonly converted to a phobia word (adding the "o" instead of the "a"). But of course, phobia-naming is a kind of wild-frontier sport where there aren't many rules and nobody's in charge.

Anyway, *ataxia* is muscular incoordination. The term comes from Greek, where *a* means without and *taxia* means order. Medically, this refers to a neurological sign in which muscle movements are not coordinated ("organized"). The term would suggest a fear of this happening, although—you guessed it—the term does not seem to actually exist in the medical or psychological research literature.

Needles (*aichmophobia*, *belonephobia*, or *tryanophobia*)

Fear of needles, pins, injections. (*See also* Injections, Vaccinations.)

Nosebleeds (*epistaxiophobia*)

Fear of nosebleeds. This phobia is never mentioned in medical or psychological research papers, and to date it's not even been blogged about except when people list random phobias that they want to cite from other online phobia lists. Were it to exist, it would probably be due to either fear of injury or pain (e.g., injuries to the nose, causing it to bleed) or to a vasovagal blood-injection-injury kind of reaction in which seeing blood or bleeding triggers the vasovagal reflex (reduced heart rate and blood pressure, fainting, etc.). (*See also* Blood.)

Pain (*algiophobia*, *ponophobia*, *odynophobia*, or *odynesphobia*)

Fear of pain. As with any phobia, it bears noting that, since most people fear pain, an excessive or unusually intense, emotional response is needed for a pain fear to be considered *algiophobia*.

Pain is, in fact, one of the more complicated subjects in human psychology and medicine. For one thing, pain is completely subjective—only the person experiencing it is able to determine how intense their pain is. An injury or stimulus that one person feels to be extremely agonizing may, to another, trigger only a mild experience of pain or no pain at all. In addition, pain levels within an individual will generally vary a great deal depending on things such as their general anxiety level, their stress level, the fears they may have about the cause of the pain, their experience dealing with similar pain, their expectations, the meaning they attach to the pain, their trauma history, their belief that they have control over the pain, and whether they are able to receive social support while enduring the pain.

Fear of pain can be disruptive in both everyday and medical settings. People may avoid new experiences, going places, or trying things because of their fear of being injured, and they may avoid going to doctors or dentists because of their fear that they will be forced to endure a painful experience. It is not uncommon for the fear of medical or dental pain to result in worsening of a person's medical or dental condition when they fail to obtain needed care as a result of their fears.

Pellagra (*pellagrophobia*)

Fear of contracting pellagra. Pellagra is a disease caused by vitamin deficiencies due to inadequate niacin and protein. It can lead to symptoms including diarrhea, skin lesions, dermatitis, dementia, mental confusion, and even death. It is rare in affluent societies except among homeless, alcoholic, or mentally ill persons, but is more common in Africa, Indonesia, Mexico, and China. While pellagra is found in various places in the world, *pellagrophobia* as a clinical condition is seemingly found only on lists of phobias.

Poisoned, being (*toxiphobia, toxophobia,* or *toxicophobia*)

Fear of being poisoned. This may refer to fear of being deliberately poisoned by others, or it may be a fear of accidental or inadvertent poisonings. It can also flow from a fear of contamination or germs, which would possibly involve primitive disgust reactions. Of course, most people would consider being poisoned to be something worth avoiding; for it to be a phobia, a person would need to be unrealistically preoccupied with the risks or fears of being poisoned. There may be a fine line between a *delusion* that involves the belief, suspicion, or sense of certainty that someone actually is trying to poison you and the fear or phobia that it might occur. The fear may be increased by books, films, or fantasies involving poisoning.

Poliomyelitis (*poliosophobia*)

Fear of contracting polio. Poliomyelitis is a disease caused by viral infection, characterized by a range of possible symptoms that can include muscle weakness or paralysis that often affects the legs. Polio was once one of the most feared of diseases, particularly after the latter portion of the nineteenth century when widespread epidemics of the disease struck Europe and the United States. (President Franklin Roosevelt was wheelchair-bound much of his life due to polio.) A vaccine for the disease was developed in the early 1950s, and now few people get the disease. Despite the once-widespread fear of the disease, there are apparently no studies of polio phobia in the psychiatric, medical, or psychological research.

Pregnancy

See Childbirth.

Rabies (*cynophobia, kynophobia, lyssophobia,* or *hydrophobophobia*)

Fear of contracting rabies. (This phobia is sometimes also listed as *cynophobia*, which is a fear of dogs). *Hydrophobia* is an old name for rabies. Literally, that term means fear of water (*hydro-*). The term became attached to rabies because rabies victims may develop a combination of severe thirst and a marked aversion to drinking water. Rabies is a viral disease that causes inflammation of the brain. It is usually fatal if not treated, and it usually is caused by the bite of an infected mammal (dogs, bats, raccoons, etc.). Since rabies is a horrible disease that kills thousands of people a year (mostly in Asia and Africa), fear of rabies is an entirely rational fear. Being careful about exposing yourself to any risk of infection (e.g., caution around wild or unknown animals, getting medical attention if bit by a strange animal) is a good precaution.

This is a good example of how realistic fears may be separated from phobias by only a fine line. The actual danger of rabies can become a phobia when a person begins to exaggerate the dangers of contracting the disease. For instance, a person may develop a fear of going any-where there may be wild animals, develop a tendency to obsess about whether they've been bitten by or exposed to any rabid animals, or begin to scrutinize their bodies for signs of bites. Sometimes people may avoid going to parks, zoos, or even visiting friends who have pets—even when they've been reassured the pets have had their rabies shots.

Rectal disease (*protophobia*, *proctophobia*, or *rectophobia*)

Fear of rectal disease.

Scratches or being scratched (*amychophobia*)

Fear of scratches or being scratched.

Skin disease or lesions (*dermatosiophobia*, *dermatopathophobia*, or *dermatophobia*)

Fear of skin diseases or lesions. Our skin being the place where we "meet" the outside world, and its importance for social acceptance and being attractive, can lead people to fear potential skin injuries. Skin conditions such as acne are common among young people, but the pos-sibility of having acne can inspire anxiety in many people. More serious skin conditions such as boils, eczema, moles, warts, or skin cancers may also be frightening. The main fears would generally be bodily threat (e.g., if the fear were of skin cancers), disgust, or social disapproval.

Stings (*cnidophobia*)

Fear of stings, such as by bees or wasps. This could be due to a fear of the pain of stings, allergic reactions, or catching diseases through something like a mosquito bite.

Suffering and disease (*panthophobia*)

Fear of suffering or disease. (Not to be confused with *panophobia*, which is the fear of anything or everything.)

Surgical operations (*tomophobia*)

Fear of surgical operations or procedures. This would generally be considered a normal or natural fear, except if it gets out of proportion (such as by triggering another problem like a severe psychological reaction or the avoidance of urgently needed treatment)—in which case the term *phobia* would more likely apply. People may fear a number of things related to surgery, beginning with the fact that, in some cases, surgeries are last resorts for someone with a very severe medical condition—meaning that the element of fear and dread is probably already present for the person (and for loved ones as well). One may also fear a wide range of things that are a part of surgery including any or all of the usual blood-injection-injury fears: needles, injury, blood, open wounds, pain—even if none of these are actually experienced. Indeed, a person's psychological fantasies about a pending surgery of their own or of someone else's may be enough to trigger strong reactions, even when the fantasies are entirely inaccurate. Fear of surgeries can also apply in dental situations or other situations involving medical procedures. (*See also* Dental surgery.)

Tetanus or lockjaw (*tetanophobia*)

See Lockjaw or tetanus.

Tuberculosis (*phthisiophobia* or *tuberculophobia*)

Fear of contracting tuberculosis. *Pthisis* is the ancient Greek term for the disease; the ancient Greek physician Hippocrates wrote that it was the most widespread disease of his era. Tuberculosis is an infectious disease caused by the *Mycobacterium tuberculosis* bacteria, which attacks the lungs and other body systems. It is often fatal. Symptoms generally include chronic coughs with bloody sputum, fever, weight loss, and night sweats. It is generally contracted by inhaling small amounts of the bacteria when exposed to infected people who may cough, sneeze, or spit particles. Treatment by antibiotics has been fairly effective in curing the disease in modern times, though there is widespread concern about the development of treatment-resistant strains of the disease and their potential to trigger new epidemics of the condition.

In the era before widespread availability of antibiotics, tuberculosis was a fairly widespread disease, and as such, it was both widely feared and, sometimes, romanticized in literature and popular culture. The notion of someone "wasting away" romantically would be an example, as were the fantasies that victims were somehow more energetic, creative, or (in the case of infected women) beautiful. Nevertheless, the fear of the disease would generally have inspired more anxiety, dread, and caution than romantic or literary feelings.

Urine or urinating (*urophobia* or *paruresis*)

Fear of urinating in public. This condition is also called by a number of colloquial terms, including shy kidneys, shy bladder syndrome, or "stage fright." This is a psychological condition in which a person has difficulty urinating in public or where they may be observed or heard. It was first studied in a survey in 1954, where researchers reported that over 14 percent of males surveyed had occasionally or chronically experienced the difficulty; more recent surveys suggest that about 3 percent of males have difficulty urinating in public. Women may have difficulty, but it occurs less frequently (though fears of germs or contamination may be more common for women using public rest facilities). The condition is listed as a form of social phobia in the DSM-IV, though it may also be considered a specific phobia. People with more severe or ongoing forms of this condition often have it for decades. It generally begins (as do most social phobia) in one's teens, but can begin at any age. See Chapter 12 for an in-depth look at social phobia.

Urophobia can complicate a person's life in a number of ways. Surveys show that at least a third of people with chronic *urophobia* report they curtail social activities, attending sporting events, and such as a result, and over half say it has affected their choice of jobs or careers. It may create problems in situations such as being required to provide urine samples in the workplace.

Vaccinations (*vaccinophobia*)

Fear of vaccinations. The traditional fears include fears of needles, pain, or contamination. In recent times there has been some fear that vaccinations cause autism, leading some parents to avoid having their children vaccinated. While this may be less a matter of a phobic reaction than a rational (whether or not an accurate) concern, such public health situations often can stir a percentage of highly anxious people to exaggerate dangers and to have more intense reactions. (*See also* Injections, Needles.)

Venereal disease (*cypridophobia*)

Fear of sexually transmitted or venereal disease. *Kypris* is the ancient Greek name for Venus, the goddess of love, who also had the honor of having her name applied to the word *venereal*. (*See also* Prostitutes in Chapter 8.)

Vomiting (*emetophobia*)

An intense, irrational fear of vomiting or seeing or encountering vomit. This can include fear of the discomfort and generally awful feeling or taste of vomiting, but may also include fear of loss of control, social anxiety, and fears related to health conditions. While most people experience discomfort related to vomit, people with a phobia may actually avoid life situations and experiences that most people wouldn't, such as pregnancy, child care, travel, socializing where alcohol might be served, or obtaining necessary medical care that might trigger vomiting (e.g., chemotherapy) or expose them to others who are vomiting. Persons with the phobia may have rituals for preparing food or eating, or they may engage in strict diets to minimize the risk of vomiting; many such persons avoid eating out entirely and report that they are underweight as a result of their difficulties.

Vomiting due to airsickness (*aeronausiphobia*)

This term can refer to fear of vomiting from getting airsick (or it may just refer to a fear of flying or airplanes, though it seems likely that this is because of the link of flying or planes with airsickness). Airsickness is a form of motion sickness that can include nausea, vomiting, and disorientation. People who are afraid of becoming airsick (either because it's happened to them before or for other reasons) may avoid flying, sometimes at great personal inconvenience. Flying may trigger other fears ranging from loss of control or fear of crashing to claustrophobia, which may exist along with fear of becoming airsick. In addition to fearing the physical discomforts, fear of vomiting in a public situation may be a form of social anxiety. (*See also* Vomiting.)

Weight, gaining (*obesophobia* or *pocrescophobia*)

Fear of gaining weight. Particularly in cultures that value thinness, fears of gaining weight or becoming obese may be common. This may be a common and healthy motivation for exercise and good diet, but may also result in excessive dieting or compulsive exercise, even to the point of people developing anorexia. Fear of gaining weight is common in both genders but is particularly common among young women. This can be a problem particularly among girls who are basically in their growth years—they may seriously damage their health by attempting to remain tinier than is healthy.

Worms, being infested with (*helminthophobia* or *vermiphobia*)

Fear of being infested by worms. This fear may lead people to avoid eating things that might cause them to ingest worms. (*See also* Parasites, Tapeworms in Chapter 4.)

X-rays (*radiophobia*)

Fear of x-rays or radiation. Radiation can be harmful and is linked to physical injuries including burns, cancer, etc. In medical settings, x-ray exposure levels are generally monitored carefully among employees, and patients are (or should be) protected against excessive exposure to radiation. Some people may fear any exposure to radiation, however, and some will actually refuse needed medical tests for fear of harmful radiation exposure.

Chapter 7

Stuff Happens: Situational Phobias

In This Chapter

- ◆ Creeped out by a situation
- ◆ List of situational phobias

When many people think of phobias, their minds go not to bugs or bears or fainting at the sight of blood, but to situations that they hope to never find themselves in. Whether it's being in an accident, going bald, or riding in a car, there are an almost limitless number of situations that people find terrifying.

In this chapter we'll explore the reasons situational phobias develop, and review a very long list of situations that can terrify.

How Situations Creep Us Out

Situational phobias are by far the largest category of specific phobias, affecting both children and adults. The diagnostic subtype of situational phobias is defined in the *Diagnostic and Statistical Manual of Mental Disorders* (DSM-IV) this way:

"Situational Type. This subtype should be specified if the fear is cued by a specific situation such as public transportation, tunnels, bridges, elevators, flying, driving, or enclosed places."

Situational phobias are quite variable in terms of the particular thing that can trigger anxiety. What they have in common is that the nature of the fear response is usually a fear of danger or injury. (You will recall that this is not always the case—some phobias tend to trigger disgust reactions, fear of having a strong emotional response like panic, or of being criticized, for instance.)

In addition to being the largest category of phobias, situational phobias are among the most common of all specific phobias. Many start in childhood, but many others seem to start on average in a person's mid-20s.

As with most specific phobias, the cause of situational phobias can vary, and sometimes it's not all that easy to tell just what triggered them. But it's suspected that some people are more vulnerable than others to developing phobias simply because their general anxiety-vulnerability is higher. In addition, histories of childhood traumas, illness, other anxiety disorders (particularly panic disorders, or having had panic attacks), or other emotional problems such as depression can all increase one's vulnerability to a specific phobia.

It's probably clear to you by now that we can develop a phobia about practically any situation that a person can be in. There are several theories to explain how this can occur. One theory of how situational phobias happen is the same as with other kinds of phobias: pairing the situation with intense fear. A second theory is that situational phobias are created cognitively. In other words, telling yourself that this situation is dangerous, or imagining horrible outcomes of being there or doing that, will help you learn to fear something that didn't bother you previously.

Of course, people seldom set out to deliberately talk themselves into phobias. More likely, they accidentally expose themselves to self-talk about how awful something would be. For instance, reminding yourself before taking a drive that something awful might happen, especially if you've recently heard of a car wreck on this same road, can start to frighten you about driving.

Sometimes other people's fears can trigger our own. I once knew a psychologist who was treating a woman who had a phobia of driving over a particular bridge. The patient would share with the psychologist how she imagined her car swerving off the bridge into the river below, and in the course of their work he had to hear many such fears and imaginings from her about that horrible bridge.

Soon, the psychologist started to notice that whenever he would drive across that same bridge, he also started to imagine *his* car swerving off into the river. He began to have a mild phobia just by being exposed to hers. Phobias are indeed contagious!

While this psychologist immediately realized what was happening and so guided his thinking in more benign directions, this isn't as easy for most people to do. For one thing, few people realize at the time it's happening that other people's fears are being absorbed and becoming their own. It's not easy to make the connection between having a conversation about a particular situation and, later, starting to fear the situation yourself.

Real Danger!

Often, the "phobic infection" is spread to children by other children or adults. Kids can scare each other with their tales of this or that awful thing happening, and other kids (especially younger kids) can start to believe it. Parents and other adults may not do this deliberately, but it's all too easy for their fears to be spread to their kids. If dad is afraid of heights, sooner or later his kids will realize this, pick it up, or sense it, and they will start to have their own fears.

Another way of developing a situational phobia is by traumatic experiences in that situation. For instance, many people develop short-lived fears of driving after they've been involved in a car accident. While most people get past this within a few days or weeks (particularly if they get out and drive again as soon as possible), a minority become permanently afraid (and may even have other related spreading phobias such as the fear of being in cars, fear of being around traffic, etc.) as a result.

Let's look at some situational phobias. Remember, in some of these situations, a small amount of due diligence or caution is called for. But for the most part, these are not generally dangerous situations—as long as you don't get all phobic about them.

Situational Phobias

Abuse, sexual (*agraphobia* or *contreltophobia*)

An excessive and persistent fear of sexual abuse. Sexual abuse in childhood has been linked with a variety of emotional difficulties including anxiety disorders and depression in adulthood. An ongoing, adult fear of sexual abuse may not be as conscious or widespread as other difficulties because adults lack the vulnerabilities of children. Adults can generally control their relationships and avoid potentially abusive situations, so the actual conscious phobia of abuse may be less prevalent (there are, in fact, few or no articles in the professional psychological literature on this particular phobia). Another outlet for fears of sexual abuse can be an exaggerated fear that children may be at risk in what are actually safe situations; some critics have expressed the concern that a society's fears of childhood abuse may result in children having few normal connections with nonparental adults other than teachers, because adults may fear that any contact or interest in children may be misconstrued as abusive behavior.

(Note that *agraphobia* is often mistaken for *agoraphobia*—see Chapter 11.)

Accidents (*dystychiphobia*)

Fear of accidents. As a normal, mild fear, concern for accidents is generally healthy. But a person may develop a more extreme and unrealistic fear, either because of traumatic experiences or some scary near-misses on a job, while driving, etc. Or they may just develop an intense focus on possible dangers as a way of focusing a more general case of anxiety. In any case, this phobia can lead people to become hyper-careful and overly meticulous, and they may worry about possible accidents that they cause or that might occur. Fears may include being injured, injuring others, or causing damage to property. It may lead to avoiding certain jobs, routes, activities, or dangerous-seeming situations.

Alone, being (*autophobia, monophobia, isolophobia, phobophobia,* or *eremophobia*)

Fear of being alone. Fear of being alone is a fairly common fear, and some surveys suggest that it may be among the most severe of phobias. We are social creatures by nature, and most (but not all) people tend to prefer both living with life partners or family—or at least the frequent support, contact, and general companionship with others. Some people with social phobia may at times feel caught between phobias if their fear of exposing themselves to criticism or rejection by others clashes with their fear of being alone or isolated. Social contact and support generally does provide a protective function for people both emotionally and physically; being alone can trigger fears of both loneliness and of not functioning as well. People may also feel more vulnerable to things such as crime, poverty, or the lack of help in emergencies if they are alone. Fear of being alone can actually become a self-fulfilling prophecy if it leads a person to become so anxious, so obviously needy and desperate, that they undermine their own efforts at reaching out to others for friendship or relationships.

Atomic explosions (*atomosophobia*)

Fear of atomic explosions. Well, who isn't afraid of that? However, particularly during times of increased international tension (or in order to win public support for policies said to be essential to preventing a mushroom cloud event), fears of atomic explosions may be heightened, and a vulnerable percentage of the population may become truly ill with worry about this possibility. Fears can include those of the explosion itself and its aftermath, including specific fears such as of radiation or radiation sickness. Fears may also include the worldwide effects of a global thermonuclear war—or even of a single explosion and its effects on life and the environment.

Automobiles, being in moving (*motorphobia* or *ochophobia*)

Fear of being in moving cars or of driving. This is a common fear after accidents, but people may develop this phobia for other reasons. Some speculate that fears of driving may be related to agoraphobia (see Chapter 11), particularly if they involve being far from home or away from one's familiar environments. People may fear particular driving situations: being the driver, being the passenger (particularly if loss of control makes one anxious), or driving in certain environments: rush hour, busy freeways, isolated country roads, unfamiliar locations, etc. Many people in rural areas develop a great deal of apprehension about driving in cities, where both the unfamiliar routes and the denser, faster moving traffic are very different than their usual driving environments.

Baldness (*phalacrophobia*)

Fear of becoming bald. This can include fears related to losing one's youth, not being attractive anymore, or to medical causes such as cancer treatment. In other words, the two typical fear categories of health and safety and social approval can each contribute to concerns and fears of baldness. (*See also* Bald people in Chapter 8.)

Bathing (*ablutophobia*)

Fear of bathing. Comes from the Greek *ablute*, meaning *to wash*. Small children may be frightened of bathing for various reasons, including the novelty of the situation or discomfort (soap in the eyes, too-warm or too-cold water shocking them, etc.). Some online sources say it's also more common in women, but there are no published studies showing this to be the case. Fears of discomfort, harm due to water exposure, etc. may be part of the reason for the fear. It seems likely this fear may be or have been more common in cultures where washing frequently is less common and so would have been more of a novel and inconvenient experience; it may also be associated with fears related to unsanitary water supplies and risks of harm that may result.

Beaten by rods or sticks (*rhabdophobia*)

Fear of being beaten with rods, sticks, clubs, etc. From the Greek word *rhabdos*, or *rod*. This fear can include fears of pain or physical injury, loss of control, humiliation, punishment, or—most likely—all of the above. Such fears are probably most common in people who have suffered traumas in the form of actual abuse, whether as children or as victims of police misconduct, torture, etc. These fears may also be common in those who have been vicariously victimized by seeing others beaten or who know that beatings are possibilities in their culture or community.

Blushing *(erythrophobia, erytophobia,* or *ereuthophobia)*

Fear of blushing. This seems to be related to social phobia and the fear of being observed, criticized, or embarrassed by one's blushing. People who fear being seen blushing are generally very focused on their own emotional reactions (which might be another phobic vicious cycle, since focusing on how anxious one is tends to increase anxiety).

Bound or tied up *(merinthophobia)*

Fear of being bound or tied up. This fear can be related to claustrophobia, or it can flow from fears of being injured, helpless, assaulted, or sexually assaulted. Loss of control, possible humiliation, or fears of robbery or death are all possible things that can go through the mind of someone with this fear.

Bridges, crossing *(gephyrophobia)*

Fear of bridges, being on bridges, or crossing bridges. This fear may be related to fear of heights or to being stuck or trapped on a bridge (similar to claustrophobia). Some people may develop panic symptoms on bridges if they try to drive or walk across. People with this fear may drive considerable distances to avoid certain bridges, and there are reports of people who become unable to leave islands on which they live because of their fear. In some metro areas with a number of bridges, traffic authorities or law enforcement may provide assistance to people needing to cross bridges.

Buildings, being close to high *(batophobia)*

Fear of passing a tall building. Thought to be related to fears of heights, falls, or looking up.

Buried alive or cemeteries *(taphephobia* or *taphophobia)*

Fear of being buried alive or fear of cemeteries. Readers of Edgar Allan Poe's horrific short stories (such as "The Premature Burial") are familiar with this fear, though it's no doubt less common in modern times. Before the availability of modern medical techniques and diagnostic devices, it was sometimes difficult or impossible to know whether some individuals had died or were merely unconscious or comatose, particularly if their breathing and heart rates were greatly slowed. Reports were common of bodies being exhumed that showed clear evidence that the individual had in fact been presumed dead, was buried or entombed, and then woke inside their coffins and began clawing frantically to escape. In modern times, and where medical resources would make it nearly impossible (though not unheard of) to accidentally bury a still-living individual, this fear would more likely be stirred up by movies (e.g., *Kill Bill, Part 2*) or stories portraying premature burials. The fear is most likely a near cousin of claustrophobia, along with fear of the dark, helplessness, suffocation, panic, and death. (*See also* Confined spaces.)

Car or vehicle, riding in (*amaxophobia*)

Fear of riding in a car or vehicle. Can include fear of bodily injury, loss of control, claustrophobic-like fears of being trapped or enclosed in a vehicle and unable to leave, agoraphobic-style fears of getting too far away from one's safe home base, and trauma-based fears such as of being in an accident. (*See also* Automobiles, being in moving.)

Ceremonies religious (*teleophobia*)

Fear of religious ceremonies. This phobia can include fears of participation in a public event, which might be a form of social phobia (e.g., not knowing how to behave appropriately or as expected in church, temple, mosque, or powwow ceremonies, or fear of being seen, judged, etc.). It may also include fears related to the contents of the religion itself, such as fear of displeasing a higher being or God, fear of being untrue to one's core beliefs, etc. It may also relate to superstition, to broader fears of the unknown, or to ultimate concerns such as death, life after death, hell, demons, etc.

Change or making changes (*neophobia* or *topophobia*)

Fear of change is *neophobia*; fear of making changes in one's life or situation is *topophobia*. Most people (and many animals) naturally fear disruptions in a familiar situation, whether it's a home, relationship, or job. Anxiety about change starts young, and many children have anxious reactions when offered a new food (or even when their peanut butter sandwiches are cut a different way!—see Chapter 13). This kind of fear can continue into adulthood, and in fact it's probably true that many people stick with unhealthy or undesired lives (homes, neighborhoods, jobs, partners) because they are, without realizing it, terrified of change and the associated risks. Fears can include a dread of major changes like jobs or partners, but it can also apply to minor changes in one's life or routine. The psychological study of resilience is largely about how people adapt to change. (*See also* Decision-making.)

The fictional TV detective *Monk* is afraid of many things, but difficulty coping with change seems to be one of his most pervasive fears. See Appendix B for a link to the full list of his phobias.

Child, bearing a deformed (*teratophobia*)

Fear of bearing a deformed child. Some people may be reluctant to have children for fear that the child won't be healthy or will be handicapped or deformed in some horrible way. This fear can be triggered by bad experiences, concerns about one's genetic background, childhood or family fears and attitudes about children, or by having been exposed to stories or images of parents in this situation. The fear may develop during pregnancy or may lead a woman to avoid becoming pregnant. (*See also* Childbirth in Chapter 6.)

Coitus (*coitophobia*)

Fear of coitus, sexual relations, or the act of sexual intercourse. Sexuality is one of the most powerful of human experiences—so many opportunities for developing fears of various aspects of it exist. It may be associated with fears of painful intercourse or general discomfort about sexuality that can be connected with fears or memories of trauma or abuse. It may also cause feelings of disgust (that sex is somehow dirty) or guilt. Fears of pregnancy, impotence, contracting AIDS or other sexually transmitted diseases, or having strong emotional reactions to sexual intimacy can underlay this fear. Fears can involve variations of social phobia, such as when a person develops performance anxiety or is afraid of being criticized for their physical appearance, sexual performance, etc. Loss of control of one's body or emotional or physical responses (such as connected with orgasm) can be frightening for many people. Young or sexually inexperienced people, or people raised in sexually uptight or repressive cultures, may be particularly fearful of sexual activity. It's worth noting that fears of emotional reactions can include both fears of unpleasant feelings and of overly pleasant ones, such as, say, if a person is afraid of falling in love with their partner or of liking sex—or sex with a particular partner or someone of a certain gender—too much.

Computers, or fear of working on computers (*cyberphobia*)

Any fear related to computers or to working on computers. For a long time there was a mystique about computers and the vast powers they were believed to have, and indeed many science fiction stories and films were based on the premise that, at some point, computers might take over the world and turn against their human builders. In more recent times, when computers are more familiar to most people worldwide and even small children are adept at using them, they may be less frightening, but other fears (such as of having one's personal data stolen, of being hacked, or of being monitored via one's computer) may at times keep computers on one's radar as possibly threatening or dangerous. People may also fear breaking them, messing things up, losing data, or being overwhelmed by the complexity of their computers. A severe fear of unrealistic threats or dangers—believing that your computer is spying on you or plotting against you—would be more of a delusion than a phobia, although it's worth noting that hackers, phishers (who trick people into sharing personal data such as bank account info), and surveillance by government agencies are all, in fact, real threats to virtually anyone who uses the Internet.

Confined spaces (*claustrophobia*)

Fear of confined spaces or of being trapped in confined spaces. This is an extremely common fear. It can include not only fears such as of being inside a tiny space like a shower, elevator, or phone booth but also of being inside anything where the walls seem close, such as airplanes, buses, or cars. People who are claustrophobic may react with rising anxiety and the feeling that a space is getting tighter and tighter in many related situations, ranging from feeling trapped when walking in the Grand Canyon or inside the "canyons" of tall buildings in Manhattan. Sometimes even articles of clothing, sleeping bags, blankets tucked too tightly under a person's feet, or anything that restricts movement (like being in the middle of a movie theater row or sitting in too-small theater seats) can trigger claustrophobic sensations. Feelings of anxiety, a desire to get free, or fear of the anxiety increasing into a full-blown panic attack may all occur.

Contamination (*molysmophobia* or *molysomophobia*)

Fear of contamination with dirt or germs or of infection. This fear includes situations that people may feel make them particularly vulnerable to contacting germs or contamination. Some people will avoid going to public places (or to certain kinds of places such as movies, supermarkets, or zoos) or avoid contact with farm or domestic animals (such as avoiding petting a cat or dog) because of their perception that these places or situations are more unclean than others. This is not entirely inaccurate, since many environments may be a bit hazardous (such as public restrooms, kindergarten classes full of kids with colds, or hospitals)—but when a person is not able to go to such places without extreme anxiety, their realistic concern has crossed over into phobic territory. (*See also* Infection in Chapter 6.)

Cooking (*mageirocophobia*)

Fear of cooking. A person can fear being confused or overwhelmed by new recipes or cooking tasks. They may have a kind of socially phobic fear that their cooking will not please others, that they will seem inept or incompetent, or that they're not trying hard enough because their potluck recipes aren't as elaborate as others. There may be elements of disgust phobias, for instance in tackling unfamiliar foods or seemingly icky items. There may be concerns about not knowing how to handle a particular food item, whether it's cleaning fresh-caught fish, preparing a frozen turkey, or learning how to handle tofu. A person may also fear being injured or burned, such as by handling pressure cookers, sharp knives, etc.

Criticized, being severely, or criticism (*enissophobia* or *rhabdophobia*)

Rhabdophobia can refer to a fear of severe criticism as well as to a fear of being beaten with a rod or stick. Fear of criticism (but without the beating part) is referred to as *enissophobia*; this term is also used to refer to a fear of sin (or of having committed sin—*see also* Sin).

Most people find criticism to be at least uncomfortable, and a substantial number find it to be extremely painful. For the latter in particular, the thought of being criticized for their actions, words, or even for being themselves fills them with dread. This is related to social phobia (see Chapter 12)—the fear of being critiqued or evaluated by others. It can also be related to realistic, if exaggerated, fears that the criticism is based on some actual or perceived failings that will jeopardize the person's career, relationships, or other important part of their lives. Criticism can also be humiliating, particularly if others get to hear about it or witness it; it can reduce a person's status and make them seem less valuable or competent in others' eyes. Adolescents are particularly vulnerable to criticism, but many people of all ages can find it deeply disturbing.

One of the problems with criticism is that it can undermine one's sense of control or competence, leaving a person less sure of their skills or, more broadly, of their very value or likeability as a person. As a result of this fear, many people go to extraordinary lengths to avoid criticism, including by becoming perfectionists (in anything from their work to their attire) or else by learning to avoid taking risks that might expose them to criticism—which may cause them to miss out on jobs, avoid recreational opportunities, or undermine their education (when they, say, don't take the risk of speaking up in class).

Crossing streets (*agyrophobia* or *dromophobia*)

Fear of crossing streets. This can be due to a fear of being injured or hit by cars or trucks, or it could be a variety of agoraphobia, since streets or crosswalks may be open spaces where one may feel more vulnerable or less protected. Many children are firmly trained that crossing streets is hazardous, and at times this fear may linger into adulthood.

Crowded public places (*agoraphobia*)

The fear of open places or open public places. This is a more complex fear and is further discussed in Chapter 11. But if a person had a fairly specific fear of *crowded* public places that didn't involve the kind of pervasive phobia that is discussed in that chapter, they would still technically be described as agoraphobic. This can include a fear of crowds because of the noise, chaos, confusion, or a sense of being observed; it can also include a fear of losing control of one's emotions or of having a panic attack in such settings.

Crowds or mobs (*demophobia, enochlophobia,* or *ochlophobia*)

Fear of crowds or mobs. This fear can be a variant of agoraphobia, but large crowds can also be perceived as dangerous physically, unpleasantly loud, and chaotic.

Mobs is less of a neutral term than *crowds* and tends to be associated more with aggressive, out-of-control, or violent groups of people. One may speak of a "crowd of onlookers" but would not refer to a "mob of onlookers," while one might refer to an "angry mob." One might, then, be unafraid to be part of a crowd but fear being swept up in the actions of a mob.

Dancing (*chorophobia*)

Fear of dancing. Much of this fear is probably similar to social phobia in general: the fear that one may look foolish, be critiqued, or be laughed at because they don't know how to dance. The imaginary critics may be dance partners or onlookers. Some people also fear messing up or doing things wrong and so may build up an image in their minds that there is a right way to dance—and thus be afraid of making errors. This fear may also be triggered by discomfort with emotional self-expression, with situations involving possible criticism of one's body or attire, with flirtation or dating-related situations, or agoraphobic-type concerns about being in a strange, unprotected, open place like a dance floor. The result of this specific phobia is that many people generally avoid dancing or situations where dancing may be expected (weddings, for example).

Dark places (*lygophobia*)

Fear of being in dark places. Fear of the dark is a fairly fundamental, universal human fear. Like many situational phobias, it may trigger fears related to physical danger. The risk of becoming lost or disoriented, of being hurt on unseen obstacles, and of threatening persons or animals lurking in the darkness are all both realistic and the raw materials for countless panic-causing fantasies, films, and stories. Darkness also seems to have a somewhat disorienting effect on many people because of the absence of cues as to their location—or even as to which directions are up or down. Since the majority of information used by sighted persons to process the world is visual, the sudden loss of visual information can create a form of stress in which the brain literally lacks data to analyze; in turn, this form of stress triggers the emotion centers of the brain and anxiety results. Many or most children are afraid of the dark, and people whose parents were not as helpful as needed in responding to their anxieties may be at higher risk for developing *lygophobia*.

Decision-making (*decidophobia*)

Fear of making decisions. Having to make decisions almost always involves some anxiety, though for most people, this is a manageable level of tension. But for some people, decision-making can trigger waves of anxiety, which are often caused more by the absence of any movement on the problem than by the presence of conscious anxiety symptoms. People who fear making choices may tend to cope with the problem either by procrastinating or by avoiding advancement to levels of responsibility which will require a lot of decision-making. Of course, this tends to merely create other, often larger problems. Indecisiveness may also contribute to relationship stress when partners or friends become impatient with the decidophobe's lack of input, enthusiasm, or energy for choosing a restaurant, activity, or life change. Much of the work of counselors is often helping people finally make important life decisions. (*See also* Change or making changes.)

Defeat (*kakorraphiophobia, kakorrhaphiohobia, kakorrhaphobia,* or *kakorrhapiophobia*)

Fear of defeat or failure. Defeat can threaten everything from death to injury to social humiliation. Some people find the prospect of defeat or failure to be so uncomfortable that they avoid any kind of situation where they might be perceived to have been defeated—whether they are playing a game, participating in an athletic contest, or standing up for their opinions or rights (or the rights of others).

Dependence on others (*soteriophobia*)

Fear of being dependent on other people. Many persons believe that they must, above all else, maintain their independence; they may fear that depending on others for material support or emotional nurturance is a sign of weakness or personal failing. Some fear of dependence is actually a form of social phobia: the belief that one will be judged or criticized for needing anything from others. A balance of dependent and independent attitudes and behaviors is generally the best and healthiest middle ground; some cultures value independence and self-reliance more highly, whereas others see the reluctance to rely on others as a form of antisocial or maladjusted personality.

Depth (*bathophobia*)

Fear of situations involving depth or deep dimensions. For instance, one may fear going into the deep end of a pool; a scuba diver might develop a fear of being in deep water. The fear seems to be related to being deep or far down in the water; of being far down, in something such as a mine shaft or tunnel; or of being deep inside something. Sometimes the word seems to be confused with the fear of heights or high places (*acrophobia*). As usual, nobody has actually published research on this fear, so it's not clear how common it is.

Dining or dinner conversations (*deipnophobia*)

Fear of dining or dinner conversation. This can involve a socially phobic fear of being criticized for either what one says or perhaps how one looks while eating; in some cases it might involve a fear of choking on food while eating. People may often feel awkward or embarrassed in dinner situations, particularly with strangers or in formal situations. They may prefer to avoid dinners with others entirely, or they may freeze up or try too hard to converse—in which case their awkwardness can become another of the socially phobics' many self-fulfilling prophecies. (*See also* Public speaking, Speaking.)

Dirty, being (*automysophobia*)

Fear of being dirty, filthy, or contaminated. This can be due to fear of criticism or humiliation because others perceive one as dirty and unacceptable; it can also possibly be due to feeling unclean and related more to a disgust feeling.

Disorder or mess (*ataxophobia*)

Fear of disorder, untidiness, or messiness. This fear may be related to a sense of loss of control or to a discomfort with mess that is related to a disgust feeling. Extreme difficulty with mess and constant vigilant cleaning up or tidying can slide more into a kind of obsessive compulsive disorder (OCD). Some people may also avoid relationships with or visits to others whom they consider to be too disorderly or messy to tolerate.

Doctrine, challenges to (*heresyphobia* or *hereiophobia*)

Fear of heresies or of challenges to accepted doctrines, theologies, faiths, or beliefs. Some people have powerful reflexive reactions to anything that seems to threaten or challenge their cherished beliefs, whether this is in a church, political, or even scientific setting. This may relate to fear of loss of control, since people tend to feel that their world is under better control if everyone agrees to the fundamentals; this may also relate unconsciously to their sense of self. Generally, people with this kind of fear tend to want to flock together with like-minded individuals, to challenge or even obliterate dissent (and historically, dissenters—even if it took burning them at the stake), and to have their beliefs reinforced. Some people believe that much of the violence in the world is based on this kind of anxiety.

Dreams (*oneirophobia*)

Fear of dreams. Throughout history, people have viewed dreams with a mixture of fear and awe. They have been seen as omens, as threats, as mysterious portals to some other world or state of being, and as the place monsters come from. Many children wake at night terrified of something they dreamt, and adults may also, at times, fear the messages or images of dreams. In actuality, dreams are harmless, and virtually all healthy humans (and probably most mammals) dream at night, often many times. (We only recall a small percentage of our dreams, as a rule.) There are many theories of dreams, bolstered by medicine and psychological research, including the belief that dreams may at times be a form of "offline processing" of memories or that they may be a form of problem-solving. Psychoanalyst Sigmund Freud believed that dreams had complex functions including psychological wish fulfillment and protecting sleep. (*See also* Wet dreams.)

Drinking (*dipsophobia*)

Fear of drinking, particularly alcoholic beverages. This term generally refers to a fear of alcoholism or becoming alcoholic; alcoholics who are trying to remain sober may develop a healthy fear of taking the "first drink." Children of alcoholic parents may also protect themselves from developing drinking problems by developing a fear of alcohol, and many who do not become alcoholics themselves do so by avoiding all alcohol.

Duty or responsibility, neglect of (*paralipophobia*)

Fear of neglecting one's duty or responsibilities. In some cultures, to neglect one's responsibilities to one's family, community, or employer is to feel tremendous shame or guilt and to lose face in one's community; it may even be considered a failing that justifies, or even demands, suicide. Most cultures have notions of what one's responsibilities or duties are; these may be more or less flexible, more or less realistic, and may fluctuate depending on external situations. (For instance, during wartime, it's more often thought to be the duty of young men—and sometimes women—to enlist in the military.) A person may have conflicting external or community responsibilities, which can create a *psychological* conflict for them as well—for instance, a pacifist or member of a pacifist religion may be very conflicted during wartime about military service.

The major fear may often be related to the same kind of fear of criticism or judgment that triggers other social phobia—that one has failed in the eyes of important members of one's community. At times, this may indeed have (or be perceived to have) real-world consequences for the group and/or for the individual. Some people, however, can develop such a fear of failing that they avoid responsibilities, telling themselves or others that they are not adequate to the tasks or that it's not really their jobs to deal with the problems. Others may develop elaborate systems to conceal their perceived failings or may become exhausted by obsessive overwork as they try to live up to their duties as they see them. All of these behaviors can have serious consequences for their careers, relationships, finances, and health.

Eating (*phagophobia*, *sitiophobia*, or *sitophobia*)

Fear of eating. Generally, fear of eating or swallowing is called *phagophobia*, while fear of eating or food may be called *sitophobia* or *sitiophobia*. People may fear swallowing because of concerns they may choke, ingest poisons, or ingest unhealthy foods. This may, at times, really be a fear of vomiting or of discomfort with swallowing. The focus here is on the act of swallowing. People may resort to liquid diets, taking in only certain foods, finely blending food, or cutting food into small bites. In other cases, this may actually be a social phobia—the fear is really about swallowing or choking while being seen by others; one may also fear that one will choke or have difficulty eating because of the presence of others. The latter fear may lead a person to always try to eat alone or to avoid eating in the presence of other people.

In *sitophobia* or *sitiophobia*, the fear may be of the food itself; this may be an aversion to new foods or to specific foods. It is also possible to have a fear of eating foods that are forbidden by one's religion; in some cases, persons who accidentally do eat the forbidden foods may have strong reactions of nausea or vomiting.

Empty room, empty spaces, voids (*kenophobia*)

Fear of voids, empty rooms, or spaces. This fear is possibly the opposite of claustrophobia. Whether it be an empty room or an empty stretch of landscape, anything we're accustomed to seeing filled or inhabited or bounded (by walls, mountains, crowds) can seem eerie or strange when the same place appears empty. It may trigger disorientation, or, hard-to-articulate anxieties about that missing *something*, such as a sense of "unreality."

Failure

See Defeat.

Frightening situations, preferring (*counterphobia*)

Deliberately choosing to become involved in situations or activities that are actually frightening in order to ward off, deny, or overcome one's fears. People doing this might not feel consciously afraid of the activity; in fact, they may feel exhilarated or very absorbed in the sport, job, or activity and may even become something of an expert in it. Some believe that a degree of counterphobic behavior is involved, or maybe required, in order to participate in sports such as skydiving. However, while this may have once been thought to be a kind of pathology or neurosis by classical Freudians, it may be equally or perhaps more positively viewed (at least when not excessive) as a healthy thing. Some psychologists have in fact argued that some degree of difficulty or threat is part of what makes some activities fun, absorbing, or interesting. However, when people take unnecessary risks, persist in dangerous activities they're clearly not enjoying, or feel unable to stop engaging in risky behavior, the possibility of unhealthy counterphobic motives should be considered.

Fire (*arsonphobia* or *pyrophobia*)

Fear of fire. Fire was considered one of the basic elements in ancient science (along with water, air, and earth); it was both mysterious and an object of fear and awe throughout history. In modern times, fears of fire generally revolve around fears of being burned or of losing control of a fire either outdoors (campfires, trash fires, etc.) or indoors (candle, cooking fires, being in a fire, etc.).

Flashes (*selaphobia*)

Fear of bright or sudden flashes of light. Glare, sudden flashes of light, or bright lights may be aversive or unpleasant; flashing lights may trigger seizures in epileptics, so it's possible for one to imagine that they are a threat. Some people avoid driving at night because of difficulty tolerating or compensating for bright headlights.

Flogging or punishment (*mastigophobia*)

Fear of flogging or punishment. This can include fear of pain or injury, but it can also include the humiliation that can be a part of undergoing flogging or other public (or even private) punishment.

Flying (*aviophobia*, *aviatophobia*, or *pteromerhanophobia*)

Fear of flying. There are so many reasons a person can fear flying that it's always worth asking what particular parts of the experience are most troubling to the aviophobe. Traditionally, the very notion of being high off the ground with nothing but air underneath is what people assume fear of flying is about, but even that can include several fears. Different people may really be reacting to different fears: fear of heights, the sense of vertigo looking down, becoming airsick, or plane crashes (with injury or death likely). Some people don't mind flying once the plane is up in the air but fear takeoffs or landings. People may also be afraid of claustrophobia inside a small aircraft cabin and may feel trapped there. Young children or toddlers may have problems with air pressure changes and so fear ear pain; older passengers may also fear the clogged ears and partial deafness that lasts through the first day of their vacation—or else may fear being trapped in a plane next to babies screaming because of ear pain.

In recent years, the air travel experience has been blemished with further reasons for fear, including terrorists and hijackings, but it may also seem as though the transportation industry went out of its way to invent new reasons to fear flying: the fear that an airline may strand passengers on the ground for hours in an overheated, unventilated plane; fears of flights being cancelled or delayed; or fear of being stranded in some strange airport. There's also the fear that there will be no water or food available on a plane; fear of contracting colds or other airborne diseases due to poor ventilation of recirculated airplane air; fear of blood clotting in the legs due to sitting in tight, cramped seats for hours at a time; fear of not being able to store or fit one's baggage on the flight, or of having it lost, stolen, or rummaged through by baggage handlers; the fear that one will have to undergo pointless, humiliating searches by rude officials; or fear of encountering mysterious no-fly lists at the airport. Many people, as a result of such concerns, prefer trains or driving to their destinations when possible.

Foreign languages (*xenoglossophobia*)

Fear of foreign languages. People may experience disorientation, confusion, or fear being unable to converse; the latter fear can have elements of social phobia in the sense of feeling critiqued or evaluated negatively because of one's inability to speak the language well.

Forgetting or being forgotten (*athazagoraphobia*)

Supposedly, the fear of forgetting, being forgotten, or being ignored. The term *athazagoraphobia* is currently listed in the online dictionary Wiktionary on their list of possibly-made-up phobia terms, and it is not listed in any of my over 12,000 scientific reference publications and articles. But whether the term is valid or not as an actual clinical-level fear, there are many less severe cases of individuals having fears related to forgetting or to being forgotten or ignored. In the case of forgetting, people may fear that they will forget particular things, events, etc.

Everything from a locker combination to an ancestors' language may be something that a person can fear losing. Many people, particularly in middle age, begin to notice and worry about the mild incidents of forgetfulness that they fear may signal the onset of Alzheimer's disease. And of course, being forgotten by lovers or others of importance may be very troubling to romantics and narcissists in particular.

Freedom (*eleutherophobia*)

Fear of freedom. It may seem absurd to imagine being afraid of freedom, since many people are raised to believe that freedom is always a good thing. But some people find freedom threatening; it may be much more comfortable to have fewer choices or to be told what to do. Some long-term convicts learn to feel at home in the structured and predictable world of prison and may deliberately get reincarcerated after brief attempts to make it on the outside prove more difficult than they can handle. A classic psychology book by Erich Fromm is entitled *Escape from Freedom* (Holt Paperbacks; Owl Book edition, 1994). In it, Fromm explores the reasons many people may choose political solutions, religions, or other identities or authoritarian moral values that exchange freedom for conformity and the illusion of being safe.

Friday the 13th (*friggatriskaidekaphobia* or *paraskevidekatriaphobia*)

Fear of Friday the 13th. *Friggatriskaidekaphobia* comes from the name of Frigg, a Norse goddess—Friday was named for her; then we have *triskai* and *deka* for three and thirteen. *Paraskevidekatriaphobia* is derived from the Greek terms *paraskevi*, or Friday, and *dekatreis*, or thirteen (ten and three). Friday the 13th has only been scary for about a hundred years, when somebody got the brilliant idea of combining their fear of 13 with their fear of Fridays (a traditionally unlucky day, by some accounts). Some researchers say that between 18 and 21 million people in the United States alone are affected by the day. Some are reportedly so fearful they stay in bed, and so there are estimates that millions of dollars are lost in business on that day. As to whether it truly is more dangerous to travel on Friday the 13th, scientific results so far are mixed: a British study found more hospital admissions due to traffic accidents on that day (for which they blamed people's increased anxiety), while a Dutch study found fewer (because people are supposedly more careful on the road). But a study of driving in Finland found that traffic fatalities varied with gender: men were 2 percent more likely to die from an accident on Friday the 13th, but women were 63 percent more likely. Taken as a whole, the results seem to suggest that Friday the 13th is a good day to save your money and do your driving in Holland. (*See also* 13 [number] in Chapter 9.)

Gaiety (*cherophobia*)

Fear of gaiety or happiness. Some people may have a kind of superstitious belief or assumption that if they let go and express happiness or really celebrate, it will either predict or bring about some terrible consequences. Others fear letting go emotionally in front of others for fear of being criticized or not being accepted; this would generally seem to be a form of social phobia (see Chapter 12).

Gloomy places (*lygophobia*)

Fear of being in gloomy places.

Good news (*euphobia*)

Fear of hearing good news. As with fear of gaiety, sometimes people have the superstitious fear that good news is actually bad news waiting to happen. Most likely, this would suggest an underlying difficulty with generally anxious or depressed outlooks on life.

Growing old

See Old age.

Halloween (*samhainophobia*)

Fear of Halloween. *Samhain* was a Celtic festival that, along with the Christian All Saints Day, morphed into the Halloween festival celebrated on October 31 in the United States. Fears of Halloween may have roots in childhood experiences of being frightened either by spooky stories or by encounters with people in frightening costumes. Some people may dread having to deal with the tricks—or simply the encounters with trick-or-treaters. Others may fear feeling pressured to attend Halloween gatherings in costume, which may feel uncomfortable and even humiliating to socially phobic people. Still others may have superstitious or religious objections to the holiday and so link it in their minds to notions of evil or the occult.

Harmed by bad persons (*scelerophobia*)

Fear of being harmed by bad persons (burglars, etc.). This fear may stem from actual traumatic experiences of being harmed, or it may come about more indirectly as a result of childhood abuse or neglect. These traumas may not exactly match the feared experience but might set the psychological basis for feeling highly vulnerable. People may also develop this fear through being exposed to stories or films involving harm, assault, or abuse. It's important again to distinguish between realistic and valid fears of strangers or dangerous persons and the more constant, exaggerated, or out-of-control fears that may impair a person's ability to function, live in certain areas, or interact with others when they are actually safe. (*See also* Burglars, Robbers or being robbed in Chapter 8.)

Heat (*thermophobia*)

Fear of heat. This can include fear of overheated environments or climates. A history of heat exhaustion or having experienced a great deal of heat-related stress may leave a person feeling more sensitized to heat, and there can be a kind of claustrophobic feeling of being trapped in a hot climate or environment. In the days before air conditioning was common in the United States, many more people possibly feared the heat of summer (you'll recall that the populations of more southerly states were only able to rise to their current levels after air conditioning became widely available).

Heaven (*ouranophobia* or *uranophobia*)

Fear of heaven. The concept of heaven or the actual existence of such a place or state of being may be feared or viewed with discomfort. This may be due to fears of the idea of being judged worthy of heaven or due to a discomfort with the notion of religious belief.

Heights (*acrophobia*, *altophobia*, *batophobia*, *hypsiphobia*, or *hyposophobia*)

Fear of heights. *Acrophobia* is probably the most common term for this phobia. Fear of heights, or of being in high places, is one of the most common of fears and one of the most researched. It may be the only fear that is present in almost all infants, and most people have at least a little bit of it. It's no doubt related to, or identical to, the fear of falling, which is possibly the only fear that appears to be inborn (see Chapter 13 for a discussion of the research on infants' fears). People with this fear avoid situations in which they have to be up in the air or on the edge of something, such as crossing narrow bridges, climbing ladders, or looking over the edge of a building, balcony, or cliff. They may also avoid driving or walking over bridges, or be unable to go above the lower floors of tall buildings. People may restrict where they live, avoid flying, or be unable to do simple tasks like climbing a ladder to change a lightbulb. Looking down may cause desperate, anxious, or panicky reactions. There has been some success treating this fear with "virtual" as well as actual heights exposure (see Chapter 3).

Laboratory studies suggest that people with fear of heights may use visual information more than average people do to help them maintain their balance and stabilize their posture. They may have some difficulties visually perceiving movement. The result is that they rely more on what they see to help them balance. So when they are looking down from a height, whether it's standing on a ladder or looking out a third floor window which has a lower sill, they may start to feel more teetery and vulnerable.

Hell (*hadephobia, stygiophobia,* or *stigiophobia*)

Fear of hell. This refers to fear of hell as a literal place a person may go after death, consisting of (by definition) a place of worse than the worst imaginable eternal torments. Belief in hell is inculcated in many religions, and so children, generally from a young age, are taught to fear it. People may develop such a terror of hell that they obsess about it. They may rearrange or restrict their lives in order to comply with whatever requirements their religion (or their own thinking) tells them are essential to avoid having to go to hell. Dramatic literary versions of hell have been famous through the ages, including Dante's *Inferno* as perhaps the most famous literary invention of the levels of hell. Belief in hell has been falling in recent years according to some polls—apparently to the chagrin of some religious leaders.

Home (*ecophobia* or *oikophobia*)

Fear of home surroundings. This can include fear of things in the home that might cause injury, such as water heaters, gas stoves, etc. This refers to fears of things inside the house.

Home, returning (*nostophobia*)

Fear of returning home. Many therapists work with people who avoid returning to their childhood or family home because of unpleasant memories or feelings about the place, the environment, or the family situation. People may become anxious or even ill if some situation (such as a wedding, funeral, or other event) forces them to have to return to the family home for a visit.

Homosexuality or being homosexual (*homophobia*)

Fear of anything pertaining to homosexuality, including contact with homosexuals, being homosexual, or having homosexual feelings. In many countries and times in history, the dominant culture has tended to prohibit, suppress, or persecute those who expressed any sexual attraction to others of the same gender. One of the main phobic-style responses includes discomfort with any kind of contact with someone who is, or is suspected of being, homosexual—even if the contact is merely shaking hands or talking with them. Another common fear includes having any kinds of sexual feelings, or being perceived as having these feelings, toward same-gendered persons. In traditional psychoanalytic thinking, homophobia could often be diagnosed not simply because a person consciously admitted such discomfort, but because their actions attempted to constantly prove—to themselves or others—that they were firmly heterosexual. (*See also* Homosexuals in Chapter 8.)

House, being in (*domatophobia*)

Fear of being in a house or in a particular house.

Hypnotized (*hypnophobia*)

Fear of being hypnotized or fear of sleep. People can fear loss of control, loss of their own will, or even of loss of their sense of self when hypnotized. This fear has traditionally been fed by the mystique surrounding the idea of hypnosis as a nearly magical or powerful psychological way of taking over a person's will and controlling them. The irony is that most hypnotists would agree that the more someone focuses on their fear of hypnosis or tries to avoid being hypnotized, the more likely it is that they may be talking themselves into a trance—since some theories of trance hold that it is really nothing more than highly-focused attention paired with perhaps some kind of emotionally relaxed (or else aroused) state of consciousness. Some people may also fear falling asleep or losing consciousness.

Ignored (*athazagoraphobia*)

Fear of being ignored. This is essentially the reverse of social phobia, since social phobia is often a fear of being observed, noticed, or scrutinized; *Athazagoraphobia* is a fear that one will *not* be noticed or will be ignored. Some psychologists have theorized that it is psychologically very important for us to know that we are known, remembered, and recognized by others. The fear of being ignored may include practical fears, such as that of losing an important opportunity in school, work, or elsewhere because people didn't recognize us, or it may include the fear of loneliness or lack of emotional connection with desired or important people. Some people go to great lengths to avoid being ignored, whether it's through attention-seeking gestures like speaking up a lot, dressing in stylish or dramatic outfits, or setting themselves on fire.

Imperfection (*atelophobia*)

Fear of personal imperfection. Two different forms of a fear of imperfection are OCD and social phobia fears. Both can involve fairly intense anxiety and may approach true clinical phobias in intensity. In the former, a person may have a great fear of doing things "wrong," of making mistakes, or of being imperfect in some way; this may lead them to expend great effort and much anxiety trying to make sure things are done correctly. This actually tends to be more of an OCD than a phobia issue, but it's one of those areas where there can be much overlap between obsessive and phobic anxiety. Fears of being seen as imperfect, flawed, of doing things wrong, etc., by others, are more of a social phobia issue. (Though this, too, tends to involve a fair amount of obsessing or compulsive self-protection, such as the case of a teacher who overprepares for a guest lecture to the point where she actually swamps her students with more information than was called for, motivated by her fear of not doing well in the eyes of her colleagues.)

Jumping (*catapedaphobia*)

Fear of jumping from high places. The term comes from the Greek word *kata*, meaning down, and the Latin *pedis*, meaning foot. Generally the fear would be of being injured.

Kissing (*philemaphobia* or *philematophobia*)

Fear of kissing. Most people (at least in cultures where kissing is a common means of expressing affection) enjoy kissing—a lot. But some people may develop a fear of kissing, just as they may develop a fear of pretty much any type of physical affection. This may stem from cultural or religious beliefs, concerns about sanitation or hygiene, feelings of queasiness or disgust, fear of bad breath, fear of being judged an unskillful or poor kisser, or a history of sexual trauma. Others may actually fear the emotional or relationship aspects of kissing, such as would be the case if a person felt frightened of getting into an emotional or sexual relationship.

Laughter (*geliophobia* or *gelotophobia*)

Fear of laughter. Some sources say that *geliophobia* is related to the fear of laughing; however, there are no published scientific studies as of this writing that use the term. A more recent psychological study has shown that fear of *being laughed at* is a clinically distinct phobia (for which they used the term *gelotophobia*). The latter would be related to social anxiety or social phobia.

Lawsuits (*liticaphobia*)

Fear of lawsuits or litigation. Lawsuits can often be nasty, brutish, and long. They can also be expensive and can result in major losses of money, resources, status, jobs, or community standing. Hence, people may develop a healthy fear of being involved in lawsuits. An extreme fear of lawsuits can result in overly conscientious behavior that stifles a person's freedom of action, such as by consulting with attorneys even over extremely minor, low-risk matters or by giving in to others on disputed matters even when one is giving up one's rights or legal options unnecessarily.

Learning (*sophophobia*)

Fear of learning. A person may fear having their comfortable ideas challenged by new facts or ideas and so at times may cling to what they already know to be true. Generally, such a person wouldn't describe him- or herself as being afraid of learning, but those who know the person might conclude that this is the case.

Light flashes (*selaphobia*)

Fear of flashing lights such as bright headlights at night, flashing lights at a dance or a bar, etc. The fear may be related to discomfort at being visually overstimulated. This is not a researched fear.

Locked in (*cleithrophobia*, *cleisiophobia*, or *clithrophobia*)

Fear of being locked in an enclosed space. This phobia is similar to claustrophobia, though the concern with being locked in may be more important than the discomfort with the sense of enclosure itself. This fear can trigger severe anxiety at even the threat of being locked in; people may wish to avoid any situation where they may feel unable to escape, though they may not mind being inside a room, building, or vehicle as long as they know that they can exit any time they want. (*See also* Confined spaces.)

Loneliness (*eremophobia* or *eremiphobia*)

Fear of loneliness. While some people fear solitude or being alone (see Alone, being), loneliness is different—it refers not to the external reality of having no other persons around but to a feeling. Some people can feel lonely even in a crowded room or when they are with their friends—particularly if they feel the need to hold back secret feelings or thoughts or if they feel that they are not being understood, appreciated, or invited into relationships. Fear of loneliness is mostly a hazard if it leads a person to compromise some of who they are in order to have a connection with "somebody—anybody."

Looking up (*anablephobia* or *anablepophobia*)

Fear of looking up. This fear may be related to *acrophobia*, fear of high places. However, it doesn't seem to have been studied, documented in the research, or even described by an anablephobic on a blog somewhere, so it possibly doesn't exist.

Loud noises (*ligyrophobia*)

Fear of loud noises. It is a normal human and animal response to be startled by sudden loud noises. Sudden noise can trigger physiological responses including increased heart rate and respiration and the release of adrenaline and other stress hormones—and in general may trigger the body's self-protective fight-or-flight response system. Infants may be traumatized by loud noises, and most people find them unwelcome and unpleasant. Noises can signal danger, though at other times (such as concerts or fireworks displays) they may be meant to be pleasurable; nevertheless, for many people they are almost always aversive and undesirable. Research has shown that the perception that one cannot control or predict the noises tends to make them more aversive.

Love, sexual

See Coitus.

Love play (*malaxophobia* or *sarmassophobia*)

Fear of sexual love play or of sexual foreplay. (*See also* Coitus.)

Love, falling in or being in (*philophobia*)

Fear of falling or being in love. A person may fear the emotional disruption of loving feelings or may fear losing himself (or herself) in a relationship. Sometimes this is due to fears that the loved one may not reciprocate the feelings, but it can also be due to fears that the wrong relationship can cause problems. More common than either of these may be an unconscious fear related either to traumatic losses or rejections or to childhood-based fears of relationships related to early attachment difficulties, parental divorces, etc.

Marriage (*gamophobia*)

Fear of marriage or of becoming married. This phobia may be related to prior negative experiences with relationships or the bad experiences of one's parents or role models. It may also stem from fears of sexual intimacy, children, or adult responsibilities. Some may fear that marriage may entail a loss of freedom or may require assuming certain roles; others may fear the loss of identity. Fear of marriage is probably normal in most people to a limited degree, since it represents a major change in identity and lifestyle for most people; however, the good generally is perceived as vastly outweighing the bad. When a person is unable to anticipate as much good as bad, they may avoid marriage out of fear. (This is not the same as avoiding marriage simply because one prefers, for whatever reasons, to remain unmarried or because they prefer some other arrangements.)

Materialism (*hylephobia*)

Fear of materialism or of adopting materialistic attitudes and behaviors that subvert or undermine other beliefs or attitudes. In many cultural and religious traditions, becoming overly attached to material possessions or money is viewed as a negative and harmful attitude. A person may develop a fear that if they let themselves enjoy just a taste of the good life, they may become hooked and so give up their values.

Mirrors (*catoptrophobia*, *eisoptrophobia*, or *spectrophobia*)

Fear of mirrors or of seeing one's reflection in a mirror. Mirrors have historically been associated with mystery, including the mystery of one's soul. Seeing one's reflection has, at various times, been thought to be a dangerous experience. (*See also* Self, seeing in mirror in Chapter 8.)

Motion or movement (*kinetophobia* or *kinesophobia*)

Fear of motion or movement. Motion, such as riding in a car, standing in a bus, etc., can be associated with danger, loss of control, loss of balance, motion sickness, or being startled due to sudden changes in motion.

Moving or making changes

See Change or making changes.

Name, hearing a certain (*onomatophobia*)

Fear of hearing a certain name. This term resembles the familiar word *onomatopoeia*, which means a word whose sound resembles the sound that is being described (like *buzz* or *boom*). Onomatophobia refers in a somewhat literal way to a similar effect—namely, when the sound of someone's or something's name triggers an unpleasant and unwanted emotional reaction. For instance, the fear of hearing the name of a former lover who caused heartbreak might develop into a very powerful emotional aversion to the name. This phobia might also refer to a more ancient belief that hearing the name of certain deities might cause harm or destruction.

Narrow places or things (*anginophobia* or *stenophobia*)

Fear of narrow things or places. This may relate to claustrophobia or other fears in which a person may fear feeling or being closed in. It might also be applied to a fear that someone may feel in trying to navigate through a narrow channel or opening.

New or novel (*cainophobia, cainotophobia, kainophobia,* or *kainolophobia*)

Fear of the new or novel. Can be applied to any fear of newness, ranging from a new idea to a new car to a new boyfriend. Change triggers anxiety because it requires adapting; a person may fear losing something familiar, routine, and reliable and adjusting to something unknown or confusing, which may turn out not to be as good as hoped. It's fairly common for even good news to be greeted with a mix of positive and cautious feelings. But some people may develop such a fear of the new that they avoid it, remaining stuck in old situations that may be even less healthy or pleasurable.

Nuclear weapons (*nucleomituphobia*)

Fear of nuclear weapons. Of course, not fearing nuclear weapons would truly be insane, but an all-pervasive, preoccupying fear that absorbs a disproportionate share of a person's time, energy, and happiness might become a problem. Most people manage to maintain a balance of fear and optimism about even the most dire possibilities—nuclear war, plagues, famines, global warming, and the odds of the earth being hit by a massive meteor among them. This may or may not be rational, but it keeps most people's lives running reasonably smoothly—particularly since the odds of any of these admittedly horrible things happening are generally fairly slim. Phobias typically involve a narrowing of focus so that one particular danger eclipses other awareness. A preoccupying fear of nuclear weapons would operate that way.

Nudity (*gymnophobia* or *nudophobia*)

Fear of nudity. *Gymno-* is the ancient Greek term for naked. Many people have a strong—and some would argue, irrational—negative reaction to nudity. They may fear being seen nude (which might be a form of social phobia if it is linked with fears of being observed, scrutinized, or criticized) or may fear seeing others' nudity. This may at times be a culturally-based habit, or it may link to more fundamental discomforts regarding sexuality.

Old age (*gerascophobia* or *gerontophobia*)

Fear of growing old. Many people associate growing old with fear of illness or death; others, with a loss of attractiveness, popularity, or opportunities. In more youth-oriented cultures, aging is particularly difficult. *Old* is, of course, a variable concept; to a 15-year-old, a 25-year-old is perhaps an old person, while to someone in their 50s, a 25-year-old is just beginning their adult years. People who have a phobia of growing old may go to extreme lengths to reduce the impact of aging, whether through obsessive health care rituals, cosmetic surgery, trying to keep up with the latest trends and fashions meant for people half their age, lying about their age, or becoming depressed as none of these strategies work. (*See also* Old people in Chapter 8.)

Opinions, expressing (*doxophobia*)

Fear of expressing one's opinions. This fear most likely stems from a form of social phobia involving the real fear of being criticized, ridiculed, or humiliated because of expressing opinions. Many people find it difficult to freely say what they think or feel and so may hold back or withdraw from conversations. This can inhibit their social development and relationships.

Places (*topophobia*)

Fear of particular places.

Places, open or high (*aeroacrophobia*)

Fear of open, high places. Similar to *acrophobia*.

Pleasure, feeling (*hedonophobia*)

Fear of pleasure. This fear may refer to particular pleasures, such as sexual pleasure, a good meal, or a massage, or it may refer to anxiety about pleasure in general. Some people keep themselves more or less chronically uncomfortable and this, for them, can become the norm—a safe, familiar way to be. Anything that disrupts that status quo can be threatening in the same way that a child may fear any kind of change. Others may have philosophical, superstitious, or religious objections to indulging in too much pleasure; they may equate it with being too worldly and thus not spiritually attuned. A Freudian interpretation might also be that any kind, or certain kinds, of pleasure are unconsciously equated with sexual pleasure, so that if someone has anxiety or guilt about sexuality, they might also suppress other pleasures to protect themselves from sexual anxiety.

Poverty (*peniaphobia*)

Fear of poverty. While avoiding poverty may be seen mainly as a practical matter, to some people poverty may also represent a lesser status, failure, or the loss of identity that may be organized around their being well off. Like many feared states or situations, poverty is generally not something most people would choose to experience, but a severe dread of poverty can become an overwhelming focus that distorts a person's life. Many people in the generation who survived the Great Depression of the 1930s developed lifelong fears of crushing poverty like they had endured—it was a traumatic experience that left many of them frightened of trusting banks, spending money even on necessities, and starvation.

Praise, receiving (*doxophobia*)

Fear of being praised. People who fear praise may fear being in the limelight or having others notice them. It may not be the praise itself but the fact of having others noticing them that is frightening, if being observed, scrutinized, or judged creates anxiety. This may be because praise may not feel deserved; the person may feel that if others look carefully, they will see the person's perceived flaws—and the praise may turn to criticism.

Precipices (*cremnophobia*)

Fear of precipices. Similar to acrophobia (fear of heights), the fear of precipices may be based on a fear of falling from a cliff and being injured or killed, fear that a cliff might collapse, or fear that one may develop vertigo or dizziness. A person with this fear would be expected to avoid standing near the edge of a cliff or to avoid going near any such area whenever possible. (*See also* Heights.)

Progress (*prosophobia*)

Fear of progress. This term might more often be used by a person to describe someone else if the latter person seems either to fear or resist what the former person feels would be positive changes or progress. (*See also* Change or making changes.)

Public speaking (*glossophobia* and possibly the other terms)

Fear of public speaking. This is a very common fear. A person may have no difficulty talking to friends or co-workers but be stricken with terror at the thought of speaking up in a group, at a public meeting, or at an event. Making speeches tops many lists of common phobias. This is similar to (or a variant of) social phobia, in which people fear being seen, evaluated, criticized, or judged negatively for their faults, errors, or what they may say. Many people fear public speaking because they are afraid that others will find their opinions to be wrong or criticize them for expressing certain thoughts or ideas. Many people avoid any opportunity to speak up in public and may refuse invitations or social engagements if there is a risk of being asked to speak up, even in something as minor as making a toast.

Punishment or flogging (*mastigophobia* or *poinephobia*)

Fear of flogging or punishment. *Mastigos-* is the ancient Greek word for whip. Both terms refer to fear of punishment, though the former is the more commonly used term.

Railroads or train travel (*siderodromophobia*)

Fear of railroads, trains, or traveling by railroad or train. As with fear of air travel or traveling in cars, a person may develop the fear of train travel. This might be based on a fear of being harmed, losing control, large or fast-moving vehicles, etc.

Rape (*virginitiphobia*)

Fear of rape. This is possibly an unfortunate term, since it translates to the fear of the loss of virginity. This may hearken back to an earlier age and set of attitudes implying that virginity need somehow be connected with sexual assault (as though the only persons capable of being raped are virgins, for instance). As with many phobias, there can be a fine line between entirely reasonable fears or concerns and phobias. The fear of sexual assault is not, in itself, a phobia and is not at all neurotic or pathological. Even in the safest societies, a shockingly high percentage of women (and sometimes, men) are sexually assaulted at some time in their lives, and the effects of such experiences are often severely traumatic psychologically and medically. Individuals may develop a phobic level of morbid preoccupation with rape that exceeds their actual risks; this preoccupation, even if accurate, tends to magnify their fear and the potential psychological damage they might experience. This kind of phobia may develop due to prior traumatic experiences that the phobic individual or others have had. Childhood sexual abuse histories, high general levels of anxiety, or life circumstances such as visiting or living in a strange and unfamiliar environment may heighten these fears.

Religious ceremonies

See Ceremonies, religious.

Responsibility *(hypengyophobia* or *hypegiaphobia)*

Fear of responsibility. A person may fear any responsibility or only certain kinds of responsibilities (such as new, unfamiliar ones). They may fear responsibilities that might expose them to others' scrutiny or criticism or responsibilities that may leave them feeling trapped in a life or situation they don't want to be in. Other people may feel inadequate or ill-prepared for whatever the responsibility is, or they may fear that the sacrifices involved are too great. Implied in these fears are social phobic fears of being judged or criticized, fear of loss of control, or fear that certain responsibilities may result in painful costs to the person. (For instance, a sea captain may feel responsible for going down with the ship but may prefer to take that last seat in the lifeboat.)

Responsibility or duty, neglecting

See Duty or responsibility, neglect of.

Ridiculed, being *(catagelophobia* or *katagelophobia)*

Fear of being ridiculed. Fear of being ridiculed can be related to a desire for approval, the admiration of others, or status; ridicule would be the very opposite of these satisfactions. In many societies, a person's status (or the approval and respect of others) is not just a pleasant situation but a matter of survival—to lose respect may mean losing out on the cooperation and assistance of others, the loss of work or support, or even the loss of protection against enemies. In such societies, ridicule may be a life-threatening catastrophe. But a phobia would be, by definition, an excessive fear of ridicule—fear that is greater than any actual threat or danger that ridicule might cause. This may lead a person to avoid being noticed by others, avoid doing or saying anything risky, or covering up one's errors or perceived flaws. (Fear of being ridiculed is also a key part of social phobia; see Chapter 12.)

Riding in a car

See Automobiles, being in moving.

Road travel or travel (*hodophobia*)

Fear of road travel or of travel in general. This can include fears related to riding in automobiles but can also include fears of other forms of travel (such as trains or even backpacking). Travel can be unpredictable and a person can imagine (and may experience) all sorts of dangers that can fuel phobias. As a result, a person may avoid travel, require various kinds of reassurances (such as never traveling alone), or become highly anxious or panicky at the prospect of having to travel. This may involve related fears such as agoraphobia or social phobias—for example, a person's fear may be partly rooted in the dread of being out in exposed or public places by themselves, of being overwhelmed or panicking in public, etc. Other fears may include loss of control, physical danger, loss or theft of one's money in a strange place, simply becoming lost or disoriented, etc. (*See also* Automobiles, being in moving; Flying; Railroads or train travel.)

Ruined, being (*atephobia*)

Fear of ruin or of being ruined. This phobia can include fears of financial or social ruin, humiliation, or failure.

School, going to (*didaskaleinophobia* or *scolionophobia*)

Fear of going to school. Many small children develop school phobia, which can in effect be a form of separation anxiety; it may actually be related more to separation from the safety of parents and home than to anything about school. Other children may develop a fear of the novel and frightening school environment. This fear is most common among elementary-age children. (See Chapter 13 for more about phobias in children.)

Sex (*genophobia*)

Fear of sex. This phobia can include fear of lovemaking or coitus, or it may refer to more broadly-defined fears such as fear of any reference or allusion to sex or sexuality, open discussions of sex, or even the fear of the word *sex*. Some people may develop a strong negative reaction to any references to or thoughts of sex—even including references to its existence at all. This may be the result of childhood experiences, cultural or religious training, or traumas. In Victorian times, the legs of tables and pianos were often draped with fabric because of the "sexual" connotations of uncovered furniture "legs." This led psychoanalyst Sigmund Freud, an astute observer, to speculate that there seemed to be an unhealthy preoccupation and discomfort with sex on a culture-wide basis, which, he theorized, was the leading cause of his patients' neuroses. (*See also* Coitus.)

Sexual intercourse

See Coitus, Sex.

Sexual perversion (*paraphobia*)

Fear of sexual perversions or paraphilias. Many people are comfortable with sex provided that it falls within a culturally approved-of form. Paraphilias are sexual preferences or tastes that traditionally have been considered outside the norm, such as sexual fetishes or interests in bondage. Historically, earlier generations of mental health professionals tended to view paraphilias as a form of mental illness—much the same way as they viewed homosexuality as mental illness. In more recent years, many mental health professionals have been revising those assumptions, and images of sexually unconventional behaviors such as bondage, domination, submission, and such are more common in the culture. But some people may have extremely anxious reactions to these kinds of images or ideas; they may avoid images or references in the media and may perhaps have a strong preoccupation with the "sickness" of nonstandard sexual expression.

Sin (*enosiophobia, enissophobia, harmartophobia, harmatophobia, peccatiphobia,* or *peccatophobia*)

Fear of sin or of having committed an unpardonable sin. The fear of committing (or of having committed) a sin which could not possibly be pardoned is a reference to various biblical or other religious concepts that emphasize concepts of sin, forgiveness, hell, etc. Since the terms above are generally defined as written, fear of "having committed ..." instead of "of committing," it's worth noting that technically this would probably be more of an obsession. One can really only fear something that might happen in the future; if you can't let go of something that happened in the past, it's an obsession. Of course, if the fear is really of being damned because of having committed an unpardonable sin, then we're back in business. (*See also* Hell.)

Single, staying (*anuptaphobia*)

Fear of staying single, of never being able to find a marital partner, or of wilting away at the ripe old age of 28 or so. (This is the opposite of *gamophobia*, which is the fear of marriage.) It is a common fear among young people, particularly once they've passed whatever age by which they feel they should have met Mr. or Miss Right; it can be exacerbated once their friends are all married or engaged. While common, this can still be a source of considerable anxiety and torment for people, particularly if they feel that they are particularly unlucky, unattractive, or undesirable or that there just aren't enough of the right kinds of partners out there. Some of the fear may be of helplessness, loneliness, isolation, or lack of benefits of marriage or children, while some people may also fear the pressure or criticism of friends, relatives, or peers if they somehow can't find a way to marry. Some psychologists have written that American culture in particular tends to have a distorted overvaluation of marriage and ignores the fact that many people have extremely satisfying lives as single persons.

Sitting down (*cathisophobia, kathisophobia,* or *thaasophobia*)

Fear of sitting or of sitting down.

Situations, certain (*topophobia*)

This is a generic term for fear of certain situations or places; it may also refer to stage fright. (*See also* Stage fright.)

Sleep *(somniphobia)*

Fear of sleep or sleeping. This may be related to a fear of helplessness, nightmares, dying while asleep, or giving up control; some people may have medical conditions (such as sleep apnea) that leave them fearful either of interrupted or unpleasant sleep or of experiencing danger, illness, or even death while sleeping.

Solitude

See Alone, being.

Space, closed or locked in

See Confined spaces, Locked in.

Speaking *(glossophobia, laliophobia, lalophobia, or phonophobia)*

Fear of speaking or talking. This fear may represent a social phobia response related to fear of being criticized for what one says, or it may simply be a fear of being heard. This phobia may also be related to a fear of hearing one's own voice or a fear of stuttering. It may also include fear of talking on the phone. *(See also* Public speaking.)

Speed *(tachcophobia)*

Fear of speed. One may be terrified of driving, biking, or flying at high speeds, generally due to fear of loss of control, injury, or death.

Stage fright *(topophobia)*

Fear of going on stage, speaking, acting, or performing in front of others. This is a common fear among even successful public speakers, actors, musicians, and others who may perform in front of audiences, as well as among children expected to read their essays or reports in front of the class. People commonly fear that they will make mistakes or be thought inadequate when performing in front of others and so may avoid the opportunity to do so. Extreme stage fright can interfere with a person's social life and even livelihood; even highly accomplished musicians, actors, and politicians have at times sought professional help or had careers undermined by this fear. Others may abuse drugs or alcohol in order to be able to reduce their anxiety sufficiently to perform, which is usually successful only for a short time before it begins to make the fear, and possibly their performances, worse. (*See also* Public speaking, Speaking.)

Stairs (*climacophobia*)

Fear of stairs or of climbing stairs. This can be a fear of falling, unsafe stairs, or heights. It may perhaps be a fear of being physically unable to climb stairs or of having a heart attack due to climbing them.

Standing (*basiphobia, basophobia, stasiphobia,* or *stasibasiphobia*)

Fear of standing, or of being unable to stand because of the possibility of falling.

Stealing (*cleptophobia* or *kleptophobia*)

Fear of stealing. This is attributed to the idea that you might fear stealing something and then either be caught or feel guilty; it implies that there is actually a fear of losing control (like a kleptomaniac). Possibly, it may be that the act of stealing itself is avoided and controlled due to the fear of being caught or punished.

Stooping (*kyphophobia*)

Fear of stooping. One could fear becoming dizzy, falling, bumping one's head, etc.

Streets (*agyrophobia*)

Fear of streets. One may fear being in the street and being seen by others, being hit or injured by vehicles, fear of crowds, etc.

Streets, crossing (*dromophobia*)

Fear of crossing streets. One may fear being hit by a moving vehicle or the openness of being in the middle of the street, similar to agoraphobia.

Stuttering (*psellismophobia*)

Fear of stuttering. This may be partially a social-type fear in the sense that if a person has a problem stammering or stuttering, the pressure to control it may trigger higher levels of emotion that, in turn, make stuttering or stammering more likely.

Suffering and disease (*panthophobia*)

Fear of suffering and disease. This is a morbid preoccupation with one's fear of possible illness or other forms of suffering. It may be linked with depression or increase the chances of developing depression.

Tests, taking (*testophobia*)

Fear of taking tests. This is a common fear among students of all ages, from early childhood through adulthood. The fear is usually based on a combination of concerns: fear that one will not do well on the test, fear of the unknown or loss of control (e.g., imagining that you can't predict or won't be able to handle the questions you are asked), fear of freezing up or not being able to answer questions, fear that you will forget what you've already learned during the test itself, fear of poor grades, or failing. Fear of failure may inspire additional fears, because the consequences of failure may include social embarrassment, criticism by parents or teachers, and loss of grades—which can lead to decreased chances for advancement and may affect the ability to be accepted into certain colleges, graduate schools, or professions. Since in many cultures the consequences of poor test performance for one's life can be huge, it's no surprise that tests often trigger massive anxiety among students. Generally, a moderate level of anxiety may actually help students by motivating them to prepare well for tests, but the vicious cycle of test anxiety is that too much anxiety generally lowers test performance, which fuels even more anxiety on the next test, lowering performance still more, and so on. Generally, normal test anxiety becomes a phobia when students notice that their test performance is poorer because of their fears, when they totally freeze up and go blank during tests or have other negative experiences, especially if this starts to happen repeatedly. Many schools, colleges, and psychologists have special test anxiety programs or clinics to help students manage their test anxiety.

Thinking (*phronemophobia*)

Fear of thinking. This phobia can include fear of thinking about certain topics or of developing unacceptable opinions. This may also be a term applied to someone with whom we disagree; we may assume that if they would only think about it, they would surely come around to our way of seeing things.

Tickled, being (possibly by feathers) (*pteronophobia*)

Fear of being tickled by feathers. *Ptero* comes from the Greek term for winged or *pteron* for feather. This may be related to experiences of excessive tickling (whether playful or malicious) during childhood. While some people find tickling to be amusing fun, others find it extremely uncomfortable and more akin to pain than pleasure. In fact, tickling has been used as torture by military and government officials against criminals, enemy combatants, and spies. Some people see themselves as very ticklish while others hardly notice it; neither extreme is necessarily phobic. But if a person develops a conscious fear of being tickled, particularly if it leads to problems such as avoiding sexual play with a partner for fear of being touched or tickled, it could become phobic. More likely, the term is likely to be used to simply describe a level of fear of tickling that falls short of an actual anxiety disorder. (*See also* Feathers in Chapter 9.)

Tied or bound

See Bound or tied up.

Touched, being (*aphenphosmphobia, aphephobia, chiraptophobia, haphephobia, hapnophobia, haptephobia, haptophobia,* or *thixophobia*)

Fear of being touched. Being touched is a common everyday experience, yet a surprising number of people find it to be uncomfortable or even highly aversive. Some people, such as those with autism or forms of autism such as Asperger's syndrome, may react with extreme distress if touched by others; some people, such as victims of sexual assault or abuse, may likewise find touch, or touch by persons associated with their trauma (e.g., males, for a female victim) to be upsetting. Other reasons for touch phobia can include an obsessive-compulsive fear of becoming contaminated or soiled, fear of sexual intent, stimulation, or feelings, or ingrained cultural fears or prohibitions against touch. Some cultures inculcate or reinforce this fear for reasons related to status, sexual purity, or to maintain boundaries. Persons from different cultures may find it difficult to negotiate or to understand the different unspoken rules about the types and amounts of contact permitted between strangers or acquaintances.

Some people react negatively even to seeing other persons touching. Medical patients may permit touch by their doctors or other health staff, yet there may even there be differences based on culture or gender. Being touched may trigger emotional reactions, even if the person is not conscious that this has occurred; at times this may be highly uncomfortable. Again, this may be a function of prior experience being touched; it may also be related to the culture or the gender of the person being touched or doing the touching. (One study, for instance, showed that male patients who were touched reassuringly by nurses just before going in for surgery found it to be more upsetting than not being touched, while female patients found it comforting.)

Train travel

See Railroads or train travel.

Travel

See Road travel or travel.

Trembling (*tremophobia*)

Fear of trembling. Similar to a fear of blushing, this is a fear of displaying or revealing anxiety by trembling. Fear of revealing one's emotions is a form of social phobia (see Chapter 12).

Virginity, losing one's (*primeisodophobia*)

Fear of losing one's virginity. Though it's traditionally been assumed that concerns about virginity have mainly or exclusively focused on females, in fact both females and males may fear losing their virginity or the beginning of sexual relations. For instance, if raised in cultures or religious traditions that strongly prohibit sexual relations before marriage, boys (or young men) as well as girls (or young women) may fear violating the expectations that they remain sexually pure (perhaps both physically and mentally) until they are married. However, it's still generally true that the social pressure to remain virginal have more often been applied to women than to men, and in many cultures, proof of virginity at marriage has even been considered essential. At the extreme, this might be a life-and-death matter for a young woman, since the suspicion that she had been sexual with someone before it was permitted could result in ostracism or even death.

In more contemporary cultures, particularly in cultures that place little or no emphasis on virginity (beyond protecting children from abuse and the need to avoid unsafe sex), virginity is less emphasized—though young persons of both genders will still find sexual encounters (particularly early encounters) to be emotionally and psychologically important. It's generally expected that the more stress a culture places on virginity and sexual purity, the more likely there will be people developing phobias regarding the violation of those norms or expectations.

Waits, long (*macrophobia*)

Fear of long waits. This may involve difficulty coping with the feeling of being delayed or frustrated, which sometimes triggers strong reactions of anger, impatience, or anxiety. Some people feel trapped while in lines or have difficulty tolerating crowds while waiting in public places; others have problems waiting for news, phone calls, or other personal or business situations or events to be resolved.

Walking (*ambulophobia, basistasiphobia,* or *basostasophobia*)

Fear of walking. Fears might include falling or being exposed to danger while walking somewhere; possible fears also include walking somewhere and having a panic response such as in agoraphobia (see Chapter 11) or walking in a public place and being seen, criticized, attacked, etc., such as in social phobia (see Chapter 12).

Washing

See Bathing.

Weakness (*asthenophobia*)

Fear of weakness. This is generally a fear of physical weakness, loss of strength, or loss of health, which may be associated with disease, deterioration, or even death. It can also refer to a fear of being emotionally vulnerable or weak or to weakness of character. The latter might be threatening both in terms of diminished self-esteem and because it may result in the loss of reputation or esteem by others. (The term *asthenophobia* is also used for fear of fainting; *see also* Fainting in Chapter 6.)

Wet dreams (*oneirogmophobia*)

Fear of wet dreams or nocturnal emissions. Wet dreams are sexual dreams in males that may include erections and even ejaculation while asleep. Some boys or men may fear shame or embarrassment if others discover that this has happened; people with religious beliefs that forbid sexual relief in forms such as masturbation or sex outside of marriage may also feel guilty and fear that wet dreams are sinful or wrong. (*See also* Dreams.)

Writing (*graphophobia*)

Fear of writing. This can include fear of having one's handwriting observed, criticized, or considered inadequate. This may be a form of social phobia. (*See also* Writing in public.)

Writing in public (*scriptophobia*)

Fear of writing in public. This is generally a variety of social phobia in which a person is afraid of writing when being observed by others, such as a fear of signing their names. This can at times create difficulties such as when a person has to be witnessed signing legal documents; they may avoid doing so even though this may result in delaying, or not being able to complete, some necessary legal tasks such as getting drivers' licenses. (*See also* Writing.)

Chapter 8

"Hell Is Other People": Specific Phobias Involving People

In This Chapter

◆ Why people scare us

◆ List of phobias involving people

Many specific phobias involve fear of people. While social phobia is a pervasive discomfort (discussed in Chapter 12), there are also many phobias that are more circumscribed. Sometimes a certain kind of person, or a person who represents a particular group or idea, may be spooky. Other times, the person's appearance, attitude, or occupation may give us the heebie-jeebies.

In this chapter we'll explore the reasons for these fears. Then we'll review a list of particular phobias that revolve around our fellow *Homo sapiens*.

Why We Get Scared of People

When many people think of phobias, their thoughts immediately run toward things such as snakes or heights. But above all, we are social animals, and often the most emotionally important realities in our lives are other people.

We generally have a mix of positive, neutral, and negative feelings toward others. In fact, as a therapist for many years, much of my work has involved helping people to become aware of how complicated their feelings toward others are. Even our most beloved partners or family members will sometimes inspire darker feelings in all of us. Our sweet mom or dad may sometimes be frankly annoying, and that cute baby brother may be a royal pain at times. Generally speaking, a great deal of what we call psychological maturity consists of understanding and accepting this mix of feelings we all have toward others.

Because our minds were designed to be part of a social matrix of connections with others, relationships naturally trigger these strong feelings. Most of the time, this works out just fine. It ensures that we have the support and ability to feel love for others, which keeps us sane and healthy. But sometimes things aren't so smooth. We may develop anxious feelings or even severely phobic reactions to others—not because that particular person has injured us, but because we come to believe that certain kinds of relationships or people are somehow a threat.

What form can that phobic threat take in our minds? It can be one of several things. All of these reactions have in common that they trigger fear.

For one thing, we may have a reaction to certain kinds of emotional expressions in others, such as anger. Certain classes of people may have come to represent something—danger, threat, enemies, or something foreign and therefore scary. We may have stereotypes in our minds about various groups, nationalities, or even professions that make people in these groups seem dangerous or threatening.

Reactions to people-related phobias can vary—we may feel fear, avoid the feared persons or situations, or even feel anger or antagonism. More subtle reactions are also possible: we may hardly ever think about "those people," but when we suddenly have to interact with someone in the phobic class, feelings may be triggered and affect our behavior even before we realize it's happening.

Prejudice and *fear* may also tend to go together. Many of the phobia terms listed in this chapter actually refer as much to prejudicial or negative attitudes toward certain groups of people as they do to literal fear. For instance, to say that one is homophobic, xenophobic, or has a dose of *Russophobia* may not necessarily mean that one is literally frightened (certainly not in the sense of a clinical anxiety disorder) of homosexuals, people from different countries, or Russians. Rather, it probably refers to one's negative attitudes—often a blend of dislike, poor understanding of that group or culture, and stereotypes or prejudices about them. But since there is often a fine line between a prejudice about people from a different group (or of a gender, or what have you) and actual fear or anxiety, and given my desire to include and define as many phobia terms as possible here, I am including these terms in this chapter.

People-Related Phobias

Anger (*angrophobia* or *cholerophobia*)

Fear of anger. It's very possible that fear of anger is, at least partially, an inborn fear. We now know that most people are extremely sensitive to the mood states of others; researchers using brain scan technologies have shown that when a person is feeling a certain intense feeling, another person who is interacting with them will also have powerful shifts in their own brain functioning *whether they realize it or not.* Anger may mobilize the fight-or-flight response of higher nervous system arousal and the release of stress hormones such as cortisol and adrenalin, in order to prepare one to cope with danger. Indeed, being around a person who is often angry is generally stressful for others.

But an anger phobia is an even stronger reaction. This may be due to generally lower thresholds for stress or may be a result of traumatic experiences (possibly in childhood). A person who grew up around angry, frightening, or abusive parents may learn to be extremely frightened whenever someone expresses even mild levels of anger. At its extreme, this can lead them to avoid relationships with others as a way of staying out of the line of fire that frightens them so.

Bald people (*peladophobia*)

Fear of bald people, or of being bald.

Beautiful women (*calignyephobia*)

Fear of beautiful women. Since beauty, and particularly female beauty (whether fair or not), tends to be highly idealized in many cultures, beautiful women can tend to become idealized. Men and women may both feel mixtures of envy, desire, awe, and anxiety when around very attractive women. For instance, men may imagine that such a woman would never be interested in even talking with them, much less in responding to overtures to get acquainted or to develop a relationship. This fear of rejection can then morph into a fear of the woman herself. There may be few actual, anxiety disorder-level phobias of beautiful women, but lesser levels of anxiety are quite common, which may cause much difficulty and discomfort for the women themselves. (*See also* Beautiful women in Chapter 10.)

Bogeymen (*bogyphobia*)

Fear of "bogeymen" or of imaginary supernatural creatures such as ghosts, goblins, apparitions, or devils.

Bolsheviks (*Bolshephobia*)

Fear, dislike, or prejudice regarding Bolsheviks or Communists. Particularly during the mid-twentieth century, many people in the so-called free world feared the threat of international Communism; at times this may have had hysterical or exaggerated dimensions to it. An individual who focuses intensively on this threat and generalizes it such that any Communist is perceived as dangerous would have this phobia.

Bums or beggars (*hobophobia*)

Fear of hobos, bums, or beggars. Fears can include the belief that strangers are potentially poor, desperate, and/or dangerous, or it may be related to fear of threat (whether to a person or property) or fear of the deterioration of civic order, depending on the situation and the values of the phobic person.

Burglars (*scelerophobia*)

Fear of burglars or of being harmed by evil or bad persons. (*See also* Robbers or being robbed; Harmed by bad persons in Chapter 7.)

Children (*pedophobia*)

Fear of children. Many people feel anxious around children, feeling that they aren't good with children or that children may be hard to manage, understand, or interact with. Increasingly, people also avoid interacting with children that they don't know well because of societal paranoia about child abuse, a fear which has led to documented instances of strangers refusing to help lost children for fear they'll be accused of abducting or hurting them.

Chinese people or culture (*Sinophobia*)

Fear, dislike, or prejudice regarding Chinese people or culture.

Clowns (*coulrophobia*)

Fear of clowns. While clowns generally attempt to be viewed as entertaining or funny, many children (especially at a young age) find the unusual and strange appearance of clowns to be frightening. This may, however, be one of those fears that is growing since the term has been coined relatively recently; there seems to be more discussion of clown phobia in recent years as people clown around on the Internet about their phobias, real or constructed.

Corpses (*necrophobia*)

Fear of corpses. This is not at all an unusual fear, and most people have at least some discomfort with seeing a dead body. In modern culture, few people have as much exposure to bodies as in earlier generations, when much of the work of funeral preparation was done by family members. Fears include the rational fears of possible infection, disgust-phobia reactions to the sight of unusual-looking bodies, reactions to the different, unnatural-seeming appearance of a friend or loved one's body, and the fear of disease and one's own death that a dead body may stir up.

Crowds *(demophobia, enochlophobia,* or *ochlophobia)*

Fear of crowds. Depending on the fear, this may be a rational or a not-so-rational fear. Crowds can be dangerous if they are panicking, for instance, and in crowds there may be a greater potential for being accosted, groped, or having one's pocket picked. Many crowd situations involve high-decibel noisy events, chaos, confusion, and other forms of overstimulation that many people find aversive. Some people may experience social phobia and may feel more vulnerable to criticism or to being observed or scrutinized in crowds. *(See also* Crowded public places, Crowds or mobs in Chapter 7.)

Deformed people *(teratophobia)*

Fear of deformed people. This is probably a fairly common fear that may be more intense in children or in people living in cultures—especially cultures that either stigmatize disabilities or differences or that have fearful superstitions or beliefs about disease/deformity and see it as a threat. Most of the harm resulting from such beliefs and fears generally falls upon the "different" person, who may face rejection and even threats by others.

Demons *(daemonophobia* or *demonophobia)*

Fear of demons. This is a fairly self-evident fear, assuming one believes in demons. Psychologically, demons are given credit for vast supernatural powers and totally evil natures. There is much to fear in that; many superstitions and mainstream religions grow up around ways to supposedly control, manage, or ward off demons.

Dentists *(dentrophobia)*

Fear of dentists. This may include fears of pain, being criticized for poor dental hygiene or failure to floss, or fears of the bad news that one needs expensive or painful work. Some point out that a person's teeth and mouth are fairly sensitive and also part of the head, which is closer, perhaps, to our sense of self than, say, our hands or knees. It's possible that, because of this, dental work may feel more like a threatening intrusion than many other kinds of medical-related care. Dental phobias are very common, and the result is that millions of people tend to avoid dental work until it is to the point of being urgently needed.

Many dentists advertise that they specialize in helping those with dental phobias, though of course almost all dentists have to deal with that on a daily basis. I've never heard of a dentist who specializes in working with tough, non-scaredy cat patients. (*See also* Dental surgery, Dentists in Chapter 6.)

Doctors (*iatrophobia*)

Fear of doctors or of going to the doctor. Similar to dental phobias, people may fear any or all of these issues related to doctors: pain, hearing bad medical news, authority figures (doctors being, traditionally, among the most authoritative of authority figures), expense, illness, medical care making a condition worse, misdiagnosis, inconvenience, demands that lifestyle choices or preferences be changed, sickness, blood-injection-injury situations, and/or death. There can be elements of social phobia (including fear of being judged, being seen naked, being criticized, or being unable to explain or ask questions) and of our biggest, ultimate existential fears (death, dying, dealing with health insurance companies). (*See also* Doctor visits in Chapter 6.)

Dolls (*pediophobia*)

Fear of dolls. One may fear any kind of humanlike object because of its eerie appearance; dolls with their staring eyes may sometimes trigger a feeling of being observed or that there is something alive in the doll. Scary TV shows and films such as the old *Twilight Zone* series frequently featured evil, staring dolls that threatened people or caused them harm. (*See also* Puppets, Ventriloquist's dummy.)

English people or culture (*Anglophobia*)

Fear, dislike, or prejudice regarding English people or culture.

Foreigners or strangers (*xenophobia*)

Fear or prejudice regarding foreigners or strangers. This fear is the generic term under which various specific examples (such as *Anglophobia* or *Sinophobia*) would fall. It's not uncommon to fear people from what seem to be foreign or strange lands. For centuries, people have told tales and spun legends about other cultures, stories which were sometimes rooted in actual fact but other times merely imagined. Fear of strangers can be rooted in fear of danger, such as when one believes the foreigner may be warlike, threatening, carry diseases or, more subtly, may carry dangerous ideas, beliefs, or faiths that threaten one's own culture. Other fears may be related to more visceral feelings such as disgust, such as when one hears that the eating, bathroom, sexual, or other habits of the foreigner are different and seem odd or repulsive. Persons who have been traumatized by wars or who have had vicarious traumatizing experiences through hearing the propaganda of one's own government or culture may develop intense fears of certain foreigners. The best cure for *xenophobia* is generally to get to know some people and make friends with people from those cultures.

French people or culture (*Francophobia*, *Gallophobia*, or *Galiphobia*)

Fear, dislike, or prejudice regarding French people or culture.

German people or culture (*Germanophobia* or *Teutophobia*)

Fear, dislike, or prejudice regarding German people or culture.

Ghosts or specters (*spectrophobia*)

Fear of ghosts, specters, etc.

Girls, young, or virgins (*parthenophobia*)

Fear of young girls or virgins. *Parthenos* is the ancient Greek term for a virgin. Some fears of girls are related to fears of sexuality; some may believe that young girls are pure and vulnerable and so fear corrupting them, while some are adults fear appearing to have, or actually having, sexual attractions to young girls. (In the latter case, a Freudian might say the actual fear is of one's own feelings, not of the objects of those feelings.)

God or gods (*Zeusophobia*)

Fear of God or gods. This term was named for the Greek god Zeus. Most cultures with beliefs in God or gods tend to have belief sets that encourage fear of said god(s). All-powerful beings are often believed to require appeasement, and even people who say they believe only in infinitely loving gods (or a single infinitely loving and well-meaning God) often include beliefs in that god's anger and rage—and they may believe that this god will create eternal torments for those who displease him (or her, or it). Many people spend their lives living in fear of those torments or retributions and spend much energy trying to please or appease the feared god(s).

Greek people or culture (*Hellophobia*)

Fear, dislike, or prejudice regarding Greek people or culture.

Homosexuals (*homophobia*)

Fear or prejudice regarding homosexuals (or of becoming homosexual or the unconscious fear of having homosexual leanings or desires). People may fear seduction (or attempts at seduction) by homosexuals or may develop fears of the intents of homosexuals; other times, there may be fear of contamination by homosexuals so that a person may fear even shaking hands with a gay or lesbian individual. (*See also* Homosexuality or being homosexual in Chapter 7.)

Islam

See Muslims or Islam.

Japanese people or culture (*Japanophobia*)

Fear, dislike, or prejudice regarding Japanese people or culture.

Jealousy (*zelophobia*)

Fear of jealousy or of feeling jealousy. One may feel that jealousy is an inappropriate emotion or that it might betray one's own feelings of inadequacy or failure compared to another.

Jewish people or culture (*Judeophobia*)

Fear, dislike, or prejudice regarding Jewish people or culture.

Kissing (*philemaphobia* or *philematophobia*)

Fear of kissing. This may include fear of violating norms of proper behavior, fear of sexual arousal, feelings of disgust or discomfort at kissing, or fear of the social or relationship consequences—for instance, kissing and developing feelings for someone other than a spouse or partner. One may also fear contamination by oral contact with another, such as fears of catching colds, venereal diseases, or even AIDS.

Men (*androphobia, arrhenphobia,* or *hominophobia*)

Fear of men. Both males and females may fear men, whether due to specific fears such as of violence (e.g., if one has been assaulted by men in the past) or due to concerns or attitudes about men, maleness, what men think or do, etc.

Mothers-in-law (*pentheraphobia*)

Fear of mothers-in-law. Tension or even overt hostility sometimes happens between sons-in-law or daughters-in-law and their spouses' mothers, particularly if one fears being criticized or judged harshly by his or her spouse's mom.

Muslims or Islam (*Islamophobia*)

Fear, dislike, or prejudice regarding the Islamic religion or Muslims.

Old people (*gerontophobia*)

Fear of old people or of aging. Some may fear old people because of the belief they may be critical, rejecting, or difficult to understand or relate to; others may fear them out of discomfort with the results of aging (such as seeing them as in pain or ill) or because they represent mortality or the loss of youth. (*Gerontophobia* is also used to refer to the fear of growing old; *see also* Old age in Chapter 7.)

Opposite sex (*heterophobia* or *sexophobia*)

Fear of the opposite sex. Adolescents in particular may feel anxiety about being in contact with the opposite sex, and at times this may escalate into a severe fear of rejection, of being criticized or seen as somehow not adequate, or being evaluated. This fear can continue into adulthood, particularly if the person develops a tendency to avoid making contact or interacting with members of the opposite sex. At times this fear can become extreme and make it impossible for the person to pursue relationships, dating, or even platonic friendships with members of the opposite sex.

Parents-in-law (*soceraphobia*)

Fear of one's parents-in-law. (*See* Mothers-in-law and multiply by two.)

People (*anthropophobia*)

Fear of people. Many people fear people; this may often be actually a form of social phobia if the fear is mostly organized around the anticipation of being criticized, judged, observed by others; others may develop a notion that, in general, people can't be trusted or will always try to cheat you (or similar beliefs). Often these feelings flow from experiences of injury or trauma at the hands of one or two persons, then generalizing those experiences to people in general. People with this kind of fear may become loners and even seek to live in isolated areas far from others.

People in general or society (*sociophobia*)

This is another term for fear of people, though the implication here may be that society—people along with their general rules, expectations, or cultural norms—is the frightening thing. For instance, if someone feels alienated from the norms of their society, they may fear being ostracized or an outcast, whereas a more general fear of people may revolve less around society than around fears of injury, being taken advantage of or cheated, etc.

Politicians (*politicophobia*)

Fear of politicians. Politicians often develop fairly negative reputations, individually and collectively, for offenses (real or imagined) such as dishonesty, corruption, or ideological sins if they disagree with one's own views. This is more likely to be an aversion or dislike than a severe anxiety disorder, though some people may have a kind of intense anxiety if they have the chance to meet or shake hands with a politician for the same reasons people may fear authority figures of other sorts.

Pope (*papaphobia*)

Fear of the pope. This phobia may occur if said pope is viewed as a powerful figure with either magical or special spiritual powers.

Priests or sacred things (*hierophobia*)

Fear of priests or sacred things. It's common for people who are raised in or believe in various religious traditions to view the priests or other clergy, shamans, medicine women or men, etc., with a kind of awe.

This feeling can be anywhere on a continuum from respect at one end to fear that can become terror on the other. People who develop extreme fear of the priests, sacred rites, objects, etc., may react with anxiety or fear if they are being observed, judged, or cursed by priests; they may fear touching or even looking at the sacred objects. (*See also* Ceremonies, religious in Chapter 7.)

Prostitutes (*cypridophobia, cypriphobia, cyprianophobia,* or *cyprinophobia*)

Fear of prostitutes or of venereal disease. Given the heightened risk in many locales that prostitutes and sex workers may contract or pass on sexually transmitted diseases, it's traditionally been the case that many people more or less equate prostitutes and disease; prostitutes can be feared for various reasons including the fear of disease, fear of criminal activities, fear that they may corrupt young men or undermine marriages or community values, fear that they may bring sin, evil, or destruction to a community, etc. Of course, it's generally the case that these beliefs don't apply equally to the johns or customers of prostitutes (who may have given them the diseases in the first place). It's likely that, in many cases, an underlying fear is fear of sexuality, of sexual desire, or—as some Freudians might say—fear based on the unconscious fact that prostitutes may actually represent the sexual freedom and expression that the phobic wishes they could enjoy for themselves.

Puppets (*pupaphobia*)

Fear of puppets. As with many fears of humanlike things, puppets can be very frightening to children (or even to adults if they begin to have an uncomfortable fantasy that there is something uncanny or human-like about the puppet). Sometimes all it takes for something to strike us as bizarre or frightening is for it to be just like something human … but not quite. So puppets, scarecrows, or even a highly realistic painting of a person can do the trick. (*See also* Dolls, Ventriloquist's dummy.)

Relatives (*syngenesophobia*)

Fear of relatives. A fear of relatives may be connected to family conflicts or old injuries, fear of confrontation, or a socially phobic-style fear of being judged or criticized.

Robbers or being robbed (*harpaxophobia*)

Fear of robbers or of being robbed. One may fear the loss of control, violence, injury, strangers, or death. Sometimes the fear is connected with the mystery or the unknown quality of robbers—to discover, say, that the big scary stranger who broke into your home was actually a 13-year-old looking for electronics may result in a shrinking of your fear or feelings of trauma. Fear of robbery or robbers is actually a normal and adaptive fear unless it becomes overwhelming and begins to rule your life. (*See also* Robbers or being robbed; Harmed by bad persons in Chapter 7.)

Russian people or culture (*Russophobia*)

Fear, dislike, or prejudice regarding Russian people or culture.

Satan (*Satanophobia*)

Fear of Satan. One can fear Satan or the devil, Satanic influences or evil, or threats to one's soul (or to others or to the world) from Satan; this fear can also represent pure evil, whether existing independently in the world or as manifested or flowing through the personalities of others.

Self, being seen (*scopophobia* or *scoptophobia*)

Fear of being seen or looked at. This would usually be related to social phobia, which is covered in Chapter 12.

Self, seeing in mirror (*eisoptrophobia*)

Fear of seeing oneself in the mirror. This can be due to fear that one does not look acceptable or due to mystical fears such as the idea that one's soul can be seen in a mirror. (*See also* Mirrors in Chapter 7.)

Society or people in general

See People, People in general or society.

Spirits (*pneumatiphobia*)

Fear of spirits, such as the spirit or disembodied soul of a dead person.

Stepfathers (*vitricophobia*)

Fear of stepfathers. While stepmothers may be more often viewed in negative lights, stepfathers may also be frightening. In general, it's fairly normal for stepparents to be viewed less favorably by children; they may seem strange and frightening, and the children may blame them for somehow replacing or forcing their biological parent away. Even if a child logically knows that a stepparent was not responsible for the absence of the biological parent (if, for instance, the biological dad were to die before mom ever met the stepfather), developmental psychologists may note that, on an unconscious level, the child may still feel that the stepparent is somehow responsible. Children may build up fears or fantasies of the evil intention of a stepfather.

Stepmothers (*novercaphobia*)

Fear of stepmothers. In myths and fairy tales, the wicked stepmother is a familiar figure. Stepmothers are commonly viewed with less trust and less sense of attachment than biological mothers, particularly when they are still unfamiliar to children. Like stepfathers, only perhaps more so, they can be viewed as frightening, unloving, and even dangerous by children, who may blame them for the breakup of a marriage or the loss of the child's biological mother. It can sometimes be hard for either the child or the stepmother to recapture the intensity of the mother-infant bond that develops between biological mother-infant pairs, so stepmothers may find relationships to be more difficult—making these relationships, of course, fertile ground for the projection of all sorts of fantasies and phobias.

Strangers or foreigners

See Foreigners or strangers.

Teenagers (*ephibiphobia*)

Fear or prejudice of teenagers. Adolescence is a time of high energy and dramatically increased physical strength and is also a time when many young people take risks that can put their own and others' safety in peril. People may fear wild teenagers or feel threatened by the energy, noise, sexuality, or other behavior of teens.

Tyrants (*tyrannophobia*)

Fear of tyrants. Tyrants may include ancient kings or rulers with dangerous powers, bosses in the corner office, an office manager, or even a family member. People may fear the loss of control, threats of violence, or arbitrary uses or abuses of power from tyrants (or people they perceive to be tyrannical).

Ventriloquist's dummy (*automatonophobia*)

Fear of ventriloquists' dummies. Similar to fear of puppets, ventriloquists' dummies can bear an uncanny or even frightening resemblance to a living creature—yet everyone knows that they are not really alive. People may begin to fantasize that there is something alive inside them and may project malevolent or evil intent onto these creatures. Some classic TV shows (such as the *Twilight Zone*) and movies have featured these dummies because of their inherently frightening qualities. Children in particular may come to fear them and so may avoid even looking at them. (*See also* Dolls, Puppets.)

Virgins or young girls

See Girls, young or virgins.

Wax statues

See Puppets, Ventriloquist's dummy.

Witches or witchcraft (*wiccaphobia*)

Fear of witches or witchcraft. Witches were viewed for thousands of years as threatening, powerful, potentially evil beings. Often they were thought to have supernatural powers and generally they were thought to be allied with evil, the devil, etc. Throughout history, many unfortunate women—and sometimes men—were falsely accused of being witches and tried and punished for same, perhaps because they were unusual in some way, had special skills using healing herbs or as midwives, or simply because they represented some kind of threat to others in the community.

Women (*gynephobia* or *gynophobia*)

Fear of women. Classical psychoanalysts tended to focus on the explanation that men may fear women due to a fear of sexuality, whether that involved fear of their own desire, a sense of sexual inadequacy, or a projected fear that women were somehow "castrated males" and so therefore symbolized a threat to the man's own sexual safety or identity; other fears in that theory included the idea that women might sometimes be seen either as castrating or sexually trapping men. In today's world, men may perceive women as more equals and organize less of their experience around beliefs that men are inherently stronger or better; there is also less of a focus on traditional sexual roles. Therefore, fears of women might be broader: men may fear women because of the perception that they are powerful, because of negative experiences or prejudices about women, or due to cultural beliefs. Women may also fear other women, for similar reasons of experiences, beliefs, or cultural backgrounds.

Women, beautiful

See Beautiful women.

Chapter 9

Odds and Ends: Assorted Object and Miscellaneous Phobias

In This Chapter

◆ Why fear inanimate objects?

◆ List of assorted object and miscellaneous fears

Many phobias are centered around stuff. In this chapter, we'll explore the kinds of phobias that revolve around objects, things, oddities, and assorted other topics—kind of a grab bag of horrors.

Why We Fear "Stuff"

You can develop (or perhaps *create* would be a better word) a phobia for just about anything, and humans have been creative and resourceful in the range of things they have learned to fear.

As with other kinds of phobias, most of the fears on this list are rare, and very few of them have ever been described in the medical or psychological research literature. If you bear in mind that, in order to qualify for a formal phobia diagnosis, a person needs both the phobic or anxious feelings *and* for those feelings to create some genuine distress or impairment in their functioning, probably few of the phobias on this list would qualify. In addition, as with the other specific phobias in this book, some of the phobia names or terms are more often used metaphorically. For instance, you may fear books (*bibliophobia*) only in the sense that you don't read very much and prefer video games or the Internet, but you might describe yourself as a bibliophobe to a friend and they'll know what you mean (or at least they will if they read more than you do).

So let's launch into a list of phobic odds and ends.

Miscellaneous Phobias

13 (number) (*tridecaphobia, tredecaphobia, triskaidekaphobia,* or *triskedekaphobia*)

Fear of the number 13. People may avoid anything related to the number 13 because they are convinced it's bad luck. They may not travel on the 13th and may walk around on the 13th of the month fearing the worst all day long.

Even famous people are not immune to this fear. President Franklin Roosevelt—remember, old Mister "The only thing we have to fear is fear itself"?—was superstitious about the number 13 and would avoid dinners where there would be 13 guests. (He'd have his secretary sit in to make 14.) It seems that most people, at least in the United States and Europe, are taught about this one, which may arguably make for a self-fulfilling prophecy: if you think the number is unlucky, it may affect your actions (even without your being aware of it).

While it's hardly ever been written about in the psych research, it is a well-known fear which affects lots of things. Like real estate, for instance. Nearly 9 out of 10 commercial elevators in the world don't have a 13th floor. (This could be unlucky: fire departments called to the "fourteenth" floor could miss you in a pinch!) In many cities there are no house or street numbers for 13; many airports have no terminal 13. It's said that people living on the 13th floor are calmer because they believe, or kid themselves into believing, that they're actually on the 14th floor—though there are no terms for "fear that I'm kidding myself and am really in a lot of danger." But the number 13, or at least the widespread fear of the number 13, does seem to be lucky for writers of horror novels and the makers of scary movies.

Some say that the fear of 13 has its origin in the Last Supper story, where Judas Iscariot made up the unlucky 13th diner. But historians point out that the number 13 was considered unlucky in many traditions that predate Christianity, including the ancient Mesopotamian, Persian, and Viking cultures. (The Persians, for example, had a calendar in which there were 13 astrological ages, each to last 1,000 years; the end of the 13th age would lead to the sky and earth collapsing and chaos ensuing.) In many traditions, the number 12 is thought to represent a kind of completeness—for instance, you have 12 tribes of Israel, 12 Apostles, 12 months of the year, 12 signs of the zodiac. So of course, if you add one more to something already complete and perfect …
it's just a mess! (Plus, just try to divide a birthday cake evenly into 13 slices.) (*See also* Friday the 13th in Chapter 7.)

P.S.: Hope you noticed that this book has 13 chapters. After all, somebody has to help you face your fears!

Alcohol (*methyphobia* or *potophobia*)

Fear of alcohol. It's not uncommon for people who have recognized that they have problems controlling their alcohol use to develop a healthy fear of imbibing. More often, people who grew up in families where a parent or sibling had a serious alcoholism problem may develop a fear of drinking, lest they, too, develop a drinking problem. Many children of alcoholics become lifelong abstainers, which is often a good thing since there is at least some evidence that a vulnerability to alcoholism is partially inherited. Some may keep this fear private, while other people may develop a very public and community-wide aversion to "demon rum," such as the social movement that led to Prohibition in America. (*See also* Drinking in Chapter 7.)

Asymmetrical things (*asymmetriphobia*)

Fear of asymmetrical things. While it may seem unlikely that there are actually people with a phobia for something as abstract as this, research does show that people with clinically severe obsessive compulsive disorders can have great difficulty tolerating asymmetrical arrangements of objects or other things, and it's not uncommon for such individuals to also have multiple phobias. At times, the OCD and phobia symptoms may indeed overlap. In addition, many persons with autism or Asperger's syndrome may require strict adherence to symmetry in the arrangement of everyday objects in order to tolerate being around them.

Researchers have noted that in some things, such as the brain's processing of human faces, symmetry seems to be highly valued. For instance, people are often rated as more attractive if their faces are mostly symmetrical (and lest you imagine that all faces, particularly your own, are perfectly symmetrical, the truth is that perfect symmetry is nearly impossible). In humans, judgment of symmetry may be unconsciously used to determine the health (and, thus, mating potential) of potential sexual partners—one indication of illness, and so bad breeding stock, might be disfigurement due to a lack of symmetry.

Symmetry can suggest that things around us are organized and so in control; we don't have to work hard to process objects or environments—including architectural environments, city layouts, or computer desktops—when things are fairly symmetrical, so symmetry is considered an important principle to consider in many levels of design from webpages to architecture. While perfect symmetry may be boring and understimulating, a lack of symmetry can suggest chaos and that things are out of control. Symmetry, within reason, seems to calm many people. (*See also* Symmetry.)

Automobiles (*motorphobia*)

Fear of automobiles. This can be related to fear of injury, speed, loud noises (e.g., cars backfiring or car horns honking), or travel in automobiles. (*See also* Automobiles, being in moving in Chapter 7.)

Beards (*pogonophobia*)

Fear of beards. This can include a child's fear of the strangeness of a bearded face (if it is something they generally haven't experienced) or the fear, based on stereotypes, that bearded individuals may be different (e.g., more threatening) than clean-shaven individuals. Some may fear that beards are dirty.

Beds (*clinophobia*)

Fear of beds or of going to bed. Can be related to fear of anything unpleasant associated with beds, including insomnia, nightmares, sleep disorders, sexual isolation, sexual activity, or a fear of sleep related to its association to death. Beds may also trigger fears in children for other reasons including fear of the dark or of something threatening under the bed or in the bedroom; these fears may relate to a more fundamental fear of abandonment or difficulty coping with the absence of a parent.

Bicycles (*cyclophobia*)

Fear of bicycles. People may fear riding bicycles due to real or imagined experiences of falling off or losing control. Some may fear being injured in traffic or being unable to manage pedaling a bike up a steep hill, etc. It's also possible to fear being hit by a bicycle.

Black (*melanophobia*)

Fear of the color black. One may also use a color name metaphorically to describe a strong distaste to black or other colors (for example, referring to a black mood). Black may be associated with gloom, darkness, or depression. (*See also* Colors.)

Books (*bibliophobia*)

Fear of books. One may fear the ideas contained within some books or the act of reading itself. Discussions of book phobias more often discuss the fear that governments or societal leaders may have regarding the impact that books may have on the populace (especially the young); in modern times, most book phobia-like behavior is generally organized around attempts by government or religious groups to have certain books removed from libraries or bookstores. On a personal level, many people find reading difficult or impossible (whether due to a lack of skill or experience reading) and so may look at an assignment to read a book with a form of dread or aversion. Memories of childhood reading assignments or, if one is still in school, a strong dislike of homework can be described as *bibliophobia*, though not in a clinical sense—unless, again, a child has some kind of learning or reading disorder that results in an inability to actually read well or easily. It is possible that neither the child nor his or her teachers or parents may be aware of the disorder, and so each new book assignment may become the cause of a painful series of confrontations, blame for not getting the work done, guilt, or accusations about laziness.

Bridges (*gephyrophobia*)

Fear of bridges or of crossing bridges. This may include fear of various mishaps: bridges falling down, driving off the bridge, heights, drowning in the river below, etc. (*See also* Bridges, crossing and Heights in Chapter 7.)

Bullets (*ballistophobia*)

Fear of bullets—particularly those moving rapidly through the air in one's general direction. Two different levels of experience and imagination of bullets can trigger intense fears: novices, who may be terrified of being anywhere near or even looking at, much less handling, bullets; and traumatized individuals (e.g., combat veterans or people who have been shot at or experienced shootings), who may be terrified of bullets, guns, loud noises, etc.

Cemeteries (*coimetrophobia*)

Fear of cemeteries. One may develop a morbid fear of anything having to do with cemeteries, graves, death, or dying and so have great difficulty entering or even driving past a cemetery. This fear may also be related to the difficulty people have accepting that a loved one is truly gone.

Chins (*geniophobia*)

Fear of chins. This may be related to tendencies to read personalities or character based on the shape of a person's chin; some may also have a fear of double chins or misshapen chins. The reaction may therefore be to one's own self-perception or appearance or to the appearance of others. This is highly rare or unlikely to be an actual clinical phobia, however.

Chopsticks (*consecotaleophobia*)

Fear of chopsticks. A person may fear having to use chopsticks at a meal, which may be due to a lack of skill using them and/or a fear that they will be embarrassed as others witness their lack of facility with the sticks. The fear of embarrassment or humiliation would be a form of social phobia (see Chapter 12).

Church (*ecclesiophobia*)

Fear of church, churches or, more broadly, church environments or various aspects of religion.

Clocks

See Time or clocks.

Clothing (*vestiphobia*)

Fear of clothing. This may include fear or discomfort with wearing clothing or seeing certain styles of clothing.

Cold or cold things (*cheimaphobia, cheimatophobia, psychrophobia, psychropophobia,* or *frigophobia*)

Fear of the cold or of cold things. This is most often a kind of physical aversion that may occur when someone has a greater-than-average discomfort when they touch (or eat) cold objects or go into the cold. Persons who dislike cold climates or temperatures may avoid going outdoors during the winter months or may even avoid living in colder climates. (*See also* Cold in Chapter 5.)

Colors (*chromophobia* or *chromatophobia*)

Fear or aversion to colors. Actual phobias in the form of severe anxiety reactions to colors are rare, though there is considerable evidence that different colors do stimulate psychological reactions and even may influence hormonal production in the body.

Computers

See Computers or fear of working on computers in Chapter 7.

Crosses or crucifixes *(staurophobia)*

Fear of crosses or crucifixes. This may be related to religious fears, fear of God, or other supernatural meanings. It can include fear of guilt in believers in Christianity as well. In popular literature, vampires also fear crucifixes.

Crystals or glass *(crystallophobia)*

Fear of crystals or glass. This phobia can include fears of being cut or injured by broken glass; in some cases, crystals may have mystical significance and so become objects of fear.

Dampness or moisture *(hygrophobia)*

Fear of dampness, moisture, or liquids. This phobia may relate to a feeling of disgust and may be associated with dampness-related substances such as mildew, mold, bacteria, or mosquitoes. It may also be related to discomfort with forms of dampness such as humidity, rainy seasons, or being wet or cold due to dampness.

Death or dead things *(necrophobia)*

Fear of death or of dead things. This can include a fear of dead animals, humans, or even plants.

Decay *(seplophobia)*

Morbid fear or feelings of revulsion of decaying matter. Feelings of disgust fuel many phobias; such feelings may be genetically programmed and may serve to protect us from consuming or contacting things (such as decayed vegetables or meats) that might be toxic. A person may react with extreme disgust or fear of touching, contacting, or even looking at decaying vegetables, dead leaves, rotten meat, etc. In extreme cases they may be unable to function near or around such things and so may be unable to do routine tasks such as housecleaning, gardening, etc.

Dirt *(molysmophobia* or *molysomophobia)*

Fear of, or extreme revulsion at, dirt, infection, or foul or contaminated things. (*See also* Decay.)

Drafts (*aerophobia* or *anemophobia*)

Fear of drafts. This could include the fear that one will catch cold or suffer some other kind of severe injury, illness, damage, or discomfort from drafts. (*See also* Air in Chapter 5.)

Dryness (*xerophobia*)

Fear of dryness. This fear can include fear of dry landscapes or deserts and may be related to an absence of moisture, water, or green landscape; the term might also be applied to other forms of dryness such as thirst, dry skin, etc.

Dust (*amathophobia* or *koniophobia*)

Fear of dust. This can be related to a fear of contamination or dirt; it may also relate to a fear of dust in the air triggering allergies or causing other types of harm.

Eyes (*ommetaphobia* or *ommatophobia*)

Fear of eyes.

Fabrics (*textophobia*)

Fear of specific fabrics.

Feathers (*pteronophobia*)

Fear of feathers or of being tickled by feathers. One may have a dislike or sense of disgust for feathers, whether for aesthetic reasons or because they are associated with birds or bird carcasses. Feathers may also be seen as unclean or possibly contaminated. (*See also* Tickled, being [possibly by feathers] in Chapter 7.)

Firearms (*hoplophobia*)

Fear of firearms. Firearms are of course dangerous, so that a healthy respect or even fear of them may be adaptive. Severe or morbid fear of firearms, however, may be a different matter—it may involve extreme reactions to the mere presence of firearms or even to the suspicion that firearms may be present (e.g., in a public place, someone's house, etc.). A person may fear being near, touching, or even looking at them. This may occur for various reasons, including a history of trauma, assault, or having been threatened by firearms.

Flowers (*anthophobia*)

Fear of flowers. One might fear or have a feeling of disgust or distaste for particular flowers due to their appearance, smell, or one's associations to them (e.g., due to the use of flowers in funerals).

Flutes (*aulophobia*)

Fear of flutes. This is one of the oldest documented fears—Hippocrates, the ancient Greek physician, reported on a case of a man who was terrified of hearing flute music (see Chapter 1). This can be related to seeing, playing, or even touching flutes.

Food (*cibophobia*, *sitophobia*, or *sitiophobia*)

Fear of food. *Sitophobia* and *sitiophobia* may also refer to fear of eating food. (*See also* Eating in Chapter 7.)

Foreign languages (*xenoglossophobia*)

Fear of foreign languages. This fear may stem from a fear of foreigners who may, so the phobic imagines, be talking or plotting against one. It may also include a fear of being confused or disoriented, missing out on critical information, being unable to get help, or being unable to be understood (e.g., in an emergency or when trying to find one's way). People often fear anything that represents a loss of control in their world, including the loss of the ability to communicate easily with others—having to interact in a foreign language, or being unable to do so, can result in considerable anxiety. People may also fear being judged inept or poor at speaking or understanding a different language, which leads many people to avoid traveling to foreign countries, trying to interact or converse with people while in the country, or even helping foreigners.

Garlic (*alliumphobia*)

Fear of garlic. The term may also refer to aversion or feelings of disgust related to garlic or to other pungent plants (such as onions). In popular literature, vampires generally fear or avoid garlic.

Genitals (*kolpophobia* or *phallophobia*)

Fear of genitals. *Kolpophobia* refers to fear of female genitals; *phallophobia* refers to fear of male genitals. A certain anxiety around sexual matters is not uncommon except in cultures which have more relaxed, comfortable, and open attitudes about sexuality (which would generally not describe the United States, for instance); fears of genitals can be deeply rooted in unconscious fears including a sense of mystique or even disgust at genitals different from a person's own. Since genitals are generally hidden from view, they tend to be more mysterious. Freudians used to believe (and some still do) that males and females may both unconsciously see female genitals as lacking the all-important penis as a result of childhood castration, which would trigger anxiety due to the trauma associated with such a horrible event; conversely, in Freudian theory, the possession of a penis sets one up for castration anxiety, and the sight of another male's penis can trigger aversive responses related to homophobia.

Glass or crystals

See Crystals or glass.

Gold (*aurophobia*)

Fear of gold.

Greek terms (*hellenologophobia*)

Fear of Greek terms. This can also be applied to the fear of complex terms, particularly scientific or academic terms. (*See also* Scientific terminology.)

Hair (*chaetophobia, trichopathophobia, trichophobia,* or *hypertrichophobia*)

Fear of hair. This can include fears or discomfort with touching hair or scalp, or it may be associated with things such as unclean or greasy hair, dandruff, etc. The terms may also be used in association with fears of hair loss or baldness, seeing hair in inappropriate places (such as on food or clothing), getting gray hairs, haircuts, etc.

Hands (*chirophobia*)

Fear of hands.

Holy things (*hagiophobia*)

Fear of holy things. (*See also* Crosses or crucifixes; Priests or sacred things in Chapter 8.)

Infinity (*apeirophobia*)

Fear of infinity. One may have a fear or discomfort with a lack of closure or time limits on things including one's own existence; the very concept of infinity or of being "in" infinity may trigger an agoraphobic-type response in some people.

Justice (*dikephobia*)

Fear of justice. One may fear punishment or prosecution or struggle with notions of guilt or moral judgment for one's behavior.

Knees (*genuphobia*)

Fear of knees. Phobias involving knees or other body parts are not common but are possible. People with body dysmorphic disorder, a mental disorder involving the perception that one's body is distorted, misshapen, or otherwise wrong, may develop a preoccupation or concern with the belief that there is something wrong with the shape or appearance of their knees.

Knowledge (*gnosiophobia* or *epistemophobia*)

Fear of knowledge. The notion that knowledge, or that certain knowledge, may be dangerous is an ancient one. In the Book of Genesis, Adam and Eve were warned against eating from the Tree of Knowledge, and their doing so resulted in expulsion from Eden and, metaphorically, from a state of childlike, blissful innocence. Later, Lot's wife was warned against looking back on the destruction of Sodom and Gomorrah, and when she did so, she was turned into a pillar of salt. Knowledge may be feared in several senses: one may fear that exposure to certain truths, facts, ideas, or sights may result in harm, the loss of innocence, the corruption of one's morals or ideals, or a change in one's self. One may also fear that allowing others (children, the innocent, or those who might challenge the established political or religious order) access to knowledge may be dangerous not necessarily to those who obtain the knowledge but rather to oneself or to those in power. There may be a fear that allowing others access to knowledge may provide external enemies a way to do one harm. Psychotherapists, and also ancient philosophers, have long noted that certain kinds of self-knowledge or self-awareness may prove difficult, painful, or even self-destructive, though on balance, most models of philosophy and psychotherapy have tended to view self-knowledge as ultimately beneficial, maturing, and empowering.

Large things (*megalophobia*)

Fear of large things. One may feel frightened by the large size or the object and fear injury. There may also be a potential to feel overwhelmed, or perhaps even claustrophobic, near large objects.

Liquids (*hygrophobia*)

Fear of liquids, moisture, or dampness. (*See also* Dampness or moisture.)

Machines (*mechanophobia*)

Fear of machines. Fears can include general feelings of being intimidated, overwhelmed, threatened, or confused by strange or new machines; fear of injury while operating machines also may be a concern. Machines may be noisy and unpleasant; one may fear being unable to handle or manage a machine or that it may break or not operate, etc.

Many things (*polyphobia*)

The fear of many things, or state of having multiple phobias. In fact, it is relatively rare that an individual has just one phobia; generally the presence of one phobia means that a person may have several other phobias as well. Having more than just a few phobias would be the most likely point at which this term would apply.

Meat (*carnophobia*)

Fear of or disgust for meat. Many phobias are based on feelings of disgust; one may dislike eating, handling, smelling, or even looking at meat and so may develop a strong aversion to it.

Memories (*mnemophobia*)

Fear of memories. A person may have unpleasant or even traumatic memories that they try to avoid being conscious of, discussing with anyone, or ever referring to. This is actually a fairly common side effect of traumatic experiences, and at times a person's memories may in fact be so painful that they unconsciously suppress all awareness of even having them. This situation is more often classified as a post-traumatic stress disorder than a phobia.

Metal (*metallophobia*)

Fear of metal. Generally credited to discomfort with certain physical characteristics of metal such as its appearance, shininess, coldness, or heaviness.

Mind (*psychophobia*)

Fear of mind-related processes. This may include a fear of thinking or memory. (*See also* Memories.)

Mirrors (*eisoptrophobia*)

Fear of mirrors or of seeing oneself in a mirror. Some people may fear or have discomfort with their appearance; others may have certain superstitions about seeing themselves or seeing mirrors. (*See also* Self, seeing in mirror in Chapter 8.)

Missiles (*ballistophobia*)

Fear of missiles or of projectiles such as bullets or spears. (*See also* Bullets.)

Moisture

See Dampness or moisture.

Money (*chrometophobia* or *chrematophobia*)

Fear of money. One may have a fear of dealing with money in general or may fear the corrupting impact of money or wealth; fear of success, fear of financial difficulty or failure, or fear of financial responsibility may also be part of this phobia. One may also fear germs on much-handled money, which may lead a person to avoid touching currency or to wear gloves when handling money.

Moon *(selenophobia)*

Fear of the moon. Most cited fears of the moon involve various super-stitions, ranging from fears of how the moon may influence human behavior to more ancient or mystical fears of the moon's significance or influence in a spiritual sense.

Mushrooms *(mycophobia)*

Fear of mushrooms. Certain mushrooms are poisonous if eaten, which can lead to either an appropriate sense of caution or else to a severe phobic reaction of avoidance, revulsion, or panic at the thought of eat-ing, touching, or even seeing mushrooms.

Music *(melophobia)*

Fear of music. Music may trigger emotions that one finds unpleasant or may be associated with memories or relationships that one finds painful to think about. Since some music has historically been associated with cultural shifts or different cultures or generations or social groups, one group's statements of "identity" or their use of music to challenge the established or mainstream society has been viewed with fear or dislike by others.

Myths, stories, or false statements *(mythophobia)*

Fear of myths, stories, fabrications, or false statements.

Needles *(aichmophobia* or *belonephobia)*

Fear of needles. Generally this is a variant of the blood-injection-injury phobias covered in Chapter 6, but one may also fear any needles, whether medical, sewing, or other, which may be due to fear of injury.

Noise *(acousticophobia)*

Fear of noise. Noise may be uncomfortable or painful and may disrupt one's concentration or functioning; many people dislike the stimula-tion of very noisy environments. Having been exposed to a great deal of unpleasant noises or noisy environments may trigger an aversion to noise that becomes intense at times. (*See also* Noises, loud.)

Noises, loud (*ligyrophobia*)

Fear of loud noises. Loud noises trigger startle reactions and may activate the fight-or-flight system of hormonal changes (such as increased adrenaline, the release of stress related hormones such as cortisol, increased heart rate and respiration rate, and other changes in the body's muscular, digestive, and other organ systems). Most people (particularly infants who do not understand what is happening) find sudden loud noises unpleasant—unless they feel they have some kind of control over the noise or that they can tune it out.

Numbers (*arithmophobia* or *numerophobia*)

Fear of numbers. This is generally a fear related to calculations, math problems, or of having to understand numbers in some form. Some people have learning disabilities which can make even reading numbers difficult; more commonly, people may have much more difficulty understanding numbers, performing calculations, or grasping mathematical ideas than they have dealing with verbal tasks such as reading or spelling. Fear of tackling numbers may itself be difficult, but doing this in front of others (teachers or peers) may trigger considerable anxiety among children or adolescents in particular; the fear of numbers may blend with the fear of being tested, humiliated, or embarrassed in front of others because of one's numerical difficulties. Fear of numbers or of dealing with numbers may adversely affect progress in school or choice of career.

Opinions (*allodoxaphobia*)

Fear of others' opinions. The fears may include hearing threatening ideas, being pulled into an uncomfortable situation of disagreeing with others, being proven wrong, or being unable to hold one's own in situations involving differences of opinion.

Opinions, expressing (*doxophobia*)

Fear of expressing one's own opinions. If a person's main fear is of expressing their opinion, the most likely fear is of being criticized, humiliated, or of having others become angry, or critical of one's opinion and, by extension, of one's self. This latter fear is a variety of social phobia, which involves fears of being critiqued or evaluated by others.

Paper (*papyrophobia*)

Fear of paper. This can include fear of or discomfort with touching, seeing, or handling paper. It may also include a fear of paper cuts.

Philosophy (*philosophobia*)

Fear of philosophy. One may fear or be uncomfortable with the academic discipline of philosophy in general. This phobia may also refer to a fear of a particular philosophy, set of ideas, or beliefs; a person may find them uncomfortable, threatening, or repellant to a preferred philosophy or outlook.

Phobias (*phobophobia*)

Fear of phobias. This can more broadly include the fear of fear itself. Many people have enough insight to know that developing certain fears can be much more dangerous to one's functioning than the actual things that are feared. For example, a rock climber or equestrian would generally be aware that if they allow fears of heights or falling (off the mountain or a horse) to take root in their thinking, they would function more poorly in their sport and would be at greater risk for injury or death. (Much of the science of sport psychology is organized around helping athletes to manage their anxiety levels when thinking about their sports.) One may also have a fear of any strong emotion because it may cause discomfort to lose control of oneself.

Pins and needles (*enetophobia* or *belonephobia*)

Fear of pins and needles. This can include the fear of injury or of being pricked or stuck. It may also be related to a fear of blood, pain, injections, etc. The phrase "being on pins and needles" refers to a feeling of tension or anxiety.

Plants (*botanophobia*)

Fear of plants. Some people may feel revulsion or disgust at particular plants; others may fear particular plants if they are perceived as being dangerous, poisonous, or unpleasant in other ways (e.g., if they have an unpleasant smell that makes one ill or uncomfortable). Some fears relate to old superstitions about certain plants.

Poetry (*metrophobia*)

Fear of poetry. Some people have discomfort with poetry due to difficulty understanding or reading it; other people find poetry uncomfortable because it may stir up various emotions or images they find uncomfortable. Some males or cultures in general may find poetry to be a feminine activity and so avoid it so as to avoid appearing unmanly.

Pointed objects (*aichmophobia*)

Fear of pointed objects. Generally this fear would be related to being injured by the pointy objects.

Property (*orthophobia*)

Fear of property. One may fear that owning property may bring unwanted responsibilities, whether financial or in the form of having to work on, monitor, or maintain it. Others may feel discomfort with the association of property ownership to wealth and success.

Purple (*porphyrophobia*)

Fear or aversion to the color purple. (*See also* Colors.)

Razors (*xyrophobia*)

Fear of razors. Generally this phobia is related to fear of injury, such as of being cut, nicked, or perhaps assaulted with a razor. Since it is fairly easy to cut or injure oneself, particularly with certain kinds of razors (for instance, razor blades or straight razors), one may develop powerful blood-injection-injury phobias after a razor injury. Some people may also develop a fear of razors due to seeing others cut themselves in person or in a film; others may fear assault by evil or murderous persons using razors. People may develop an extreme reaction even to touching or looking at razors.

Red (*erythrophobia*, *erytophobia*, or *ereuthophobia*)

Fear or aversion to the color red, or fear of blushing. (*See also* Colors; Blushing in Chapter 7.)

Religion or gods (*theophobia*)

Fear of a particular religion, multiple religions, religions in general, God, or gods.

Rooms (*koinoniphobia*)

Fear of rooms. This generally refers to a fear of rooms full of people; this would then be a variant of social phobia.

Rooms, empty (*cenophobia* or *centophobia*)

Fear of empty rooms. This would also include a fear of empty places; this is seen as a variant of agoraphobia (see Chapter 11).

Running water (*potamophobia*)

Fear of running water. (*See also* Rivers in Chapter 5.)

Sacred things or priests (*hierophobia*)

Fear of sacred things or priests. (*See also* Priests or sacred things in Chapter 8.)

School (*didaskaleinophobia* or *scolionophobia*)

Fear of school. *Didaskaleinophobia* is often listed as fear of going to school. Many children, particularly younger children, are said to have school phobia, but as with most phobias, it's especially important to assess what the actual fear is about. Children diagnosed with school phobia have more often been found to have difficulties tolerating separation from the reassuring presence of their parents and of their more familiar and comfortable home. Some children may express fear of going to school when the actual fear is of just one particular event or worry—not the entire school experience. This fear may be of anything from a scary school bus ride, a bully or dog they have to pass on the way to school, a particular teacher or class, or simply the feelings of confusion or anxiety that something in the school day may trigger. With very young children, even something like a single lesson, a reprimand from a teacher, or a "weird" lunch can trigger anxiety. It is important to try to understand what the fear is about in order to help a child overcome it—see Chapter 13 on children's phobias for more information and tips for dealing with school and related phobias.

Scientific terminology (*hellenolophobia*)

Fear of complex scientific terminology. While few people tremble and have panic episodes when faced with a long Greek or Latin term, people may feel easily overwhelmed when confronted with school lessons or other situations in which they are expected to read, write, pronounce, or learn long, unfamiliar terms. (*See also* Greek terms.)

Semen (*spermatophobia* or *spermophobia*)

Fear of semen. This phobia can be due to fear of impregnation, the possibility of disease, or more commonly, the same kind of disgust reactions that are common when dealing with bodily fluids, unfamiliar body processes, or issues related to sex. This discomfort may be more common in young people who are just beginning to understand sexuality and bodily processes; in males, it may be related to homophobic feelings. For both male and female partners, it may result in avoidance, disgust, or discomfort with sexuality.

Sermons (*homilophobia*)

Fear of sermons. Sermons are speeches generally organized around a religious topic, lesson, or theme. Some people may be uncomfortable with any discussion of religious topics; others may fear the feelings of guilt, shame, or fear that some sermons may stir up. Still others may prefer not to be challenged or to have their current ideas contradicted. After the famed Puritan preacher Jonathan Edwards gave his famous sermon "Sinners in the Hands of an Angry God" in 1741, legend says that the congregation was full of terrified weeping, fainting, and swooning people who had been powerfully moved and frightened by his dark vision of an angry God and the torments of Hell. It's possible that some of them may have been vicariously traumatized by the experience.

Shadows (*sciophobia* or *sciaphobia*)

Fear of shadows.

Shock (*hormephobia*)

Fear of shock. The term is used to refer to shock in the metaphorical sense of being unpleasantly surprised and overwhelmed at a sudden discovery or bad news; it also refers to a fear of electrical shocks.

Slime *(blennophobia* or *myxophobia)*

Fear of slime. Slime is one of the most common substances to trigger fairly primitive disgust reactions. Slime is not actually one thing, of course—it is any substance that is moist, slippery, and viscous.

Slopes, steep *(bathmophobia)*

Fear of steep slopes. This phobia may be related to fear of falling, injury, sliding, or losing one's footing (on snow, loose rock or gravel, or other slippery, sloped surfaces). It may also be mixed with fear of heights in general.

Small things *(microphobia* or *mycrophobia)*

Fear of small things.

Sourness *(acerophobia)*

Fear of sourness. Like other taste fears, this can be related to disgust. People may have vague fears of sour things being toxic or poisonous (which is also related to the "disgust" reaction), or they may merely fear discomfort in the sense that they may dislike the taste. Children often react strongly against sour tastes. (*See also* Taste.)

Stairways *(bathmophobia)*

Fear of stairways. (*See also* Slopes, steep; Stairs in Chapter 7. Note that the term for the fears is the same.)

String *(linonophobia)*

Fear of string. As with many items on phobia lists, this one is dubious. It does not appear in the medical or psychological databases (though neither do most phobias), nor does anyone currently describe an actual fear related to string on a current search of Internet blogs (though, again, neither does anyone blog about most phobias). Fear of string, unlike most phobias, seems pretty implausible, though as is true for all phobia terms, it's entirely possible for someone, somehow, to develop some kind of fear of string.

Symbolism (*symbolophobia*)

Fear of symbolism. People may learn to fear certain symbols due to their historical or emotional importance or connotations (e.g., the swastika or religious symbols), or they may fear the underlying reality that a symbol may represent, whether that is a government, religious, superstitious, or magical reality.

Symmetry (*symmetrophobia*)

Fear of symmetry or symmetrical things. Symmetry means having exactly identical parts facing each other or on each side; it refers to balance and pleasing proportions. However, some may find symmetry to be distasteful aesthetically. In that sense, a fear of symmetry would be more of a metaphorical than a psychiatric use of the term. (*See also* Asymmetrical things.)

Taste (*geumaphobia* or *geumophobia*)

Fear of taste. This would generally include a disgust-type reaction to certain tastes and a fear of having to taste those items again. It may also be a fear based on other associations or meanings of importance to the individual.

Technology (*technophobia*)

Fear of technology. People may react to technology with fear, rejection, or revulsion if it seems new or threatening, if it is strange and unknown, or if it seems dangerous. Technology may result in changes to ways of doing things that result in difficult changes in work processes, job losses, or reduced (instead of improved) operations. Many people who have romantic notions of the "good old days" may resent technological changes that seem inferior to the older ways of doing things or that may seem to replace warmer, more humane, or esthetically pleasing methods with colder, more impersonal, or ugly systems. People may also fear being overwhelmed by the complexity of new machines, computers, or methods for doing tasks and may link technology with threats to their own livelihoods. (*See also* Machines; Computers or fear of working on computers in Chapter 7.)

Teeth (*odontophobia*)

Fear of teeth. One may most commonly fear being bitten, though a disgust reaction (or other form of discomfort) with teeth might also occur.

Telephones (*phonophobia* or *telephonophobia*)

Fear of telephones. One may express a fear of telephones that is based on fear of technology, fear of being eavesdropped upon or wiretapped, or fear of talking to others on the phone (the latter being a form of social phobia).

Theaters (*theatrophobia*)

Fear of theaters. Some people may fear theaters because of a number of things, ranging from crowds to dark open spaces to strangers in dark spaces; others may fear movies or plays because of the content or the kind of often powerful emotional stimulation a film or play may provide.

Theology (*theologicophobia*)

Fear of theology. Some people may dislike, loathe, or fear theology or religious ideas and theories in general; others may have a particular fear of certain ideas or beliefs because they seem threatening, sacrilegious, subversive to one's preferred beliefs, or misleading to others or to one's society. This may link to other fears such as fears of the sacred or of sacred objects, priests or clergy, mystical aspects of religions, or God (or gods). It may also be related to feelings of guilt or blame that may flow from theological ideas. (*See also* Priests or sacred things in Chapter 8.)

Time or clocks (*chronophobia*)

Fear of time or of clocks. One may fear having too little time or be troubled by the passage of time; this may be related to becoming old. One may also feel that time is inadequate for a certain purpose and so be frightened as the clock runs out.

Vegetables (*lachanophobia*)

Fear of vegetables. This is generally similar to other fears of food, which can be due to disgust at the unfamiliar or at eating things that one imagines to be strange; some people may fear that vegetables may taste funny or unpleasant. Children may fear—or have strong aversions to—vegetables, particularly those that taste less pleasant to children because they have different taste sensitivities than adults.

Wealth (*plutophobia*)

Fear of wealth. Some may fear the corrupting effects of becoming wealthy on oneself; others may fear that the wealthy will abuse their power and injure others. Many people have traditionally associated wealth with corruption or evil (though the wealthy generally associate it with having been virtuous.)

White (*leukophobia*)

Fear or aversion to the color white. (*See also* Colors.)

Wine (*oenophobia*)

Fear of wine. More broadly, this is a fear of the effects of alcohol, imbibing, or drunkenness. (*See also* Drinking in Chapter 7.)

Wooden objects (*xylophobia*)

Fear of wooden objects or of forests. Traditional fear associated with fears of the magical properties of wood, trees, forests in some (e.g., Celtic) traditions. (*See also* Forests or woods in Chapter 5.)

Words (*logophobia* or *verbophobia*)

Fear of words. This can include a fear of certain words due to their threatening, magical, sexual, or other nature (e.g., a fear of swear words); it may also include a fear of speaking or of hearing conversation, speeches, uncomfortable truths, etc.

Work (*ergophobia* or *ponophobia*)

Fear of work or of exertion. One may fear the physical threats or exhaustion due to work—or simply the discomfort of work.

Yellow (*xanthophobia*)

Fear or aversion to the color yellow. (*See also* Colors.)

10

They Only Sound Like Phobias

In This Chapter

◆ What's a real phobia and what's not?

◆ List of dubious, humorous, and spam phobias

As you know by now, a phobia can be many things. It can be a mental disorder, something so severe that it interferes with someone's day-to-day functioning. Those phobias may be formally diagnosed as anxiety disorders, according to the *Diagnostic and Statistical Manual of the American Psychiatric Association* (DSM-IV).

Other phobias are also real, but not severe enough to be diagnosable under the DSM-IV. An example might be a fear of snakes in people who don't live anywhere near snakes and never actually see them. They hardly ever have to think about or confront their fear, and the fear doesn't really bother them all that much or interfere with their life. Rather, they just may live with the knowledge that snakes "ick them out" if they see one in a movie or zoo. These "out of sight, out of mind" phobias are still real phobias but are not very disruptive, and they are not classified as anxiety disorders.

There are other ways of using the term *phobia* that don't really amount to actual phobias in either of these senses. In this chapter, we'll explore some of those other kinds of things called phobias.

Is It a Real Phobia?

By now you're aware that a real phobia is a strong fear of something, provided that the fear you experience is out of proportion to the severity of the actual danger. But beware of counterfeits! Not all phobias are real! Sometimes people use the word *phobia* to refer to something different than a fear. For instance, sometimes people confuse phobias and superstitions. Sometimes the word *phobia* gets used as a kind of *metaphor* or figure of speech to refer to a dislike of a certain thing—or even just a political or aesthetic difference of opinion about a subject. Sometimes people invent humorous phobia terms. Finally, there's the sneaky case of "spam phobias."

def•i•ni•tion

A **metaphor** is a literary device, a figure of speech, used for comparing one thing to another by using a word or a phrase to characterize something that is not literally true. To say, for instance, "I was so angry that I blew up" is a metaphor.

All of these uses have added to the collection of phobia terms, and most lists of phobias and books on the subject don't distinguish between valid phobias and these fake phobias.

Superstitions

Sometimes there's a fine line between a phobia and a superstition, and at times the two can overlap. If you feel uncomfortable because a black cat just walked across your path, it's probably just a superstition. But if you stop dead in your tracks when the cat passes and change your direction entirely as a result, I'd call that a phobia—particularly if you do it more than once, experience real fear if you are forced to try to cross the cat's path, and feel much better once you get the heck away from that scary cat.

Many phobias may start out as superstitions. Somebody decided that the number 13 was unlucky and passed the story on. You hear about it, perhaps during some raw, impressionable youthful moment, and it takes root inside your brain. "Watch out for 13!" Pretty soon, you are afraid to fly or drive on the 13th. If you have to stay on the 13th floor of a hotel, you don't sleep a wink all night out of fear.

The other thing about superstitions, of course, is that they tend to be contagious. People seldom invent their own superstitions—they are cultural products. That's why, for instance, that very few hotels anywhere in the world have a 13th floor! See the listing for 13 (number) in Chapter 9 for more.

Metaphors

People sometimes have invented and used phobia terms metaphorically. The *Oxford English Dictionary* lists several examples of phobias used as metaphors (if you look up the term *-phobia*, which they define as "forming nouns with the sense of 'fear of ___' or 'aversion to ___'"). One example, from a writer in 1811 named Anna Seward: "He is a very laconic personage, and has upon him the penphobia." Similarly, one might talk about a politician stirring up "tax-o-phobia" or a tired student having "termpaperophobia."

But as is the case with superstitions, a phobia term used metaphorically could plausibly turn into someone else's real phobia. All it would take would be an alert, questioning mind and a vivid imagination. ("Hmm ... I wonder why people might fear pens? I suppose you could poke yourself in the eye. Or you might write something you lived to regret ... what if I wrote something that somebody misread and thought it was a libelous statement and sued me ... and then my life would be ruined ... uh-oh!")

Of course, it can also be the case that one person's metaphor is already another person's actual fear. Going back to the *Oxford English Dictionary*, one of their examples of metaphorical-style phobias concerns cancer phobia. It's a quote from a 1997 newspaper story on cancer screening: "It was immediately obvious that screening isn't very accurate, that an abnormal smear is rarely anything to worry about but we've sown the seeds of Big C-phobia anyway." While this example uses *Big C-phobia* as an example of a made-up term, the parallel truth is that many people do live in terror of the possibility of getting the Big C: cancer.

Spam and Other Nonphobias

Spam phobias are phobias that are neither real anxiety disorders nor metaphors nor jokes, but those that are generated by online search engines. In some cases, various lists of phobias are actually nothing more than copies of other such lists or of entries from books. In other cases, unusual or even fictional phobia terms may trigger responses from some websites that purport to offer expert treatment for whatever phobia term is entered in the list.

(Almost all specific phobias are treated in pretty much the same way; thus, if the site is marketing a real clinic or treatment, they may actually treat your "fictionaldiseasephobia" if you show up. As long as you can actually show that you have some specific fears, you can get it treated—based on the oft-repeated truth that a person can develop a fear of just about anything.)

Other examples of non-real phobias can include the use of phobia terms to characterize hostile or discriminatory attitudes towards people or things. For instance, some of the terms listed in Chapter 8 are often used to characterize prejudice. For example:

- *Homophobia*—A deep-seated fear of homosexual feelings in oneself, or else fear, dislike, or prejudice toward homosexuals

- *Sinophobia*—Fear, dislike, or prejudice toward Chinese people or culture

- *Islamophobia*—Fear, dislike, or prejudice toward the Islamic religion or Muslims

- *Gynophobia*—Fear, dislike, or prejudice toward women

Humorous Fictional Phobia Terms

A palindrome is a word that is spelled the same forward and backward. So what would a fear of palindromes be? *Aibohphobia*, of course—a word that's spelled the same backward and forward. I'm not sure who coined it, but it's pretty hard to imagine someone actually having a fear of words based on their spelling. This is an example of a humorous phobia, a phobia term made up as a joke.

While it's generally considered rude, impolite, and tacky to joke about serious illnesses, people seldom hesitate to make phobia jokes. As I've mentioned before, I was struck while discussing this book with folks by how many times people went from serious discussions of the pain of phobias to humorous comments about them. Maybe this suggests something unkind in human nature, but I think the utter irrationality of phobias is part of the reason for our mixed reaction to them. After all, even people who have phobias usually know that their fears are exaggerated and out of proportion to reality. And sometimes, the best defense against such fears is humor. There's even some good science behind this—if you're laughing, it's hard to be trembling in fear. This is similar to the relaxation dynamic I discussed in Chapter 3. The idea is that having a different emotional reaction than fear when you're exposed to a threatening object, such as finding something funny in the "threat," makes the fear go away.

How to Know If a Phobia Is Real

It's not always possible to know if a phobia is real, or if it is simply another example of someone having patched some Greek, Latin, or English term to the suffix -*phobia*. This can be frustrating if you need to know for sure about some phobia word.

At times during the writing of this book, I've begun to develop symptoms of a phobia of my own, which I'm hereby christening *neophobophobia*—a phobia book writer's fear of yet another new phobia term. (I'll lay odds that it turns up in the online phobia lists shortly.) That's because after awhile, a writer of a book on phobias begins to dread having to do a lot of research to figure out what a phobia actually consists of—or if it's real at all.

The problem, you see, is you may often have no real clues to help you. The fact that a phobia term appears on some online list means nothing. The lists are just collections of phobia terms that other people have coined—most of the lists are just copies of other people's lists. But even professional books or research may not help, since only a very small percentage of specific phobias have actually been written about in professional medical or psychological research journals. (I would say that fewer than 5 percent of the phobias in this book are listed in the professional research based on my review of the professional databases. That doesn't mean they aren't described by some books [or other sources] written by professionals, only that there may be no published research articles or findings of studies on them—which is a different matter than, say, someone writing a book like this one.)

Finally, plausibility may be an imperfect guide to determining whether a phobia really exists. Consider the phobia mentioned by Hippocrates in ancient times—a man who had a fear of flute music, but only if he heard it at night! Weird, right? But given Hippocrates's reputation as an accurate medical reporter—and perhaps the very implausibility of such a phobia—I'd personally have to say I believe him. He was apparently as puzzled as we might be by such a fear, but it sure sounds like it was real to Hippocrates's patient, the poor afflicted Nicanor.

So how can you tell if a phobia term refers to a real phobia? Sometimes you can't, and that's the way it is. Life is hard.

But before dismissing something as a fake term, just remember that a person can develop a phobia of just about anything, because phobias are essentially mental constructions. If you can imagine flying monkeys, or that a porcelain candleholder might burn you if you touch it, you can develop those particular fears.

Phobia Science

Ultimately, phobias are a lot like dreams. In a dream, anything is possible. You can walk through walls, bunny rabbits can talk to you, and you can fly. In a phobia, innocent little otters can be terrifying, strong bridges may collapse under you, and just being looked at by another person may seem life-threatening. People can be scared of things that don't exist as surely as they can be scared of things that do exist but that aren't really dangerous. And people can be scared of ideas, of concepts, or of things only at certain times or under certain conditions. In short, anything goes in Phobiatown.

So if someone says they have a certain fear (and they seem to be serious—not joking around or using the term metaphorically), maybe they do. If you are looking online for verification (I hesitate to say *proof*) of a phobia's existence, check out the blogs (e.g., use Google's blog search tool). People generally blog about anything, and so if they have a fear of butterflies or moths or hot days, they write about it.

That's pretty much the rule of thumb of practicing therapists, by the way. If a client comes to me and says, "Doc, I have this fear …", I will tend to believe them.

So let's look at some examples of counterfeits—phobias that aren't real phobias. At least, I don't think they're real phobias—yet.

Examples of Metaphorical, Joke, or Spam Phobias

8 (number) (*octophobia*)

Fear of the number 8. This appears in multiple Internet phobias lists. While one might plausibly decide to fear any number, letter, or object in existence, there is no evidence for this one other than on the Internet.

666 (number) (*hexakosioihexekontahexaphobia*)

Fear of the number 666. This term is a pretty literal translation from the Greek of six hundred sixty-six fear. If you have a fear of just saying it, try breaking it down into parts: *hexa* (six in Greek), *kosioi* (hundred), *hexe* (six again), *konta* (ten, or *six tens*), *hexa* (just that last six), and *-phobia*.

Actually, this isn't really a phobia of a number but of what it represents. This one comes from the New Testament, where 666 is given as the number of the beast—whatever that means. This is the exact quote, from the King James Bible: "Here is wisdom. Let him that hath understanding count the number of the beast: for it is the number of a man; and his number is Six hundred threescore and six." (Revelations 13:18) Some Christian believers say it's connected with the Antichrist and so should be taken as a literal prediction of things to come during the so-called *end times*. However, most biblical scholars and historians say it probably represented something to do with the Roman Empire. But the number has been featured in many popular movies about demons, end times, and spawns of Satan, so its fame lives on. Internet rumors reported that many women tried hard not to have babies on June 6, 2006, while others pointed out that, with changes in the calendar hundreds of years ago, the actual date to watch was probably sometime in 2002.

There are no references or reports of the phobia actually existing in the more than 12,000 references on phobias that currently exist in my medical and psychological databases. So medically and psychologically speaking, the phobia may not even exist; more likely it should be sorted into the superstition (or urban myth? rural myth?) pile.

Beautiful women (*Venustraphobia*)

Fear of beautiful women. While there is actually another term for the fear of beautiful women (see Chapter 8), and the fear is sometimes genuine, this term was specifically designed as a humorous term in a 1998 article in the BBC news. The term is a combination of *Venus trap* and *phobia*.

Ducks, watching you (*anatidaephobia*)

The fear that "somewhere, somehow, a duck is watching you." This is a joke phobia from a Gary Larson "Far Side" cartoon.

Palindromes (*aibohphobia*)

Fear of palindromes. The term is itself a palindrome (a word or phrase that is spelled the same backward or forward, as in "A man, a plan, a canal, Panama!"). This is a joke phobia.

Peanut butter sticking to the roof of your mouth (*arachbutyrophobia*)

Fictional or joke fear of peanut butter sticking to the roof of one's mouth. This term was supposedly first invented by author Peter O'Donnell in a novel in 1985. Some online clinics promise to cure it and all other phobias, which should come as a relief to the peanut growers of the world.

Phobias, new *(neophobophobia)*

A self-help book writer's fear of new phobia terms—or of finding another new phobia term that has to be defined. A joke phobia made up by yours truly as an example of how the game is played.

Rat, great mole *(zemmiphobia)*

Fear of the great mole rat. This is another leading cause of those "Hey, does this really exist?" blog postings. Not in the medical or psychological literature, it doesn't. Neither, perhaps, do great mole rats—though there are such things as (ordinary size and properly humble) mole rats.

Temporal displacement *(anachrophobia)*

Fictional fear of temporal displacement, invented by Jonathan Morris in a *Doctor Who* novel.

Words, long *(hippopotomonstrosesquipedaliophobia)*

Fear of very, very, very long words. This term is interesting and there are various histories of it given, but the etymology is clear as river mud. Take a deep breath: *hippopoto-* refers back to hippopotamus, which has been used as a basis for words meaning *large* since the mid-nineteenth century (in the word *hippopotamine*); this itself comes from the Greek term for hippopotamus, which was literally *river horse*, or *hippo-* (horse) combined with *potamos* (river). *Monstros* in the middle is from the Latin *monstrum* for *large* or *evil omen*. *Sesquipedal* means *a foot and a half long word*, from the Latin *sequi* meaning *one and a half* and *pedal* from the Latin *pes*, meaning *foot*—then of course, we add the *o* as glue and the *-phobia*, and there it is. Easy as pie! It is, of course, a joke term, despite the fact that there are probably many students who do fear having to learn to spell very long words.

Part 3

When Phobias Get Serious

While all phobias are quite serious to their owners, in many cases the phobia is specific enough that you can avoid having to deal with it much of the time. But there's a huge difference in these phobias: their complexity, pervasiveness, and ability to disrupt your life is considerable.

In this part we review two major phobia-related anxiety disorders that can wreak havoc with a person's life. With agoraphobia, a person may be frightened of leaving the house, being in public places, or even the intensity of their own fears. Persons with social phobia often live in constant fear of being criticized, observed, or evaluated by others. Finally, we look at the phobias that can afflict children.

Chapter 11

The Aggravation of Agoraphobia

In This Chapter

- ◆ What agoraphobia feels like
- ◆ What is agoraphobia?
- ◆ The cause of agoraphobia
- ◆ Treatment and recovery

So far I've been discussing specific phobias, meaning phobias that center on a particular object or situation. But sometimes a person's fears can be much broader. They may happen in a variety of situations or settings; therefore, the toll they take on the person's life may be much larger than specific phobias.

In this chapter you'll learn about one of the most painful and debilitating big-ticket phobias—agoraphobia.

A Snapshot of Agoraphobia

It started innocently enough. One day Suzie went outside, got in her car, and drove to the local mall to shop for some clothes. While walking down the aisle past the cookie store and enjoying the warm, chocolate-chip smells, she began to feel strange. Suddenly she was afraid—very afraid. More afraid than she'd ever imagined feeling. Her heart was pounding, her hands were shaking, and she wanted to cry or scream. Was it a stroke? A heart attack? She felt spacey, like she might faint or just twirl around and collapse.

With great effort she managed to get herself over to a bench and sat down. She felt terrified that people would look at her, but also felt she needed help. After a few minutes, a mall security guard stopped by and said she looked sick, and asked if she was okay. Suzie said she just got dizzy, but asked the guard to walk her back to her car. Once she was inside her car she felt calmer, and after a few moments of rest, she carefully drove home.

For days Suzie worried about whatever it was that had happened at the mall. But after that, she didn't think about it much—until, that is, the next time she had to go there a few weeks later. She put the trip off, afraid to risk … whatever. She knew it was silly, but she just kept finding excuses not to do her errands at the mall.

A week later, she went to a safe place—the grocery store. And it happened again … suddenly she felt that terror coming over her. She really noticed the pain in her chest and the weird, spacey feeling this time, and so she began to fear she was having a heart attack. But again, once she was in the car, she felt a bit calmer … except now she was worried about whether she might have an attack while driving home. All the way home she imagined herself suddenly passing out or having a stroke, and her hands shook until she had safely parked the car in the garage and was seated at her kitchen table.

A year later, even after reassurances from her doctor that her heart was fine and that this was an anxiety problem, Suzie was more afraid than ever. In fact, her fears had grown more pervasive. Like a spreading set of spiders' webs that might cover the entrances of every place Suzie usually went, she suddenly felt frightened of going to the movies, shopping, or even driving. Bit by bit, Suzie had become a prisoner in her own home because of her agoraphobia. It is only when her husband or sister go with her places that she feels safe.

What Is Agoraphobia?

Agoraphobia is the fear of being in a situation where you might panic, lose control, or have a severe emotional reaction and where you are afraid you won't be able to control the situation, escape, or get anyone to help you. People with agoraphobia generally have experienced either full-blown or partial panic episodes or panic attacks in which they suddenly felt severe, almost unbearable fear. The fear in ago-raphobia is basically that you may have another such attack—and have it somewhere you won't be able to get away from.

> **def•i•ni•tion**
>
> **Agoraphobia** is a strong fear of having panic attacks, which keep a person from going places where he or she might have those attacks or lose control emotionally.

Agoraphobia is technically not a diagnosis in the *Diagnostic and Statistical Manual of Mental Disorders* (DSM-IV), because there are two different kinds of diagnoses that involve the term. In one diagnosis, the main focus is panic disorders—the history of more than one episodes of panic attacks. If you have had a bunch of panic attacks, you may be diagnosed with the panic disorder label. At that point, you may be diagnosed as having your panic disorder with or without the agoraphobia part, depending on whether your panic episodes have made you afraid of going various places for fear of having panic attacks.

It's also possible to have a diagnosis of agoraphobia without panic disorder. In this situation, your agoraphobia is a problem but your panicky moments aren't technically full-bore panic disorder level.

If you feel that the distinction between "panic disorder with or without agoraphobia" versus "agoraphobia without panic disorder but with a pretty darn close set of panic symptoms" is confusing, you're not alone. Many mental health professionals feel that the diagnoses in DSM-IV are cumbersome and hard to distinguish from one another. Practically speaking, if you have a fear of losing it out in public, and if losing it in the past has involved panic symptoms like sudden and extreme fear, shortness of breath, trembling, fear of heart attacks or fainting, feeling spacey, etc., you're pretty likely to be agoraphobic.

> **Phobia Science**
>
> It's estimated that between 8 and 10 percent of us will have at least one panic attack in our lives. About half of the people who have panic attacks develop agoraphobia.

Conditions That Resemble Agoraphobia

It's not always easy to diagnose agoraphobia with certainty. Even psychologists and physicians may be unsure what the real problem is, since many of the same difficulties can crop up in agoraphobia and in a variety of other psychological conditions. Here are some related problems that may resemble agoraphobia:

◆ **Panic disorder without agoraphobia**—You can have one or more panic attacks (or partial attacks) but never develop the agoraphobia itself. This is not uncommon. The main difference would be that despite having had some panic episodes, you don't become afraid of going out, driving, or doing other things like that. While panic attacks are unpleasant, this is a much less debilitating situation than letting the agoraphobic symptoms take hold.

◆ **Social phobia**—Social phobia, discussed in detail in Chapter 12, is a fear of interpersonal situations, being judged or evaluated by others, and such. It can resemble agoraphobia since in both cases you may fear going out to social events, public places, or performing in front of others; it may affect your ability to go to school or work, to visit family, or to participate in class. Since in both cases you may avoid a number of situations or places, the two conditions look similar. The key difference is that the focus of anxiety in social phobia is being evaluated, criticized, or observed by other people; with agoraphobia, the major fear is of the loss of control, panic, or other intense *feelings*—not of what others may think about you. However, the two conditions can sometimes overlap or develop in the same person, so the distinction is not necessarily cut and dried.

◆ **Specific phobias**—Both agoraphobia and specific phobias may lead you to avoid particular places or situations. The main differences are that, with agoraphobia, the fear is focused on avoiding panic, losing control, and so on; also, agoraphobia tends to spread to various locations in a person's life instead of being confined to just one or two particular situations. In contrast, a specific phobia, such as fear of driving, may be limited to just that one situation. So being in the mall or a movie theater may not be scary, but getting to the theater is what terrifies. Also, specific phobia fears may be related to things other than losing control or having a panic disorder—such as fear of being in a car crash, being pulled over for speeding, getting lost at the mall, getting mugged, etc.

◆ **Generalized anxiety disorder** (GAD)—While agoraphobia may involve high states of anxiety in many situations, you generally don't bring it home with you. Most of the time, agoraphobia victims may feel fairly normal as long as they can stay in whatever environment or situation feels safe to them—so you may feel fine until you are pressured into having to leave the house. In a generalized anxiety disorder, you may feel anxious pretty much all the time. Whether you are home or out, you are thinking about things that frighten you or preoccupied with your worries. (See Chapter 12 for more about generalized anxiety disorder.)

◆ **Depression**—Just as with agoraphobia, depressed individuals may avoid going anywhere, may often feel anxious or frightened, and may have panic attacks. From the outside, the two conditions may look pretty much the same; what the outsider sees is that you no longer come to school or go shopping, you seem anxious and frightened, you aren't yourself and seem unhappy, etc.

While many people with agoraphobia do develop severe depression as well, the core conditions are different. The major focus in depression is not on avoiding panic or the loss of control when outside one's comfortable areas; a sad or depressed mood is more central than fear of panic. In addition, while agoraphobics are mostly uncomfortable when they have to leave their safe home base, in depression the bad feelings are generally present most of the time; in fact, getting out for some fresh air or going to a movie is more likely to make a depressed person feel better rather than more anxious. In depression, the most common feelings are sad, black, or empty moods, loss of energy, feelings of hopelessness and helplessness, the anticipation of bad things happening, feelings of worthlessness, and so on.

The Impact of Agoraphobia

The case of Suzie is similar to what happens to many people with agoraphobia. It can gradually spread and interfere with living your life in many different situations. Some people can't go out to shop, go to movies or restaurants, or drive places by themselves. While some people with agoraphobia are only bothered by the problem from time to time (or can manage the anxieties fairly well) others are literally housebound by the condition.

Real Danger!

Agoraphobia is often the most disabling of all anxiety disorders. If you can imagine how your life would be affected if you felt suddenly unable to go about your usual routine, unable to go places or see people, you realize the toll agoraphobia takes on both individuals and on society.

According to *The Encyclopedia of Phobias, Fears, and Anxieties* (see Appendix B), five major categories of problems are known to flow from agoraphobia. The following statistics show that men and women have different rates of these problems, but in both cases, the impact of the condition is severe:

1. **Work restrictions**—In one study, it was found that more than 40 percent of men and 14 percent of women were unable to work because of the impact of agoraphobia.

2. **Social restrictions**—Both men and women frequently lose touch with friends or family, or are unable to develop new friends or relationships, because of their agoraphobia.

3. **Personal psychological effects**—People generally develop other psychological problems as a secondary result of the agoraphobia— everything ranging from low self-esteem to loneliness to severe depression.

4. **Travel limitations**—People may fear leaving home or familiar situations, driving, being in public places, etc. This may limit their ability to apply for jobs, complete routine errands, enjoy recreational opportunities, etc.

5. **Marital and family problems**—Agoraphobia tends to increase marital tensions, and many people feel it adversely affects their children as well.

The costs to society are also immense. Many people end up on disability for the disorder, which limits their participation in the workforce, deprives society of their energies and talents, and exacts a financial toll on society in the form of disability compensation, lost earnings, and medical costs.

What Causes Agoraphobia?

For a long time, the phenomenon of agoraphobia was poorly understood. Part of the confusion no doubt flowed from the fact that the condition was, from the start, poorly named.

As with most phobias, the name *agoraphobia* is a combination of two Greek words. Of course, *-phobia* means fear, flowing from the name for a mythological, terrifying Greek god named Phobos. No problem there.

The problem was the term *agora*. In ancient Greece, the agora was the marketplace. An agora would be the place in a village or city where the citizens came to do many of their public activities. So it was where you might go to shop for dates or fish at the market stalls, to grab a cup of wine and chat with your friends, or to meet with others to transact business or hear a speech. In other words, the ancient agora was not all that different from a modern shopping mall or public square.

The name *agoraphobia* suggests that the thing a person is afraid of is the agora itself. It is more or less like calling the person a mall-phobic. And it makes a bit of sense—if your agoraphobia first emerged at the mall, and you are now afraid of going to malls, then you have mall phobia. Except that the fear often spreads, and then it's not just the mall—it's also the movies. And the street in front of your house. And driving. And walking in the park. In short, the fear isn't really organized around a specific place like the mall at all. Your fear is of something else. What, then?

"Fear of Fear Itself"

Some years ago, researchers began to realize that the real fear of many agoraphobics was actually fear that they might have more of those horrible, unpredictable panic attacks while they were out at that mall. Suddenly it got clearer that the real fear of many agoraphobes is the fear of fear itself—which may not make sense unless you consider the big picture.

First of all, a panic attack is extremely painful. It is really one of the most unpleasant experiences a person can have. A panic attack feels like extreme fear that doesn't quit, that seems to go on for an eternity— even if it's really just 10 minutes or so. It's coupled with a host of physical symptoms that are both super uncomfortable and that resemble or suggest severe medical emergencies. (Many people who have them end up being rushed to the ER because they can resemble a heart attack.)

Second, a panic attack is generally unpredictable. You may be fine at the mall, then next time everything blows up and you are lying on the bench in a cold sweat. Then you get through the mall five times with no problem ... then it hits again.

In short, the cause of agoraphobia is having a panic attack, and then becoming terrified that you might have more of them. So if you have a panic attack at the movies, at the mall, or while driving, the first thing that happens is you don't ever want to go to the movies, the mall, or to drive again—the fear is that intense. You are afraid of having more periods of fear.

How Agoraphobia Starts

Agoraphobia generally starts somewhere between early adolescence and the late 20s or early 30s, though you can develop it at any age. Many more women than men develop the condition. Some scientists feel it's more likely to develop during times of stress or among people who have had other anxiety problems.

The condition generally begins after a person has one or more panic episodes or attacks. Studies suggest that the most common place to have a first panic attack is not the agora or open-air market; rather, they tend to happen in a car more commonly than anywhere else—about 15 percent of people have their first one while driving somewhere. Other common places can include restaurants, at work, public places, at school, in stores, on bridges, or while on public transportation.

After the panic episodes, some people fairly quickly begin to be afraid that they may have more of those horrible episodes if they go out again. Other people incubate their agoraphobia for a long time, maybe even for months or years, before they begin to have the most powerful symptoms—until one day, they realize they just can't face going out in the car, to the mall, or to school anymore.

What happened? After the panic episodes, the person may experience increasing feelings of vulnerability. The panic episode was truly horrible—like the worst case of being sick in public that you can imagine. The sense of vulnerability becomes very powerful—you feel that there is nothing you can do to prevent the horrible feelings from happening. Even thinking of going out may trigger panic.

So the person decides they aren't going; they can't handle it—not yet, anyway. Not today. And so they cancel their plans and their anxiety drops. Behavioral psychologists might say that this decision, and the resulting drop back into their comfort zone, essentially reinforced or rewarded the avoidance. Not going out because of the fear may have literally made the fear problem worse.

> **Try This!**
>
> With almost any anxiety disorder, you increase the risk of getting agoraphobia the more you avoid whatever it is you're a little bit afraid of. Fears feed on themselves. The best prevention for developing any phobia is to confront, as best and as often as you can, whatever it is you're afraid of.

How Agoraphobia Is Maintained and Strengthened

Of course, once you are in this "avoid and reward" loop, agoraphobia gets ever harder to control. Every time you recall your anxiety at the mall and so decide not to go there, your reduction in anxiety may make the anxiety problem that much stronger. Your own self-protective reaction can become the chains that bind you.

People who get caught in this agoraphobic loop also experience other things that stress them further. Their anxiety and avoidance may start to spread to other areas. Soon they're worrying about not just the grocery store where they had their panic attacks, but also the mall, the cafeteria at work, being in their car, or that long ride across the bridge. They may believe their spouses or friends blame them for not trying hard enough to change, or they may feel that their doctor or nurse isn't being supportive enough. The sense of conflict with others, whether it's real or imaginary, tends to create more isolation—so they are cut off from the essential support they need. Marital conflicts may worsen, relationships with friends may vanish, and jobs may become difficult or impossible to get to.

Every time another of these losses or conflicts occurs, it stresses the person still further. The stress may result in even more episodes of panic, more phobias, and more depression. The only thing the person may have *less* of is self-esteem.

The Natural Course of Agoraphobia

There is no typical journey through agoraphobia. Some people find that the condition goes away, seemingly by itself. Others may have long periods when they are symptom-free only to find that the condition returns at some point.

Most commonly, agoraphobia tends to get worse over time unless people get help with it. In addition, people with agoraphobia are more likely than average to develop secondary problems such as other phobias, generalized anxiety disorder, obsessive symptoms, or depression. They may have more frequent mental symptoms such as derealization (the odd sense that nothing seems real) or depersonalization (the sense that they aren't real), etc.

Reduced sexual satisfaction and interest are common, and these in turn further stress already-stressed marital (or other) relationships. Partners or spouses may become frustrated because the agoraphobic is not reliably able to run errands, do chores, or go out without needing to make the occasional emergency call from the mall or work when a panic attack happens. In addition, if working becomes limited or impossible, the family may face additional financial stress due to the agoraphobic's lost income. Finally, a partner may resent or get burned out from being the sole source of emotional support of the agoraphobic partner; this may happen as other friendships are lost, or become impossible to rely on, due to either travel difficulties or strains in the friendships as the agoraphobia takes over the person's life and attention.

Alcohol and drug abuse problems are very common among people with agoraphobia. In fact, a large percentage of alcoholics have difficulty getting sober because their drinking may have started as a way of coping with chronic anxiety. As they try to live without the assistance of alcohol (or other drugs), their anxiety may start to build, leading them to consider returning to the relative comfort of chronic alcohol overuse. In addition, people who have spent a long time trying to manage their anxiety with alcohol or drugs may have lost many of their coping, relating, and problem-solving skills—so their stress levels trying to make it as sober people may be much higher than average. Ironically, there is much evidence that the initial feel-good effects of alcohol, barbiturates, marijuana, minor sedatives, or other drugs may be temporary and illusory. In fact, anxiety levels, along with depression and other symptoms, may tend to increase as a result of chronic substance abuse.

People with chronic agoraphobia may become disabled; they may be unable to work or attend school. Many apply for disability benefits, which may be difficult to obtain given the fairly strenuous requirements of government disability agencies or private insurance companies. In addition, though few people on disability for anxiety conditions may wish to admit it, there is some reason to speculate that being paid for being agoraphobic may tend to prolong a person's difficulties.

Treatment and Recovery from Agoraphobia

On average, a person will wrestle with agoraphobia on their own for 10 years before they seek professional help for their problem. In many cases, it's only the long, slow erosion of support and functioning, and perhaps the end of marriages or jobs, that prompts a person to seek help. It's also the case that much help-seeking is put off because of the same kinds of anxiety that keeps the person from going to the dentist or the mall—fear of the discomfort that may result.

That is a shame, though. Many people can be helped to at least reduce their agoraphobic symptoms, and a sizeable number manage to eliminate the problem with skilled help from therapists.

A person needing assistance can consult with a physician, psychiatrist, psychologist, social worker, counselor, or nurse to at least begin getting the treatment they need. Generally, help starts with a thorough assessment, which should ideally include getting a physical exam to make sure there are no medical conditions that might be complicating the person's agoraphobia (or even, rarely, causing it). In addition, a thorough psychological evaluation, which might include some psychological testing, may help identify some of the things that contribute to the condition.

There are many treatment options that may help a person with agoraphobia. (These are basically the same approaches that were discussed in Chapter 3.) Learning to identify the specific situations that trigger panic attacks, for instance, may be a good first step. Learning to understand the mechanics of panic anxiety and how anxiety works in general are also important.

Many people benefit from learning some specific anxiety management skills, such as systematic relaxation techniques that help reduce tension and help to maintain (or return to) a mentally calm state of mind. While that is harder to do in mid-attack, the ability to deliberately calm yourself down even a little can be a powerful first step in feeling that you have control over the panic. Even if you do start to lose control in a scary situation, it may not be so horrible if you have learned (and maybe even practiced a number of times) how to sit down on the bench at the mall and calm your heart and breathing down.

> **Try This!** _____
>
> One easy way to reduce your anxiety level is to focus on taking some long, slow, deep breaths. Get into a comfy position, close your eyes, and take 10 very deep, slow breaths. Practice this daily and it will work better and faster over time. Working with a therapist, taking a course in meditation or yoga, or looking at an online video or a book on meditation can help you increase your skill at relaxing and reducing your tension. The main thing to note is that it does take practice!

Treating panic and fear of particular places may require exposure training, in which you learn to manage anxiety in safer-feeling locales and then gradually expose yourself to the places you most fear. Doing this at a deliberately slow rate, using support and guidance from your therapist along the way, never overwhelming yourself, and just taking on the exposure at the rate you can handle it can gradually help you to learn to be comfortable in places you've previously avoided.

Another part of the treatment is learning about panic disorders and agoraphobia. Many people are helped considerably just by coming to understand that their vague, hard-to-define terrors are merely a fear of losing emotional control—not fears linked to heart attacks, pending insanity, or some vague, mystical, deadly danger out there somewhere.

Other approaches include developing skills at managing your thinking. Cognitive behavior therapy, for instance, can be very useful in helping you to develop skills at identifying things that run through your mind and may trigger anxiety. Once you have learned to capture such thoughts, they become more manageable using the techniques your therapist will teach you.

Since people with agoraphobia tend to have the condition a long time, they often need help straightening out the shambles the condition has made of their lives. Therapists can often help with this as well.

Some people find self-help in support groups to be very useful. An agoraphobia support group is a good place to learn about the condition and to get support and empathy from other people who've been there and who won't make you feel ashamed for your fears. You may even find one or two people to go out and practice new anxiety management skills with.

Finally, many people find that psychiatric medications can help them develop improved anxiety regulation. Medications that may help include tricyclic antidepressants, monoamine-oxidase inhibitors, and antianxiety drugs (such as Xanax). The best place to get information on what meds can help is your local psychiatrist, your physician, a psychiatric nurse, or if you live in a state where they're licensed to provide meds, a psychologist.

The Least You Need to Know

- ◆ Agoraphobia is the fear of being in a situation where one might panic, lose control, or have a severe emotional reaction and where they are afraid they won't be able to control the situation, escape, or get anyone to help them.

- ◆ Agoraphobia is the most disabling of all phobia and anxiety disorders, causing problems for most people in their work, school, social, marital, and family lives and reducing their freedom of movement. The costs to society are high as well.

- ◆ Agoraphobia generally starts after a person has had one or more panic episodes while driving, in a mall, or other public place. They become terrified of losing control and having another such attack, so they become afraid of going out.

- ◆ While there are many treatments for agoraphobia, the average person waits a very long time before getting help.

- ◆ Treatment for agoraphobia is complex since it involves treating the panic episodes as well as the various fears of going places (or other fears that have grown up around the panic); behavioral therapy, cognitive behavioral therapy, and medication treatments may all be helpful.

Chapter 12

Social Phobia

In This Chapter

◆ Defining social phobia

◆ Social phobia—a common affliction

◆ Why be scared of people?

◆ Conditions that resemble social phobia

◆ How social phobia hinder and hurt

◆ Coping with social phobia

Social phobia can be one of the most difficult phobias to deal with. As with agoraphobia, discussed in the previous chapter, in social phobia the things you fear tend to be everywhere. After all, if your phobia is about snakes, but you don't live in a tent in a snake-infested jungle, the phobia may not affect your life very much. But our lives are often "infested" with people and the need to deal with them. And while we may not feel any desire to ever again see a snake, even the most socially phobic among us longs for companionship, approval, and connection.

A bit of anxiety around other people is pretty normal and may even be healthy and adaptive. But when your anxiety crosses the line into social phobia, it's painful and can undermine your friendships, school and work functioning, and even your physical well-being.

In this chapter we'll talk about social phobia, why they happen, and how they feel. And we'll discuss state-of-the-art approaches to shrinking and even eliminating the fear of other people.

What Is Social Phobia?

Social phobia are among the most common phobias. The condition is also one of the most serious, because it can have a bigger impact on your life than many other phobias.

The *Diagnostic and Statistical Manual of Mental Disorders* (DSM-IV) lists social phobia (like all phobias) under the category of anxiety disorders. You may be socially phobic if you have some of these symptoms:

- ◆ You have an intense fear of social situations. This includes situations where you may have to perform in front of others or where you'll feel that you are being evaluated for how you act or who you are. You may be afraid of being humiliated or embarrassed or of showing others just how scared you are. This fear has to persist— a single episode doesn't qualify.

- ◆ Whenever you are in the social situations that you fear (or even if you anticipate being in one), you get anxious. The anxiety can even include panic attacks.

- ◆ You realize that this fear is unreasonable—more than normal or more than the situation actually merits. In other words, there are situations where being afraid of being embarrassed might be pretty normal—for instance, performing in public when you're not sure you have learned the dance or speech, taking a big oral exam, or interviewing for a job would trigger the heebie-jeebies in most of us.

- ◆ Your anxiety is so intense or uncomfortable that it causes you to avoid the situations that trigger it—or else, if you go, you feel awful and may not be able to endure it. (Cold sweats, anyone?)

♦ Your anxiety messes things up, like your routine, your school or work functioning, relationships, and your social life, and/or you are very concerned, upset, or distressed by the fact that you have the phobia.

In other words, you've got a social phobia if you are afraid of some (or all) social situations, become anxious (ranging from mild anxiety to mega-anxiety) when you are in them, and understand that your fear is above and beyond. And this fear does cause you some problems.

Children can also be socially phobic, though it is diagnosed differently (see Chapter 13).

How Common Are Social Phobias?

Social phobia, or social anxiety disorder (its other official name) is hands-down the most common of the anxiety disorders. You're more likely to catch this one than fears of snakes, dogs, horses, or the agora discussed in the last chapter. Studies show that all in all, about 5 percent of the people in the United States will have problems with social phobia in their lifetime—1 in 20 of us.

Social phobia usually starts out as a young person's problem. You're most likely to develop a case of social phobia just before or during your teens. About half of the people in one study reported problems by age 11, and 8 out of 10 people who develop the problem do so by age 20.

Depending on where you live or who you are, your risk may also vary. For instance, in one major survey it was found that having a low income or being Native American tended to increase the risk of developing a social phobia. Asian, Hispanic, or African American individuals had a lower risk. You're also more likely to have the problem if you live in a less-populated area. Possibly, being in a quieter, smaller neighborhood gives you more opportunities to avoid people, which may tend to increase your risk.

Even though most people develop social phobia by mid-adolescence, the average person with a social phobia avoids getting treatment for it. Only about 1 in 5 people with social phobia go for treatment, and even they tend to wait until their late 20s to seek help, on average.

> **Real Danger!**
>
> Once you get a bad case of social phobia, you tend to hang onto it. Most people with the condition tend to remain socially phobic for nearly two decades! Of course, this doesn't mean you can't get help right away. Your odds of getting over the condition are dramatically increased if you seek help with a therapist or other health-care expert when you realize two things: you have the problem, and it's not going away on its own.

Why Do We Get Scared of People?

As with other phobias, socially anxious individuals are just "too good" at learning something about danger. In other words, they have a stronger reaction to social discomfort, or "learn" more readily than average that some social interactions can be painful. It's not actually all that helpful being such a "fast learner," though. It really amounts to reacting too strongly to the kinds of social discomfort that everyone experiences from time to time.

Adolescence and Social Phobia

Social phobia tend to develop during adolescence. It's a time in life when young people are becoming super-conscious of the importance of peers. They are learning that going to school or hanging out with other kids carries with it many opportunities to be praised—or laughed at. Teachers may criticize your work or make you feel bad about yourself. Parents may make criticism of what you say and do—or even how you slouch in the chair—a daily part of your experience. Worst of all, other kids may criticize what you wear, what you say, how you act, or what you carry your lunch in. At a time in life when the approval of your friends is super important, not getting that approval (or even just the fear of losing the affection and smiles of friends) can be very traumatic for young people. That's probably why most people develop social phobia between the ages of 10 and 16.

One reason social phobia emerge during adolescence may be because that's the time when our thinking abilities change. During adolescence we develop a greater ability to be aware of how others think—we learn to imagine how we might look in others' eyes. This may include our being suddenly shocked if we suddenly can imagine other kids or adults evaluating or criticizing us, and that shock may trigger phobic reactions.

Thinking Processes That Increase Social Anxiety

What seems to happen in a social phobia can be best explained in terms of the thinking process that occurs. People are afraid that they are going to be evaluated and somehow criticized for their performance. They are afraid they may not measure up. The reality of this threat starts to eclipse everything else in their awareness until they feel like they're being watched, judged, and found wanting all the time.

Phobia Science
Dr. Aaron Beck, the founder of cognitive behavior therapy, has compared the experience of social phobics in a social situation to walking a tightrope. You feel, he says, vulnerable that something serious and awful will happen if you make the slightest misstep. You may freeze up and become inhibited. You feel that your safety and status are on the line and that you are being judged by critical evaluators.

The problem of social phobia is a hard one to get rid of; the very things which seem, in the short run, to defend you against your worst-case fears coming true are also the things that keep the phobia active: avoiding the situation that triggers them. If you find it uncomfortable to make phone calls or to have friends over to your apartment, you stop making the calls or inviting them. This tends to reinforce, or reward, the phobia: every time you hang up the phone without dialing, it's like giving yourself a little injection of an addictive drug. Ah!!

But in addition, there are many things that we are discovering that socially phobic individuals do in social situations that also tend to reinforce their fears. One of the most important is their tendency to selectively perceive only certain kinds of responses from others.

The Socially Phobic Brain

People with social phobia are afraid of being evaluated, and research is showing that they tend to be overly responsive to feedback from others (such as facial expressions)—especially when that feedback seems critical. For example, in a study of the brain scans of people with social phobia, their brains responded more strongly to photographs that had frowning faces than to faces that were neutral or smiling. Other people's brains respond differently; most people, looking at a bunch of faces, will respond positively to smiling faces. Neutral, expressionless faces may not trigger anything, and they may or may not respond to frowns.

Think about how that works in a social situation. You feel you are going to be evaluated by others. This is something which you feel very sensitive to, and feeling evaluated means a great deal to you—it is the thing you fear most. Because of this, you tend to respond as though you were in great danger of that evaluation. Whenever an organism expects to be in a dangerous situation, it begins to scan for signs of that danger. If a mother has to protect her baby from snakes, she starts to tune into anything that looks like a snake. If you are afraid of being evaluated, you start to notice anything that looks like an evaluation: a frowning face, for example. Someone doesn't nod and smile when you make a joke, and instead of ignoring it, you read it as a criticism.

The next thing that starts to happen in response to these perceived criticisms is a tendency to shut down. You may become tongue-tied, your voice may get quieter, and you may be unable to remember what you wanted to say. Your memory may begin to fail you, and so the dazzling speech you expected to make somehow gets lost in the back closet of your brain. Likewise, your body tends to shut down, losing your natural expressiveness. You don't make gestures, you don't smile, you don't nod your head at the attractive stranger—instead, you stiffen up.

> **Try This!**
>
> Practice your physical relaxation skills *before* you face a big social "test" situation. Whether it's meditation, yoga, deep muscle relaxation, aerobics, or some other technique, if you learn to reduce your physical tension at will, you can use that skill to tense up less when you feel on stage.

You may even start to look a little bit invisible, fading into the wood-work at the party or in the classroom discussion.

Again, this may be a genetically designed safety mechanism—but one that is being misapplied. In many situations involving interactions with larger, more threatening individuals, some scientists think that a shutdown of certain individuals was actually a survival tool. If another ape wants to be dominant, and you start making a lot of noise, it could result in your getting swatted down because you represent a threat to the dominant one. In order to survive to breed another day, an individual may need to shut down, or become a little bit less visible, in order to not attract the dangerous attention of threatening others.

The problem, of course, is that shutting down in modern social situations has just the opposite result. Instead of helping you survive or function better socially, shutting down actually tends to attract negative attention. The person who chokes while giving a presentation at work gets noticed instead of the presentation being noticed. In short, as with many phobias, the shut-down response and other things that happen when reacting phobically tend to become self-fulfilling prophecies: you become less successful in a social situation—which was exactly what you were afraid of.

Other Conditions That Resemble Social Phobia

One of the sticky things about any psychological problem is that it tends to resemble, and to morph into, similar problems. Since social phobia, like other phobias, is basically an anxiety-management problem, it can be related to all sorts of other problems that involve the two main issues at stake here: anxiety and people. For example, it can be similar to simple, garden-variety shyness, but can also be related to more serious problems such as depression and substance abuse.

Shyness

Shyness is a fairly normal psychological reaction in which a person feels some anxiety or caution when interacting with others. Almost all children have periods of shyness; this is due to the fact they don't know what is expected of them in social situations. So they tend to be anxious and cautious while they learn the rules.

In some cases, shyness lasts through adult life. As long as it's fairly mild, shyness can actually be a healthy and adaptive response to new social situations.

Most people outgrow most of their shyness, however. Sometimes people have difficulty with this; instead of learning to be more relaxed around others, they may tend to increase their anxiety up to the point of developing social phobia.

Sometimes the line between shyness and social phobia is a bit fuzzy. The main differences have to do with intensity and pervasiveness. Extreme anxiety suggests a social phobia, while a mild level of anxiety and caution in new social situations is more likely to be shyness. In addition, people tend mainly to be shy around strangers, while people with social anxiety may continue to be uncomfortable and anxious even as they get to know people or groups better.

Generalized Anxiety Disorder

A condition that is similar to social phobia is termed a *generalized anxiety disorder* (or GAD). Technically, this refers to a psychological condition in which fairly severe levels of anxiety occur often in a person's life. You can have both GAD and a social phobia, or you may be better suited for one diagnosis or the other.

def•i•ni•tion

Generalized anxiety disorder (GAD) is the diagnostic term for a kind of anxiety disorder characterized by pervasive and moderate to severe levels of anxiety. Whereas social phobia is organized around interpersonal situations, GAD sufferers are anxious in all sorts of situations—whether with others or alone.

The key issue seems to be whether or not most or all of your anxiety occurs in social situations (or when thinking of social situations). If you are fairly anxious about a number of things, live your life feeling mostly afraid of things, or just have a number of situations in life that trigger a lot of anxiety (whether or not they have anything to do with dealing with other people), you might be more likely to have generalized anxiety disorder. But if everything you are afraid of concerns interactions with others, especially when your fears seem to revolve around being seen, observed, criticized or evaluated by others, then a social phobia might be the best diagnosis.

Depression

It's not unusual for people with social phobia to have, or develop, serious problems with depression. Depression is often considered a different emotional state than anxiety. Instead of a pounding heart, dry mouth, shakiness, or an urge to vomit or flee, people with depression might experience fatigue, insomnia, and difficulty motivating themselves. Instead of shaking anxiously, they may be tearful. They may, in more severe cases, experience a severe level of flatness—a sense of not being quite alive—with difficulty concentrating and thinking. People who are depressed tend to be very critical of themselves, to be pessimistic about the future, and to have difficulty experiencing pleasure, among other things.

Both social phobia and depression are laced with misery. In some studies, it is difficult to tell whether the mood a person is experiencing is mainly anxiety or mainly depression, although there are certainly differences when we look at brain scans. But the main difference is fairly clear: in a social phobia or another anxiety disorder, the major focus is anticipation of something bad happening; the major concern in a depression has more to do with expecting that nothing good will happen. Depression focuses on negative evaluations of yourself and your experiences. "I'm having a lousy time" or "I'm a bad person" is a depression issue; "They are going to hate my speech and laugh at me" is more about expecting something awful to happen. The major focus in a social phobia is fear of being observed, evaluated by, or interacting with people in more than one kind of situation. The main problem with depression may or may not have anything to do with people, but the focus tends to be on a negative feeling about yourself and others. And again, sometimes you can have bits of both.

Introversion

Many people who are not phobic nevertheless tend to avoid social interactions. In some cases, they are simply introverted individuals. Introverts are people who generally feel more comfortable spending time by themselves or interacting with only a few people. One way of thinking about introversion is that when you are an introvert, you find your own inner resources and thoughts to be fairly satisfying; you may not need to spend as much time looking to social interactions for your satisfaction. Extroverts, on the other hand, generally prefer connecting with others and may even find themselves uncomfortable if they spend too much time alone. Neither introversion nor extroversion are pathological, and people generally fall into either one or the other category.

The difference between introversion and social phobia is the level of anxiety. In short, introverts aren't troubled necessarily by the high levels of anxiety that socially phobic individuals experience. For example, the average healthy introvert isn't particularly frightened or anxious of going to a party or making a phone call. They may simply prefer not to go or to send an e-mail instead of calling. They may get tired more easily if they spend time in noisy social situations, but they don't get shaky or frightened—they don't freeze up with anxiety.

With social phobia, the anxiety is the main reason for avoiding social situations. In fact you can be a socially phobic extrovert—someone who would dearly love to spend more time socializing except for the fears that it triggers. Or, you may be very comfortable in some social situations and go to them as often as possible (such as dealing with customers at the store or seeing friends at parties), but you may find that whenever you have to deal with an authority figure (such as a teacher or a boss) or make a phone call to a stranger, your anxiety level spikes.

Avoidant or Schizoid Personalities

The difference between a social phobia and having a *personality disorder*, which also involves avoiding people, is also a tricky one. Just as with social phobia, people with avoidant or schizoid personalities tend to be uncomfortable in social situations. They are, in many ways, quite similar to people with social phobia. In fact, the major difference between them is often the fact that people with these problem personalities generally don't see their discomfort around people as being unusual (for themselves, anyway) or something that they think needs to change.

def•i•ni•tion

A **personality disorder** is a long-lasting or lifelong pattern of thinking, feeling, and behaving that is generally rigid and inflexible; this behavior creates psychological, social, and/or vocational difficulties for a person. They generally are not aware that the way they manage relationships, or the way they think about themselves and others, keeps causing them difficulties, and so they tend not to change this pattern.

Avoidant individuals generally have higher levels of anxiety and may be uncomfortable in threatening situations (which may or may not be social situations). But this level of avoidance tends to be more pervasive, and it tends to involve a wider range of situations. Further, it may never occur to them that this avoidance is a problem at all; while social phobics know they're anxious and wish they weren't, avoidant people may see their discomfort with and fear of social interactions as natural and inevitable.

Schizoid personality refers to a tendency toward having a flat, disinterested attitude toward social relations. Generally, people with a schizoid pattern may develop lifestyles of never interacting in any way, or only in very superficial and distant ways, with others, and they may not see this lifestyle as a problem—it may not cause feelings of loneliness, longing for closeness, or a sense that there is something wrong with their lives.

So while a socially phobic person may long for connections but feel afraid of social situations, schizoid people may not have close connections anywhere in their lives—and may not really miss them, either.

How Does Social Phobia Affect Your Life?

A problem with social phobia can have a wide range of consequences on your life. Like everything else about phobias, just *how much* of a problem it is depends on a couple of things—mainly the strength of your anxiety reactions, and how widespread the problem is in your life.

Poorer People Skills

Social skills are largely made, not born. Throughout our lives, we generally improve our ability to meet and befriend new people, to negotiate differences and influence others, and to function well in school, work, and leisure situations. Whether it's school, work, dating, or learning to talk with your new baby, practice makes perfect!

This means, of course, that anything that keeps you from getting out there and practicing your social smarts will limit you! In fact, it may put you at a real disadvantage in many school, work, and relationship situations. (Imagine, say, someone who never learned another thing about dealing with people after age 10. That person would really have problems as an adult, right?)

Obviously, the more you let your social phobia hold you back, the further back you will be. In fact, socially phobic individuals do tend to have greater difficulty coping with everything from business affairs to affairs of the heart.

Less Fun

It's hard to have fun if you're sweating and shaking! People with social phobia are doubly cursed: they may know that they really want to get out and be successful with others—but they can't do it! Unlike introverts, who may not feel at all deprived if they don't go to the big office party or eat lunch alone every day, social phobics may want to go but hold back. Or they may show up, but then spend so much time feeling uncomfortable that they duck out the back door the first chance they get. Or, they get through the interview, phone call, or presentation, but never have the chance to enjoy the applause, the nice comments from others, or just the simple pleasures that come from being part of a welcoming social group.

School and Work Problems

Social phobia can impair your school or work functioning. For example, students may have a range of problems making friends, interacting with teachers or coaches, or handling situations such as giving presentations, working with others on group projects, or functioning in team sports. They may miss opportunities to get into leadership roles that they'd otherwise enjoy or be good at because they are more comfortable working alone. Asking teachers for help, calling a classmate to get an assignment, or approaching a coach for an explanation may be impossible.

Work problems may start long before the first day of employment. Some people avoid even applying for jobs they might be good at because they fear these positions will require uncomfortable kinds of social interactions. Job interviews may be occasions of sweaty handshakes, trembling hands, and awkward silences. They may even perform poorly at answering questions on topics that, when calm and alone, they are experts on. Interacting with peers, bosses, or customers may all be difficult or impossible because of the intense anxiety. Some workers hide out in their cubicle or workstation and spend too little time connecting with peers or building up their professional networks.

Real Danger!

You can make important life decisions because of social phobia problems you aren't even aware you have! Many people are so used to avoiding social situations out of anxiety that they avoid jobs, recreational opportunities, or social events they would secretly love to go for, because their anxiety gets in the way. Just ask yourself, "If I had absolutely *no* concerns or anxiety about what other people would see or how they'd react, would I want to do this?"

Other Mental Health Problems

Another problem with social phobia is that they may make you more vulnerable to other mental health problems, especially depression and chemical abuse or dependency. This certainly seems unfair—isn't it bad enough that you may have to cope with all this anxiety and the pain it causes without also developing other conditions?

But it makes a kind of dismal sense. Take depression, for instance. If I were going to coach you on how to *get* depressed, I might suggest that you do things like be less successful at school or work or that you avoid making friends who might care for you and support you. Being unsuccessful and lonely are excellent ways to make yourself less happy, right?

I might also tell you to cut yourself off from fun—don't date, and avoid parties or other social events. Finally, I'd recommend that you spend as much time as possible telling yourself how you blew it, how people see only your flaws and failings, and how much they disapprove of you.

By the time I was done giving you that treatment, you'd almost certainly be pretty miserable! And that, of course, is exactly what social phobia cause people to do to themselves. Is it any wonder that where social phobia is powerful, depression can easily slip in as a kind of second, uninvited guest?

Substance Abuse

Similarly, a social phobia can lead to over reliance on the comforts of alcohol or mood-altering chemicals. Anxiety hurts—it's almost physically painful at times. People sometimes get temporary relief from the discomfort with a beer, a shot or two, or a hit of their favorite street pharmaceutical. This is why, for instance, people have long referred to alcohol as a social lubricant—keep in mind that in any group of 20 people at a party, odds are that at least 1 has a severe social phobia, and many others are struggling with milder degrees of anxiety.

So let's be clear: occasional, in-control medicating of mild social anxiety is not uncommon and may not actually be a problem for most people. It wouldn't be a problem for anyone if there were no such things as alcohol dependency or drug addictions—and if the consequences of problem use weren't so horrendous. (That's why, for instance, pharmaceutical treatments for social anxiety that are prescribed by a psychiatrist or other qualified professional and taken responsibly are generally helpful and won't cause you any harm.)

But alcohol and other drugs create their own problems: addiction, habitual dependence, and behavior changes. Relying on these substances to help manage your anxiety may tend to reduce your ability to cope with social anxiety and social situations. Plus, when your big worry socially is that you think people are evaluating you, what could be worse than knowing that when the folks at the party (or your kid's teacher) saw you last night, you were too out of it to function at your best?

Recovery from Social Phobia

There's been much progress in recent years in learning to help people cope with social phobia. There are several effective ways to treat the problem, including behavioral and cognitive therapies, psychodynamic approaches, other forms of counseling and self-help and emotional support, and medications.

A good first step is recognizing that you may have some degree of social phobia. As I've mentioned, it's possible in milder cases to not recognize how much of your life is affected by anxiety about being evaluated by others.

If you conclude that you need to become less socially anxious, or that your social anxiety is limiting your life, there are a number of ways you can proceed. For example, you can …

♦ Try to gradually broaden your range of social activities, push yourself into some new situations, and see if you can get more comfortable.

♦ Learn some of the relaxation skills discussed in Chapter 3, especially if you have problems with physical tension symptoms.

♦ Make a list of the particular social situations where you seem to be most anxious, and try to come up with some new ways to handle them.

Of course, if your social anxiety is too difficult to manage on your own, you may need to get some help from a pro. Consider talking with a local therapist about your concerns and getting his or her input. Remember, going to see someone for a brief consultation doesn't necessarily commit you to seeing that person for treatment—sometimes just a visit or two can be very helpful. But sometimes more extensive treatment is needed, especially if your social phobia is very intense or seems to affect you in many parts of your life, or if you also have problems with depression, other anxiety issues, or substance dependency or abuse. (Chapter 3 covers treatment issues at greater length.)

While it would be too optimistic to say that all social phobia problems can be cured, the majority of people who seek help for the problem experience at least some benefit from treatment. The good news is that most people can reduce or even eliminate social phobia problems. The main thing is to have a positive attitude that you really can be less socially anxious, take active steps to address the problem, and take it one step at a time.

The Least You Need to Know

◆ Social phobia, or social anxiety disorder, is fear of social interactions with others. It's the most common phobia.

◆ The main fear in social phobia is usually a fear that you are being observed, judged, and evaluated critically by other people—so you get scared and want to avoid them.

◆ Social phobia can cause many problems in your life, ranging from loneliness, depression, and other mental health concerns to poorer functioning in school, career, and relationship situations.

◆ Social phobia can often be helped by various therapies including behavioral, cognitive behavioral, psychodynamic, and medication approaches. Most people can improve or resolve their social phobia problems with appropriate help.

Chapter 13

Phobias in Children

In This Chapter

- ◆ Putting children's fears in perspective
- ◆ Stress and kids
- ◆ Little dangers that are *big* for kids
- ◆ Phobias in little kids
- ◆ The fears of older kids

Any parent knows that a big part of caring for children is helping them with everyday fears. A very small child may burst into frantic tears when a stranger tries to hold her, even if the stranger is the same loving grandma who held her just a few weeks ago. A toddler may not be able to sleep because of the monsters under his bed. And an adolescent may go into severe panic mode because of an upcoming test.

Most of the fears of children are normal. In some cases, though, these fears are harder to grow out of. What you thought was just a phase can become a longer-lasting fear. At times, this can be the beginning of a phobia.

Many adults still have the phobias they developed as small children. Others (the majority) managed to grow out of those fears of dogs or strangers or the hundreds of other things that once scared them.

In this chapter we'll look at the world of childhood fears and phobias. To begin, let's get some perspective on how children's emotional worlds develop.

Understanding Children's Fears

The most important fact about children is that they are not small adults. Even though a child may be a whiz on the computer, know how to set the clock on your VCR, and have her own Facebook page, she thinks about and experiences the world very differently than adults. And the younger a child is, the more unlike adults she is in her ways of understanding the world, feeling things, and reacting to stressful events.

To understand a child's fears, you have to understand how he or she thinks. This leads us into the world of *developmental psychology*.

Developmental psychologists have spent many decades learning how children think about things. It turns out that, to children, the world may be a very different place than it is to adults. As adults we may tend to underestimate the differences between how we see things and how our children do, because as our minds have matured and our lives have grown more complicated, we've forgotten how things used to seem.

def•i•ni•tion

Developmental psychology is the branch of psychology that studies how people change throughout their lives, from birth through old age.

How Children Experience the World

Infants come into the world with very little ability to sort out their experiences. They can react to stimulation such as light, hot, cold, or noises. They quickly become aware of the presence of caregivers and even newborn infants seem to like gazing at the faces of people hovering over them.

As an infant begins to mature, he develops more awareness of things going on around him. One of the ways that infants get information about the world is through what we call referencing. If you approach a baby, you will notice that the baby quickly looks to his mother, then back at you—he may do this several times. The baby is using mom as a guide for how to react to your approach. If mom looks relaxed or smiles, the baby is likely to relax and greet your approach more calmly. If mom looks tense or worried, the baby may cry or fuss, using mom's cues that this is not such a good thing.

The baby learns what is safe and what is not by checking or referencing mom's reaction. (Of course, this only works if mom is around at that moment.) Because of this referencing process, parents have a big influence over how scary or safe the world seems to their young children.

Stranger Anxiety

As children grow and come to understand more about the world, they start to become afraid of things that they weren't so scared of at an earlier age. This is normal and healthy.

For instance, before they are about six or seven months old, babies will generally let anyone hold them or talk to them. But around that age, something changes. Suddenly, grandma's visits are not happy times of cuddling her new granddaughter who just coos and smiles but occasions of tears and screaming every time grandma gets near her.

What happened? Well, at about seven to nine months (give or take), the child has developed enough memory and understanding of the world to be able to recognize familiar persons. But that also means she realizes that someone else (like the grandma she hasn't seen recently) is not familiar. And so this "new" person is scary!

Babies demonstrate this by resisting, leaning away, or crying when approached by someone who is not part of their daily familiar circle. This has come to be called *stranger anxiety*.

def•i•ni•tion

Stranger anxiety is a normal fear of strangers that babies begin to show at age seven to nine months.

This new stranger fear shows that little Emma is now able to recognize Mommy as Mommy and not just another face in the crowd. She feels safe, relaxed, and happy when she sees Mommy's face because she has so many warm memories of playing, feeding, and cuddling associated with that face. But Emma is also now able to recognize that the store clerk (or an unfortunate grandma who has less frequent contact with her), is not Mommy. This is a strange face and Emma looks at it with some feelings of anxiety and concern. She is likely to be reluctant to let the person hold or even touch her and will turn away to hide her face in Mommy's neck.

This kind of stranger anxiety reaction is quite common and not a cause for concern. It is a sign that the baby is becoming mature enough to know who is familiar and who is not and to prefer the safety of the familiar.

Separation Anxiety

At about 18 months of age (give or take a few months), children generally develop another natural fear: *separation anxiety.* The child experiencing separation anxiety responds with distress and clinging to the sight of Mommy leaving. Little Emma may even react to signs that Mommy is just about to leave, such as seeing Mommy blow-drying her hair in the morning. The toddler knows nothing about work, but she knows how scary it feels to have Mommy go away; she has learned to associate hair drying and other signals of a pending separation with Mommy's disappearance.

Again, this is a positive sign of the toddler's cognitive development and her ability to understand her world and to make predictions about what is happening. It shows she can see how events are related to each other. But it can be hard on parents to have these sad scenes every time they have to leave in the morning.

def•i•ni•tion

Separation anxiety is a normal developmental process that children experience beginning at around age 18 months, when they begin to experience high levels of anxiety when they are separated from their main caregiver (e.g., their mother). Babies begin to understand that they are going to be separated from their mother, or caregiver, but do not understand that the separation is temporary, and so they become anxious. This anxiety generally begins to peak at about 18 to 24 months.

Childhood Temperament and Fears

Imagine that we are watching a group of eight-month-old babies playing on a rug together. Each child is calm, happy, and involved with the toys on the rug. Then someone's big brother comes in and runs a loud toy fire truck, its siren blaring, onto the rug. All the babies are startled. But each baby's reaction is a little different.

Little Roger stiffens, stops playing, and becomes very still with an unsmiling face. He looks around for his mom, who smiles at him reassuringly. But Roger remains subdued and tense and continues to look from his mom to the scary truck.

Little Emily shrieks, begins to cry loudly, and waves her arms about in great distress. At first she is unable to open her eyes to look for her mom because she is crying so hard. Her mom goes to her to try to calm her by talking with her and reassuring her with pats or hugs.

Little Josh shows a brief startled look then quickly searches for his mom. She points to the truck with a smile and a nod. Josh studies her a moment then smiles back at her. He now appears much calmer, and he turns to look at the truck with curiosity.

As the moms comfort or encourage their babies, we see that each baby has his or her own response style. Roger tenses up when startled and takes a long while to relax. He remains cautious, wary, and watchful despite encouragement from his mom. Even after he appears to have calmed some, Roger does not seem eager to learn more about the noisy new toy. Although Emily was badly frightened, she does calm down as her mom continues to hug and speak softly to her. When she finally gets over her upset, she may be willing to put her fears aside and play with the new toy. When she hears the toy on another day, she may react very happily and go to play with it. Josh is startled, but he calms quickly; watched by his nodding and smiling mother, he is ready to find out more about this intriguing new experience.

These different reactions of the three children are because of inborn *temperament* differences. Some babies, like Roger, react to distress by freezing up or withdrawing but can usually relax somewhat if given time. But they may take a longer time than other children to calm down, and they tend not to reach out and touch new experiences very comfortably. Others, like Emily, are highly reactive to disruptions, showing intense negative feelings and difficulty calming down. Others, like Josh, are calmer by nature, and react relatively mildly even to fairly startling events.

---

def•i•ni•tion

Temperament refers to a person's inborn emotional disposition. Psychologists use the word to refer to things such as how strongly a person reacts emotionally, how active they tend to be, etc. Many of these traits can be observed in newborns, and they often last throughout a person's life.

Outgoing children like Josh do not often develop phobias. They may become momentarily upset but usually rally quickly. They are then ready to take on new situations with gusto, meet new people, or play new games; they show a lively curiosity about their worlds.

Children with more intense, high-energy temperaments like Emily, also tend not to develop phobias. They may initially become upset, but once they calm down, they like to explore the world and take on new experiences. What is more difficult is their unpredictability. One day they seem unflappable no matter what happens, while another day every little change upsets and derails them. This can be trying for mom and dad!

Interestingly, researchers have found that babies who show Roger's response—a pattern of tense withdrawal and avoidance when faced with something new or startling—are the most likely to show later anxiety problems or develop phobias. It's important to note that not all babies with this pattern develop phobias. It is simply more common among these children than among children in the other two groups.

It appears that some infants and children, like Roger who tensed up when the fire truck appeared, simply have higher internal stress levels, even when things are going well. They seem to be so reactive to things around them that they can become overwhelmed when even a small amount of stress is added. As a result, they tend to freeze up and are often seen as shy and retiring. They tend to avoid new experiences or changes (even what seem like minor changes to adults), perhaps as a way of keeping their inner worlds more settled.

And these inborn temperament traits tend to be with us throughout our lives. Some children are simply more fearful, more outgoing, or more active by nature, regardless of what a parent does. If you have more than one child, or if you think about your own siblings, you will likely see these kinds of inborn differences in their natures.

Knowing your child's temperament can help you to anticipate his or her reactions to situations that might prove scary (such as meeting a new babysitter, starting day care or school, or even getting a new pet). This allows you to help him or her to cope more effectively. For example, although shy children like Roger will try to avoid new situations, this may not be the best thing for them.

Some research shows that being in good quality day care can help these children become a little less shy and anxious over time. Apparently having regular help from adults in how to deal with changes—along with the examples of other children who are enjoying the new experiences—can teach these children ways to calm themselves and be less upset.

Phobias and Small Children

All children have to cope with fears and anxieties as they grow. Children experience normal fears such as stranger anxiety or separation anxiety at predictable points in their development. These fears actually show that the child is on track in developing normal, healthy reactions to the world.

We've also seen that children have different temperaments and so naturally react to ordinary events with different kinds of emotions. Usually, they rely on their parents' reactions to know how to make sense of, or how to process, their fears. If the parent signals that a clanging new toy is okay, most children learn that it's safe—though different kids will have more or less trouble adjusting to the noise.

A few other things have a big impact on children's fear-managing abilities, including:

♦ **Vulnerability.** Little things are often *big* things to children. As we've already seen, a loud toy can startle and frighten a bunch of toddlers. A stranger or a strange dog can be quite terrifying.

◆ **Fantasy versus reality.** Young children cannot really tell the difference between fantasy, reality, and imagination. They are not always clear that what they see on TV, what they dream, or just what they picture in their minds is not the same as what happens in real life around them. If they can see something or hear something, then it is real—whether it seems imaginary to adults or not. Young children understand the world through their perceptions, not through ideas. What you see, hear, taste, and feel is what is real.

Indeed, real is an adult concept; all these things—dreams, stories, TV images, thoughts—are real to a very young child. And because they have limited understanding of what can and cannot hurt them, a lot of what they see or hear can be frightening for them in ways that adults may not realize. The roar of a vacuum cleaner is not too different from the roar of a monster to young ears!

◆ **Language.** Smaller children generally can't explain their fears in language the way older children can. They have not yet developed the ability to put fears or other feelings into words. So a frightened small child may not be able to talk about what frightened them in the same way that a school-aged or older child can. Instead, they may react physically to a fear—an upset stomach or an odd crying spell may be your only way of knowing that a child has been frightened by something.

One way to understand what a child is feeling is just to understand some of the things that can frighten them. Some of the common fears of small children are discussed next.

A Fear of Falling

I've talked about stranger and separation anxiety and how they appear in toddlers as they mature. An even earlier fear response, perhaps the only one present in nearly all babies at birth, is the fear of falling.

Jason is excited about his developing ability to crawl. He delights in crawling to mommy to be swept up in a hug and to see her smiles! But something seems different now. Seated on a sturdy platform, Jason looks at his mom as she coaxes him to crawl across the platform to her.

He seems eager to do so—at first. But as he rocks onto his knees, he casts anxious looks down and puckers up his face with worry. His mom calls again and beckons to him encouragingly; Jason clearly longs to go to her, but instead he rolls back into a sitting position and begins to cry. Why is he so afraid to go to his mom?

Well, although Jason is resting on a very solid piece of Plexiglas that can easily hold his weight, what he sees through the transparent flooring is a scary abyss to cross. He cannot get himself to risk it—even to get to his smiling mommy's arms. The fear of falling is inborn and unshakable. No amount of reassurance from mommy will get Jason, who cannot understand that he is on a see-through floor, to crawl off the cliff that he sees.

This interesting finding was reported by psychologists using what they termed the *visual cliff* experiment. They laid a transparent platform of Plexiglas across two supports. They also laid out a checkerboard cloth under the Plexiglas so that it ran down one of the supports and across the floor. This made a clear display of how far away the floor was underneath the platform, even though the babies could not really fall to it.

All babies have an inborn startle response to feeling like they're falling. Even very little babies will avoid crawling over an empty space, even if they are really supported, as in the visual cliff experiments.

> **Phobia Science**
>
> Those who live in cities may well have had experiences with their own visual cliff in the glass-walled elevators some buildings have adopted. The feel of the floor under their feet—when faced with that endless view of how far one can fall—offers no reassurance to those with a strong fear of heights!

Darkness and Shadows

To Mom and Dad, a basket of stuffed toys is the same—and just as harmless—whether seen during the day, by moonlight, or as a silhouette when the room is dark. But to a very young child, if the toys *look* different in the light and in the dark, then the toys *are* different.

The movement of a shadow across the room as the lighting changes outside is the same to the young child as something crawling around in the room. Fears of monsters and lurking things in the dark are active in young children—but some will fear the dark itself since it looks so different from light. If it looks different, then it is different.

Luckily, young children's belief in magical properties and the aliveness of all things makes it possible to use a stuffed bear or other toy to stand guard and keep the shadow creatures away.

New Foods

While our daily food choices may seem mundane and boring to us, to the young child every taste, texture, color, and scent is a new experience. And things that seem strange can also seem dangerous. In part, this is because the child has had enough experience to know that some things make you sick or hurt you—but she has not had enough experience to know exactly how to tell what is safe and what is not. So the young child relies on what is familiar to be a guide. Anything that looks, smells, tastes, or feels too unfamiliar is suspect. Even changing the dish the food is put in—creating a different look to it—can mean that the food is not safe!

To a very young child, a peanut butter and jelly sandwich cut into little triangles may not seem at all the same as the delicious PB&J he had before, when it was cut into little squares. Or when it was on a different plate. Or when it had grape jelly instead of apple.

All parents endure some of this, and they usually learn to pair new foods with well-liked favorites—adding puréed squash to applesauce—to coax a child into trying something new. But for some children, no amount of coaxing will work. These children develop what is called food neophobia—a phobic refusal to try any new (*neo*) foods or to accept any new presentation of a familiar food. Children with this phobia will be quite adamant about not accepting any but a few select foods, always prepared the same way. Their very restricted food choices make it difficult for them to enjoy parties, restaurants, or other situations where they are expected to eat novel or unappealing (to them) foods. Most children grow out of this.

Needles

It's a fact of life. Babies, toddlers, and young children spend a lot of time getting shots. And those shots hurt! Shots hurt adults, too, when they have to have them, but adults can understand that it is a brief hurt that leads to long-term health.

Not so the very young child. As always, perceptions or sensations trump everything else. If it hurts, it's bad! And some young children can become phobic not only of the needles, but to the sight of white coats or stethoscopes—the sights that accompany the appearance of the actual needle. (Indeed, some research indicates that up to 10 percent of adults continue to be needle phobic; see Chapter 6.)

Cats and Dogs

Pets are an important part of family life and can be valuable companions to young children. But for very young children, even ones who may have adjusted to a family pet, other animals may provoke intense fear. This is especially so when confronted by ones that seem to be moving too quickly or unpredictably.

A cat that leaps from one place to another or a dog that comes right up and licks the child's face may prove to be too startling and frightening for a young child to cope with. Romping puppies are fun for an adult to watch but may present a terror for a toddler who is trying to stay on his feet and who can't judge where the next rush will come from.

Clowns

Clowns are usually jovial, silly, endearing figures to adults. We know that when we see them on TV or in a movie, those are just images that cannot harm us; when we see them in a circus, we know that those are ordinary humans in make-up and unusual clothes. Again, we see them as harmless and fun.

But as we've seen, very young children are highly dependent on how things look. They do not make allowances for changes due to costuming or make-up. If a creature suddenly appears with a giant red nose, strange facial colorings, and huge floppy feet, it is seen as totally real and completely out of the ordinary. It can be scary as all get out! As a result, many very young children cry and feel afraid when approached by clowns, developing a lifelong phobic reaction to these figures of fun (see Chapter 8).

Helping the Very Young with Their Fears

Infants and toddlers have little ability to calm themselves down. They rely on their parents to help them. First and foremost it is important that mom and dad remain calm. Let the baby see it in their faces, hear it in their voices, and feel it in their touch.

Toddlers and preschoolers need to have limited exposure to frightening images, stories, or characters. TV or movie selections should be age appropriate, and mom or dad should be sensitive to how their child is reacting. For some children, a show about superheroes and monsters may be exciting fun; for others, it may be too frightening. Save it for when the child is older.

Similarly, a child who responds with anxiety and pulling away to a visit to Santa may need more time to grow up before being asked to approach closer and sit on his lap. Let the child stand at a distance and watch this figure while telling him about the good things Santa does. Help the child calm down and feel more at ease. The child may be much less alarmed and more ready to visit with Santa (or get closer to clowns) in another year.

For young children who have bad dreams, it is not helpful to tell them, "It's just a dream; go back to sleep." For the child, that is the same as hearing, "Yes, there are scary monsters in here, but just go to sleep." Not very calming news!

Try This!

A parent can take advantage of the child's imagination and acceptance of fantasy. Hunt for the scary animals and reassure the child you see none, then leave a stuffed animal to stand guard or leave on a night light that the scary monsters "don't like." The child will feel reassured by these concrete actions to deal with the dream animals and will be more able to fall back asleep.

Common Phobias of Older Children and Teens

Older children and teens have a good understanding of the physical world. They understand the differences between TV images and real life, between the outer appearance of someone in make-up and the real person underneath the costuming, between the thoughts and fantasies in their heads and outside events. They are therefore less likely to be frightened by these things.

But older children and teens are more aware of social concerns, such as status within a group or relationship issues. In school, they can be acutely sensitive to rejection, exclusion, failure at academics or sports, and being teased. These lay the groundwork for the two most troublesome phobias of this age: school phobia and social phobia.

It's also true that some anxiety problems from their earlier years may continue to trouble older kids. Temperament continues to play a role in how intensely older children and teens react to their experiences. Parental responses are still important. However, what their peers say and do becomes more and more important as the child moves from grade school to middle school and into high school. Rather than referencing how their parents react, older children and teens are more likely to reference how their peers react.

School Phobias

It is not unusual to hear children talk about how they wish they didn't have to go to school or hear teens tell about how they can't wait to graduate and get out of school. Vacation periods and unexpected breaks like snow days are greeted with glee. Yet most children and teens readily attend school, enjoy their learning, and look forward to seeing their friends and engaging in the various school activities.

For some, however, the thought of attending school—of just being in the building or on the grounds—is not just a chore but also a dreaded situation fraught with terrors. There seem to be a couple of major reasons that some children or teens develop school phobias, which is one of the most common phobias of youngsters.

For some, learning problems make schoolwork impossible. Seeing how hard it is for them compared to peers creates a painful sense of inadequacy. There may also be a fear of disappointing parents with poor performance. This may be too humiliating to face. For others, fear of bullying, hazing, or outright aggression makes the school feel too threatening to enter.

Churning stomach, aching head, and palpitating heart may begin to plague the student with school phobia at the sight of the school. If he or she is able to get into the building, it is not long before the student is at the nurse's office looking for a way to go home. More often, the student begins to refuse even to attend school.

Social Phobia

As we've seen, some children are temperamentally more shy and withdrawn than others and tend to avoid new situations. This is particularly seen in social settings, where these children tend to remain on the outside of a group, watching but not joining in. These are children who feel too anxious and fearful about rejection, embarrassment, or teasing to risk making new friends.

What is good-natured joshing to most children feels like painful rejection and public ridicule to the child or teen with social phobia. And the fear of facing further rejection or ridicule may create such anxiety that all social relationships or competitive situations are avoided.

The reticence of children and teens with social phobia may be misunderstood by their peers. Feeling anxious and vulnerable, they stand silently watching and never join in; thus the students with social phobia may be seen as snobbish or critical.

Poor social skills due to lack of participation in peer group activities can also make the child or teen with social phobia seem awkward or odd. This may then lead to the very teasing or ribbing that intensifies the child's fear about social interactions.

Over time, children and teens with social phobia tend to perceive social or group settings as more threatening than fun. An invitation to a party arouses dread and the conviction that something terrible will happen to them. They may not get the most out of their schooling due to reluctance to work in groups, to ask for help, or to have study buddies to support them.

Helping Older Children and Teens with Their Fears

Older children and teens who are struggling with school, social fears, and stresses may respond well to talking about what they have been through—or what they are afraid they will go through. Simply being able to express their points of view with someone can be calming. Getting specific help with developing social skills or dealing with learning problems also helps. And children and teens with school and social phobia benefit from learning strategies for soothing the physical aspects of their reactions. Using deep breathing, visualization, positive affirmations, and even just counting to 10 can all be used to help calm an anxious flare-up.

Real Danger!

It's important to help kids with their fears so these fears don't turn into phobias. While fears are natural for most kids, fears they don't master can lead them to develop patterns of avoiding new situations, not trying new things, and not fitting in. It's easier to help children avoid a problem with fears now than to have to help them overcome a phobia later.

Here are some additional suggestions for helping kids with their fears:

- Be supportive and interested in your child's experiences—be the person your child comes to when he's afraid.

- Don't pressure, shame, humiliate, or punish your child for having fears.

- Help your child develop the basic skills at handling situations so she won't be afraid, whether it's bike riding, being around animals, or talking in front of class.

- Encourage a child to confront a fear, but do it with your child's consent, and gradually; never throw a child in over his head in order to force him to overcome his fear—he may instead develop a traumatic response.

- Let your child know that everyone has fears, and encourage her to take it one step at a time—and be ready to answer the question about what your fears are!

- Remember that it's not always clear what the fear is about—it may be separation from you, not something at school, that is scaring your child—or vice versa! It may take some patient talking and sharing to figure it out.

- Let your child's teacher know about your child's fears, and ensure that the teacher is supportive and will keep it private (so the child doesn't hear the teacher announce Suzie's fear of bees to the whole class).

The Least You Need to Know

- Most children's fears are normal.

- Some of the fears children develop, such as fear of strangers or separation anxiety, are actually signs that they are on track in developing some important mental and emotional abilities.

- Children differ in their inborn temperament or emotional dispositions and so have different ways of reacting to frightening or overwhelming events.

- Very small children may develop temporary fears of things like the dark, new foods, needles, pets, or clowns. Patience and support go a long way in helping them to master these fears.

- Older children become more socially attuned, and so social anxieties and school fears are not unusual. Helping them to express their fears, providing reassurance and support, and giving occasional help with learning problems or social skills may prove very important.

Appendix A

Index of Phobias

Phobias are customarily named in one of two ways; that is, most phobias have a "medical" name, and a plain old English (or Japanese, or Spanish, or whatever your language is) name as well. The medical or technical names are most often created by combining Greek (usually), Latin (sometimes), or other term from some other language with the suffix -phobia. So, for instance, the fear of spiders, *arachnophobia*, is based on the combination of the Greek word for spider (*arachnos*) with the word for phobia. (*Phobia* is a word named for the Greek word for fear, *phobos*.) Sometimes, a phobia can also have several different Greek, Latin, or other technical terms.

In the following index of phobias, the most common English term for the phobia is written in Roman, and the technical term is written in italics. So if you want to know about your fear of spiders, you can just look up "spiders," but if you happen upon a phobia term such as *arachnophobia* and want to know what it means, you can find those terms here, too. Each term is followed by the page number or numbers where you can read more about the phobia in this book.

Appendix B

Resources

Books

American Psychiatric Association. *Diagnostic and Statistical Manual of Mental Disorders, Fourth Edition.* American Psychiatric Association, 2000.

Antony, Martin, and Richard Swinson. *The Shyness & Social Anxiety Workbook, Second Edition.* New Harbinger, 2008.

Beck, Aaron T., Gary Emery, and Ruth Greenberg. *Anxiety Disorders and Phobias: A Cognitive Perspective.* 20th Anniversary Edition. Basic Books, 2005.

Bourne, Edmund J. *Beyond Anxiety and Phobia: A Step-by-Step Guide to Lifetime Recovery.* New Harbinger Publications, 2001.

———. *The Anxiety & Phobia Workbook, Fourth Edition.* New Harbinger, 2005.

Doctor, Ronald M., Ada P. Kahn, and Christine Adamec. *The Encyclopedia of Phobias, Fears, and Anxieties, Third Edition.* Facts on File, 2008.

Gardner, James, and Arthur Bell. *Phobias and How to Overcome Them: Understanding and Beating Your Fears.* New Page Books, 2005.

Greenberg, Gary, Balvis Rubess, and Matthew Reinhart. *The Pop-up Book of Phobias.* Harper Entertainment, 1999.

Peurifoy, Reneau Z. *Anxiety, Phobia, and Panic.* Grand Central Publishing, 2005.

Saul, Helen. *Phobias: Fighting the Fear.* Arcade Publishing, 2001.

Websites

All of the following links were accurate as of this writing. Websites vary widely in their usability, accuracy, and credibility—use appropriate judgment and caution in relying on web-based information and advice.

American Psychological Association   http://apa.org. Includes links to articles about phobias and other topics in psychology, and a "Find a Psychologist" service.

WebMD topic overview: Phobias   www.webmd.com/anxiety-panic/tc/ phobias-topic-overview. WebMD is a great source of generally accurate info on phobias and other medical and mental-health–related topics.

Find a Therapist service   http://therapists.psychologytoday.com/ppc/ prof_search.php?iorb=4764. Reputable therapist search service operated by *Psychology Today* magazine.

List of all known phobias website   www.webspinning.com.au/home/ lambertj/public_html/phobia.html. A massive list of phobias.

Monk Phobia Dictionary   www.usanetwork.com/series/monk/ webexclusives/dictionary/index.html. List of phobias on site devoted to the TV detective *Monk*, who is said to have "38 documented phobias, but that number grows by the episode." The list is fairly extensive.

Museum of Hoaxes Website   www.museumofhoaxes.com/hoax/ weblog/comments/107. Discussion forum of hard-to-believe-these-exist phobias.

The Phobia List site   www.phobialist.com. Another site listing zillions of phobias.

Unusual phobias   http://unusualphobias.com. Website devoted to unusual phobias.

Unusual phobias group   http://health.groups.yahoo.com/group/unusualphobias. A Yahoo! group devoted to unusual phobias.

Index

nonreal phobias, 201, 207
  determination of real phobia,
    202, 205-206
  examples, 204
  humorous fictional terms, 204
  metaphor, 202-203
  spam phobias, 204
  superstitions, 202
nosebleeds, fear of, 106
nosmaphobia, 97
nosophobia, 97
nostophobia, 139
novercaphobia, 174
nuclear weapons, fear of, 145
nucleomituphobia, 145
nudity, fear of, 145
nudophobia, 145
numbers, fear of, 192, 207
numerophobia, 192
nyctohylophobia, 81
nyctophobia, 79

O

obesophobia, 112
object phobias. *See* miscellaneous
  phobias
obsessive compulsive disorder
  (OCD), 66, 100, 130
OCD. *See* obsessive compulsive
  disorder
ocean, fear of, 82
ochlophobia, 127, 166
ochophobia, 119
octophobia, 15, 207
odontophobia, 95, 199
odynesphobia, 106
odynophobia, 106
oenophobia, 200
oikophobia, 138
old age, fear of, 146
old people, fear of, 170

ombrophobia, 83
ommatophobia, 185
ommetaphobia, 185
oneirogmophobia, 159
oneirophobia, 130
onomatophobia, 144
open high places, fear of, 83
open places, fear of, 146
open spaces, fear of, 83
operant conditioning model, 32
ophiciophobia, 70
ophidiophobia, 70
ophiophobia, 70
opinions, fear of, 146, 192
opposite sex, fear of, 170
orbasostasophobia, 158
ornithophobia, 63
orthophobia, 194
osmophobia, 92
osphreisiophobia, 92
ostraconophobia, 70
otters, fear of, 68
ouranophobia, 137
outer space, fear of things related
  to, 78

P

pain, fear of, 106
palindrome, 204, 208
panic attacks, 10, 116, 215
  agoraphobia and, 215, 220
  definition of, 11
  fear of having, 220
  medical phobias and, 97, 100
  medications to manage, 55
  pain of, 220
  social phobia and, 228
  statistics, 216
  trigger, 221
panic disorder without
  agoraphobia, 216

U–V

W

X-Y-Z